MW00624749

(261.8+5)

234

Portland Mennonite Church
12 SE 35th Ave.
Portland, Ore. 97214

Mennocostals

Pentecostals, Peacemaking, and Social Justice

Series Editors: Jay Beaman and Martin Mittelstadt

Mission

Pentecostal and Charismatic Christians comprise approximately twenty-five percent of global Christianity (more than 600 million of 2.4 billion). This remarkable development has occurred within just the last century and has been called the "pentecostalization" of Christianity. Pentecostals and Charismatics experience Christianity and the world in distinctive ways, and this series invites discovery and development of Pentecostal-Charismatic approaches to peacemaking and social justice.

The majority of early twentieth-century Pentecostal denominations were peace churches that encouraged conscientious objection. Denominations such as the Church of God in Christ and the Assemblies of God said "no" to Christian combatant participation in war, and some Pentecostals and Charismatics are exploring this history and working for a recovery and expansion of this witness. The peacemaking aspect of the series focuses on pacifism, war, just war tradition, just peacemaking, peacebuilding, conflict transformation, nonviolence, forgiveness, and other peacemaking-related themes and issues within Pentecostal-Charismatic traditions and from Pentecostal-Charismatic perspectives. We launched the series with a twentieth-anniversary reprint of Jay Beaman's Pentecostal Pacifism--an appropriate look back to the generative years of the Pentecostal movement when many denominations believed that nonviolence was a hallmark of the gospel of Jesus Christ.

Some early Pentecostals also confronted the injustices of racism, sexism, and economic disparity. Others perpetuated the problems. Yet the Holy Spirit leads us now, as then, to confront injustice prophetically and work to redeem and restore. Pentecostal-Charismatic Christians around the world are working for justice in a myriad of ways. This aspect of the series focuses on gender, race, ethnicity, sexuality, economics, class, globalization, trade, poverty, health, consumerism, development, and other social justice related themes and issues within the Pentecostal-Charismatic tradition and from Pentecostal-Charismatic perspectives. Some authors may wish to be more directly theological. Could something be learned by exploring eschatology and social justice, prophecy and social justice, pneumatology and social justice, faith and culture, the relationship of faith and politics, church and society, or even hermeneutics from below. We understand that peace and justice are not separate concerns, but different ways of talking about and seeking shalom--God's salvation, justice, and peace.

We welcome contributions from theologians, biblical scholars, philosophers, ethicists, historians, social-scientists, pastors, activists, and practitioners of peacemaking and social justice. We encourage both original work and publication of important historical resources. We especially invite both scholarly and praxis-oriented contributions from global south Pentecostals and Charismatics, for this series seeks to explore the ways that Pentecostal-Charismatic Christians can develop, strengthen, and sustain a peace-with-justice witness in the twenty-first century around the world.

MENNOCOSTALS

Pentecostal and Mennonite Stories of Convergence

Martin William Mittelstadt
and Brian K. Pipkin

PICKWICK *Publications* · Eugene, Oregon

MENNOCOSTALS
Pentecostal and Mennonite Stories of Convergence

Pentecostals, Peacemaking, and Social Justice 12

Copyright © 2020 Wipf and Stock Publishers. All rights reserved. Except for brief quotations in critical publications or reviews, no part of this book may be reproduced in any manner without prior written permission from the publisher. Write: Permissions, Wipf and Stock Publishers, 199 W. 8th Ave., Suite 3, Eugene, OR 97401.

Pickwick Publications
An Imprint of Wipf and Stock Publishers
199 W. 8th Ave., Suite 3
Eugene, OR 97401

www.wipfandstock.com

PAPERBACK ISBN: 978-1-5326-1974-8
HARDCOVER ISBN: 978-1-4982-4629-3
EBOOK ISBN: 978-1-4982-4628-6

Cataloguing-in-Publication data:

Names: Mittelstadt, Martin W., editor. | Pipkin, Brian K., editor.

Title: Mennocostals : pentecostal and mennonite stories of convergence / edited by Martin W. Mittelstadt and Brian K. Pipkin.

Description: Eugene, OR : Pickwick Publications, 2020 | Pentecostals, Peacemaking, and Social Justice 12 | Includes bibliographical references and index.

Identifiers: ISBN 978-1-5326-1974-8 (paperback) | ISBN 978-1-4982-4629-3 (hardcover) | ISBN 978-1-4982-4628-6 (ebook)

Subjects: LCSH: Mennonites. | Pentecostalism. | Anabaptists.

Classification: BV601.8 .M46 2020 (print) | BV601.8 .M46 (ebook)

Manufactured in the U.S.A.   JANUARY 20, 2020

In honor of Alan Kreider (1941–2017)
A faithful and fellow mennocostal

Contents

Contents

List of Contributors

Jay Beaman (PhD, Iowa State University) is a retired sociologist who lives in Portland, Oregon, with his wife Rockie. He is author of *Pentecostal Pacifism* (1990) and co-editor with Brian K. Pipkin of both *Pentecostal and Holiness Statements on War and Peace* (2013) and *Early Pentecostals on Nonviolence and Social Justice* (2016). His website is pentecostalpacifism.com.

César García (MA, Fresno Pacific Biblical Seminary) was born in Bogotá, Colombia. He is a member of the Colombian Mennonite Brethren Church and has served there as church planter, pastor, and chair of the national Colombian MB Church. Since 2012, César has been serving as General Secretary of the Mennonite World Conference.

Ryan R. Gladwin (PhD, University of Edinburgh) is an Associate Professor in Theology and Ministry at Palm Beach Atlantic University. He has two forthcoming books (*Latin American Protestantism* and *Towards a Liberating Latin American Ecclesiology: The Local Church as a Transformative Historical Project*). His research interests are in social ethics, practical theology, pentecostalism, and Latin American and Latino/a theology and religion.

Martin W. Mittelstadt (PhD, Marquette University) is Professor of New Testament at Evangel University. His books include *Spirit and Suffering in Luke-Acts* and *Reading Luke-Acts in the Pentecostal Tradition*. Other publications reflect a lifelong interest in Luke-Acts, pentecostalism, ecumenism, and peacemaking. He currently serves as co-editor of the Canadian Journal of Pentecostal-Charismatic Christianity and current president of the Society for Pentecostal Studies.

Matthew A. Paugh (DMin, Wesley Theological Seminary) is pastor of St. Paul's United Methodist Church in Oakland, Maryland. A provisional elder in the West Virginia Annual Conference of the United Methodist Church, he matriculated at Anabaptist and pentecostal institutions and is completing Doctor of Ministry studies at Wesley Theological Seminary in Washington, DC.

Brian K. Pipkin (MA, Asia Pacific Theological Seminary; MAR, Azusa Pacific University) is executive assistant at Mennonite Disaster Service, an Anabaptist disaster relief organization in Lititz, Pennsylvania. He is co-editor with Jay Beaman of both *Pentecostal and Holiness Statements on War and Peace* (2013) and *Early Pentecostals on Nonviolence and Social Justice: A Reader* (2016). He attends Blossom Hill Mennonite Church in Lancaster, Pennsylvania, with his wife and three young children.

Tony Richie (DMin, Asbury Theological Seminary; PhD, London School of Theology) is Adjunct Professor of Theology at Pentecostal Theological Seminary (Cleveland, Tennessee) and Senior Pastor at New Harvest Church of God (Knoxville, Tennessee). He has authored more than a hundred articles and book chapter contributions on pentecostals, theology, spirituality, and ministry. Recent books include *Speaking by the Spirit: A Pentecostal Model for Interreligious Dialogue*; *Toward a Pentecostal Theology of Religions*; and *Pentecostal Explorations of Holiness Today: Words from Wesley* (with Randy Howard).

Gerald Shenk (PhD, Northwestern University) is a follower of Jesus who walks within the Anabaptist tradition. Studies in Virginia (Eastern Mennonite), California (Fuller), Croatia (Zagreb), Bosnia (Sarajevo), and Illinois (Northwestern) equipped him to train theological students for social dimensions of discipleship in the way of Jesus. He has taught at the Evangelical Theological Faculty in Osijek, Croatia, and at Eastern Mennonite Seminary in Virginia. His current pursuits are focused on active duty grandparenting in Virginia.

Richard E. Waldrop (DMiss, Fuller Theological Seminary) is Adjunct Professor at Pentecostal Theological Seminary. He and his wife, Janice, have served as long-term missionaries in Latin America and currently direct The Shalom Project (theshalomprojectinternational.com), dedicated to developing partnerships with schools and churches for the practice of holistic mission.

Natasha G. Wiebe (PhD, University of Western Ontario) is Adjunct Professor in the Faculty of Education at the University of Windsor. She has written about the Canadian Mennonite experience in *Forum: Qualitative Social Research*; *Journal of Mennonite Studies*; and *Narrative Inquiry*. Wiebe and her family attended pentecostal churches not far from her opa's farm in southwestern Ontario, Canada. In 2007 she began to explore the intersections of her Mennonite and Pentecostal experiences in "mennocostal" poetry published in *Rhubarb: A Magazine of New Mennonite Art and Writing*.

Menno Simons (1496–1561) was a former Catholic priest who became an influential Anabaptist religious leader in the sixteenth century. He joined with the Anabaptist in 1530 and his followers became known as Mennonites.

Acknowledgments

WE OFFER A HEARTFELT thank you to Anna Mitchell (TA for Marty Mittelstadt). She read through essays, hunted down and checked various sources, and converted a number of papers to the unique style manual employed by Wipf & Stock. She is the consummate TA.

We wish to thank our families for their support of our endeavors. Though some might see these words as necessary platitudes, we extend special thanks to Evelyn Mittelstadt and Shannon Pipkin.

Introduction

By Martin W. Mittelstadt

I GREW UP PENTECOSTAL and I learned early that we had it *right*. Nobody knew God or did church better than us. Whether this incipient elitism was more "felt than telt" I find difficult to discern. I remember more than a few preachers railing against other traditions, those facades of authentic Christianity. Though Roman Catholics often received the brunt of these attacks, Mennonites were not immune. These traditions (a bad word in and of itself) were often deemed "dead religions" filled with people simply "going through the motions," "Sunday-only Christians," and either "too progressive" or "legalistic." Growing up in southern Manitoba, a haven for Mennonites, I remember not a few conversion narratives that included the label "ex-Mennonite." Still other preachers used more careful language, but implied an elitist posture by their references to the advantages available to pentecostals; those of us full of the Spirit had a leg up on those not yet filled with the Spirit and those uninterested in or antagonistic to life in the Spirit. Such talk made it difficult for many pentecostals to acknowledge diversity.

So what changed? How did I (and others) move toward convergence? The first and most important opening for a more inclusive worldview begins with relationship. Three years at Providence Seminary in Otterburne, Manitoba, gave rise to several lifelong friendships with Mennonite faculty members and classroom peers. Though I remain grateful for my grassroots pentecostal heritage with our emphasis on the Spirit-filled life and experience, I discovered similar passion with different verbiage and thus began a nascent appreciation of my Mennonite friends. This set in motion an earnest study of John Howard Yoder's theology, and I stumbled on a seldom-cited statement that would lead me to reevaluate and enlarge my pentecostal worldview. According to Yoder,

> Within or beside apostate churches, He raises up in every age new movements of protest, witness, and fellowship. These "free churches" are marked by the duress which gave them birth: socially unbalanced, theologically unbalanced, poor, strangely structured, given to false starts and exaggeration—and of such is the Kingdom of Heaven.

He continues:

> Pentecostalism is in our century the closest parallel to what Anabaptism was in the sixteenth: expanding so vigorously that it bursts the bonds of its own thinking about church order, living from the multiple gifts of the spirit in the total church while holding leaders in great respect, unembarrassed by the language of the layman and the aesthetic tastes of the poor, mobile, zealously single-minded. We can easily note the flaws in Pentecostal theology, organization, or even ethics—very similar, by the way, to the faults of the early Quakers and Anabaptists, or of the apostolic churches—but meanwhile they are out being the Church.[1]

Mennonites spoke of the prophetic life not primarily in the sense of utterance gifts, but as a counter-cultural worldview. Their activism looked so much like the response craved by the Old Testament prophets and mirrored the early church's response to dire needs in the days after Pentecost. And in their *nachfolge* ("following after" Jesus), Mennonites sought to reenact a prophetic ethic akin to Jesus' focus on the poor, the captives, the blind, and the oppressed, all of these groups in desperate need of immediate Jubilee (Luke 4:18–19). And who can ignore the historic willingness of Mennonites to stand against the powers by way of the lowly cross? Mennonites brought together the triumph and tragedy of the Gospel. Life in the Spirit proved to be an all-encompassing life. These ideas took root in a paper I wrote some time ago entitled "My Life as a Mennocostal."

Years later, Brian contacted me about using this essay for a collection of similar stories. Instead, I volunteered to write a new chapter, a sequel to the first. I also implored him to allow me to serve as co-editor of this volume. I am grateful that he obliged me. Brian and I sought pentecostal contributors who would embody this message. As we pursued Mennonite contributors, Brian and I discovered in many ways a parallel reversal.

1. Yoder, "Marginalia," 78.

Mennonites committed to their worldview encountered pentecostals and found their lives equally enriched.

In our quest for contributors, Brian and I sought diversity. We are undoubtedly pleased with the combination of academicians and pastors, theologians and practitioners. The missionary experiences of Rick Waldrop and Ryan Gladwin in Latin America and Gerald Shenk in Croatia take readers outside a North American context. We are also delighted by official institutional reflections offered by César García, General Secretary of the Mennonite World Fellowship, and Tony Richie, not only a renowned ecumenist and local pastor, but a leading representative for the Church of God (Cleveland, TN) to the Mennonite/pentecostal dialogue. We also stumbled on the playful yet provocative literature of Natasha Wiebe; she wrote mennocostal stories well ahead of our first connection. Still others began in one tradition and migrated to the other or took the best of both to yet another tradition. Jay Beaman discovers the pacifistic heritage of pentecostals and settles among Mennonites. Brian begins among pentecostals, works for an extended season with Evangelicals for Social Action, and winds up with Mennonite Disaster Service. Matthew Paugh, our Metho-mennocostal, grows up pentecostal, receives his undergrad education at Messiah College (Brethren in Christ) and graduate degree from the Assemblies of God Theological Seminary, and eventually finds a home (at least for now) in the Methodist church. Finally, we include a chapter by Menno Simons (1496–1561), the founder from whom Mennonites would take their name. Simons wrote a moving sermon that could have easily been proclaimed in a modern pentecostal context. In the spirit of Yoder's commentary cited above, we believe this sermon remains vitally important for both Mennonite and pentecostal contexts. For this reason, we see his exhortation as a fitting conclusion to this volume.[2]

Having said this, I must share of our dismay concerning our lack of further diversity. We sought yet failed to secure additional gender, ethnic, and global south diversity. Though we found tremendous interest and support for the project, several people rejected our offer due primarily to previous commitments. I hope this volume inspires some of them—and other mennocostals—to create space for their stories among their publications.

2. Menno Simons, "Holy Apostles." Like Yoder, Menno Simons speaks of Anabaptist pneumatology in a manner not unlike that of twentieth-century pentecostals. I am grateful to Jay Beaman for first directing me to this "sermon."

On the matter of contributors, I would like to acknowledge one further person committed to this project, but not able to complete his essay. With great admiration, we dedicate this work to the late Alan Krieder. I remember the day he called to tell me about the terminal diagnosis. Alan had cancer. I and several other contributors to this project were getting to know him as a passionate ecumenist. He had only recently found kindred spirits among many at the Society for Pentecostal Studies. Though he and I began to strategize an inaugural mennocostal gathering in Elkhart, Indiana, his failing health required the postponement of this meeting. Though he and I talked passionately about his forthcoming essay on mennocostal convergence in the early church fathers, he passed away on May 8, 2017. We not only suffered the loss of an emerging Mennonite voice among pentecostals, but we grieve the loss of a gentle and loving friend. We honor the life and work of Alan Krieder.

Concerning the order of the chapters, we settled on a rather simple structure. Though we generally alternate between pentecostal and Mennonite contributors, the story-shaped nature of these narratives should not necessarily require readers to mark through the volume in a linear fashion. Having said this, we also trust that the cumulative effect of the chapters produces a coherent and plausible conclusion to the theologies and practice of our fellow mennocostals.

As you prepare to read these chapters, I must delve one more time into my pentecostal heritage. I encourage our readers to reflect upon these essays through the genre of testimony. Pentecostals view the art of testimony as a critical component of the gathered assembly. Testimonies instruct. They carry exegetical, thematic, and practical import for the people of God. Testimonies serve a liturgical purpose. Though many outsiders hear the name "pentecostal" and think first of vibrant worship, prayer, and spontaneity, testimonies prove utterly liturgical. They give rise to praise and perseverance and call listeners to an active faith. In like manner, I trust these essays testify to the role of *personal* transformation through convergence between Mennonites and pentecostals. And of course, these stories serve not only to recount individual stories, but witness—dare I say prophesy—to a growing chorus, that is to collective voices committed to the best of both traditions. Perhaps these testimonies will give us pause to hear "what the Spirit is saying to our churches." Could it be that people of the Spirit, both Mennonites and pentecostals, have a word from the Lord to and from one another? And could it be that members of both traditions not only speak to one another, but already embody integral elements of the other? Could it be that our shared views might give rise to common witness? Brian and I trust you will answer these questions in the affirmative!

Pentecost 2018

BIBLIOGRAPHY

Mittelstadt, Martin W. "My Life as a Mennocostal: A Personal and Theological Narrative." In *Pentecostals and Nonviolence: Reclaiming a Heritage*, edited by Paul Alexander, 333–51. Eugene, OR: Pickwick, 2012.

Simons, Menno. "How the Holy Apostles Practiced Baptism in Water." *Menno Simons.net.* Edited by Machiel van Zanten. https://mennosimons.net/ft096-apostles.html.

Yoder, John Howard. "Marginalia." *Concern for Christian Renewal* 15 (1967) 77–80.

1

Mennocostals in a Contextual Way

César García

It was 6:30 am when we began to pray. A well-known Colombian Mennonite pastor laid hands on me and cried out to God for my healing. A few days before, a doctor had found a tumor in my esophagus, the culmination of living for fourteen years with precancerous esophagitis involving various stomach ulcers plus a hiatal hernia. Now a tumor! Lord have mercy!

Several weeks later, sitting in the same doctor's office, she exclaimed what my skeptical mind could not believe or explain—the tumor, the esophagitis, the ulcers, and the hiatal hernia had all disappeared. Gone! "There is no medical or scientific explanation," the specialist said. "What we now see is impossible. There is nothing wrong with you. You need no further treatment and there is no need to continue with regular check-ups."

This was the specialist's conclusion after consulting with a committee of peers. Fourteen years of pain and strict care had disappeared, just like that. It made no sense, yet how could I deny being the recipient of such divine love and power? With thousands of other Mennonites in contexts of suffering and violence, I experienced God working a miracle in my life, a spectacular miracle, if I may say, in a service more akin to a pentecostal church. God had performed a miracle in my life, one more among so many that I have witnessed along with my spiritual journey. "Mennocostal"— pentecostal Mennonites—may be the best characterization of the majority of Anabaptists in the Majority World today.[1] The influence of pentecostalism in Mennonite congregations in this part of the world is an overwhelming reality. In their recent study of Mennonite World Conference churches, Conrad Kanagy, Elizabeth Miller, and John D. Roth conclude "One of the defining differences between Mennonite World Conference members in the Global North and the Global South is their experience of the charismatic gifts of the Holy Spirit, with Europeans and North Americans much less likely to identify with these experiences . . . pentecostalism is the most rapidly growing expression of Christianity in the world, and Anabaptists are not foreigners to this reality."[2]

While each church experience is unique and is closely linked to each specific context, there are three defining characteristics of Mennocostals in the Majority World. In addition, there are significant implications of being filled with the Spirit for Mennocostals living in contexts characterized by suffering and violence, contexts like Colombia.

LIFE IN THE SPIRIT MEANS TO BE CHRIST-CENTERED

A few years ago I found myself sharing Christ with a young university student. I used all the philosophical and logical reasoning possible to leave him without any excuse for not becoming a Christian. My strategy, however, did not work. Much later I came to understand that he needed more than theoretical reasoning, but rather a testimony of an authentic relationship with Jesus.

Analysts have described Colombian society as one where relationships are valued more highly than the logical and abstract reasoning or rational philosophical arguments so prized in debate, dialogue, and academia. This is most likely one of the reasons why Latin American culture, in general, has been categorized as relationship-based.[3] For Colombians, this characteristic can be summed up in the words of Spanish philosopher Miguel de Unamuno, "The letter is dead; in the letter you cannot look for life."[4] As a result, philosophy, laws, and theoretical knowledge are viewed as

---

1. "Majority World" refers to what in other contexts might be called the Global South. The "Majority World" includes Asian and European countries not geographically in the Global South, but similar in location according to infrastructure and economics.

2. Kanagy et al., *Global Anabaptist Profile*, 23.

3. Skidmore and Smith, *Modern Latin America*, 454.

4. Unamuno, *Agonía Del Cristianismo*, 101.

boring and of little use. As Colombians, we prefer celebration over study, and improvisation over research.[5]

While various evangelical denominations and independent churches emphasize and even require cognitive assent to creeds and intellectual affirmation of doctrines as necessary to enter Christian faith,[6] in contexts characterized by suffering and violence, like that of Colombia, Mennocostals emphasize a relationship with God that flows from a personal encounter with and experience of Christ. Theology and doctrine emerge as a second step that follows reflection on Christian experience and practice. Miroslav Volf concurs:

> People come to believe either because they find themselves already engaged in Christian practices (say, by being raised in a Christian home) or because they are attracted to them. In most cases, Christian practices come first and Christian beliefs follow—rather, beliefs are already entailed in practices, so that their explicit espousing becomes a matter of bringing to consciousness what is implicit in the engagement in practices themselves.[7]

Thus, while intellectual doctrinal assent and theoretical study are important for Mennocostals, they do not take first place in the worship and life of the church as they do in more conservative protestant Christian traditions.[8] "Sound doctrine"—*orthodoxy*—moves to a second plane (without implying that it loses importance) in order to give way to the search for "sound practice"—*orthopraxis*.

This emphasis on a personal experience with Christ and a vibrant spiritual relationship with God diverges from other pentecostal traditions in that Mennocostals' entire experience is evaluated in light of Jesus's life and teachings as seen in the Gospels. Imitation of Christ—his character, mission and priorities—constitutes their sound practice, their orthopraxis. Christ-centered discipleship, understood as following Jesus within a personal relationship with him, avoids the excesses and blurring observed in pentecostal streams that give primacy to experience over Scripture.

Some of these excesses are rooted in a "Theology of Glory," with its image of God as a distant, steadfast, and impassive God, free of pain and suffering, who is more comparable to a powerful monarch than a poor,

5. Puyana, *¿Cómo Somos?*, 31.

6. Bidegaín Greising and Demera Vargas, *Globalización Y Diversidad*, 258.

7. Volf, *Captive to the Word of God*, 52–53.

8. Bidegaín Greising and Demera Vargas, *Globalización Y Diversidad*, 260.

first-century carpenter. If the Jesus of the Gospels is not the center of all experience, then forms of worship and ideas about God easily emerge that do not reflect the God revealed in the person of Jesus Christ. Mennocostals' orthopraxis helps them evade this error.

The towering, twentieth-century German Protestant theologian Karl Barth insisted that when Christianity is solely based on experience, the question arises whether faith has become a purely human endeavor and God a purely human projection.[9] As Canadian theologian Douglas John Hall asserts, "Neither nature nor rationality nor experience leads the soul to conclude that the Absolute is merciful."[10] Yet the God who is revealed in Jesus Christ is astonishingly compassionate. The revealed God rescues us from our egocentric, self-centered, and consumerist way of living and resituates us in a life of renunciation, forgiveness, and love for the well-being of our communities, our societies, and even our enemies.

When Colombian Mennonites place emphasis on experience in contexts of suffering, the Bible takes its fundamental place: Mennocostals perceive the Bible to be a script that shows how to live out the teaching of Jesus in such a context. This is how they convert the Sacred Text from a propositional revelation into a constant faith practice. In a country where political discourse denies the possibility of diversity and where people who have different opinions are not respected,[11] viewing the Bible as a series of verifiable and absolute truths may not prove very useful at best, and dangerous at worst because that approach can lead to the use of violence against those who think differently. As John Roth explains, "claims to absolute certainty about faith—as expressed in carefully formulated systematic statements—could easily provide a rationale for condemning to hell all those who disagreed."[12]

For Mennocostals, a living relationship with Jesus Christ marked by experience beyond propositional truths places Scripture in the center of daily practice in a manner that accepts and promotes pluralism as part of the Gospel and that is congruent with the life and teaching of Christ. In the Colombian context, where tolerance in general is lacking,[13] using pluralism as epistemology "is not a counsel of despair but part of the Good News.

9. Karl Barth cited in Vanhoozer, *Cambridge Companion*, 30.

10. Hall, *Cross in Our Context*, 23.

11. Sánchez and Peñaranda, *Pasado Y Presente*, 394.

12. Roth, *Beliefs*, 30–31.

13. Comacho Guizado and Gutiérrez, *Álvaro Camacho Guizado*, 86–88.

"Ultimate validation is a matter not of a reasoning process . . . but of the concrete social genuineness of the community's reasoning together in the Spirit," affirms John Howard Yoder.[14]

Such pluralism finds its origin in the presence of a community, without which it would be impossible to grow in and with Christ. Our mutual experience with Jesus enriches and completes the experience of all the other members. In so doing, the priesthood of all believers and the interdependent expression of the gifts of the Spirit prove central and natural to daily life. This is countercultural in and of itself. The affirmation of life in community serves as an alternative lifestyle in Colombia, where society is profoundly individualistic.[15]

Individualism in Colombia is ubiquitous and is one of the reasons for the lack of national unity, solidarity, social consciousness, and consensus in moments when a unified community response is so urgently needed.[16] According to leading Latin American historian Marco Palacios, younger generations have lost interest in social change and utopias and express their non-conformity "by staying away from the polls and affirming the values of personal autonomy and growth."[17]

The centrality of community in the Mennonite faith experience leads to a new society, and an alternative to one that promotes individualism. Relationships in this community are marked by compassion and forgiveness as witnessed in the person of Jesus. This also calls for us to care for those around us, whether they belong to our community or not. In contexts such as Colombia, Mennocostals not only offer an alternative society, but we are actively involved in the larger well-being of our country, all of this as witness to God's love for the world. Thus, mennocostal communities also understand themselves to be called to actively be a people of reconciliation.

LIFE IN THE SPIRIT MEANS WORKING TOWARDS RECONCILIATION

Newscasts in Colombia are an interesting mix of news and sports, along with a daily dose on the lives of the rich and famous. Sports and gossip follow seamlessly after a report on a tragic event of violence and destruction,

14. Yoder et al., *Pacifist Way of Knowing*, 88.

15. Skidmore and Smith, *Modern Latin America*, 253.

16. Puyana, *¿Cómo Somos?*, 43.

17. Palacios, *Between Legitimacy and Violence*, 239.

and can often take up more time than the tragic news story that preceded. Amnesia is a hallmark of the Colombian survival, a built-in "ability" to forget and escape reality. *"Colombia se derrumba y nosotros de rumba"* (*While Colombia collapses, we party*), is a popular saying that sums up the tendency to want to ignore the suffering that afflicts us. Sports, soap operas, and beauty pageants are some of the ways in which we try to escape.[18]

Palacios explains that "Colombia offers one of the worst pictures of income distribution in Latin America, and therefore the world."[19] Economic inequality, political exclusion, and land distribution remain critical issues in Colombia. These plus the lack of opportunities have been some of the reasons for the formation of revolutionary and guerilla groups since the middle of the twentieth century.[20]

Some 4,000 political leaders have been assassinated over the last 40 years and more than 6 million people have been displaced. According to the National Historical Memory Centre, approximately 70,000 people have disappeared in violent ways.[21] Colombia remains a region of ongoing war,[22] where violence is not limited to the armed conflict. Violence permeates every sphere of society in domestic relationships, education, business, and politics.

Therefore, many people use churches as an escape mechanism in this context. Colombian Catholic theologian Jaime Laurence Bonilla suggests the response to suffering and the needs of others in countless churches is one of indifference.[23] With few exceptions, the mega churches of the large cities have no social programs and do not provide support to people in extreme need.[24] Issues of social justice are almost non-existent in such congregations. Though certain preachers frequently promise instant financial success, they fail to consider the importance of holistic transformation for the person as well as their immediate environment. These churches reject the Christian hope that Jürgen Moltmann describes as refusing to accept things "as they happen to stand or to lie, but as progressing, moving things

18. Palacios, *Between Legitimacy and Violence*, 239.

19. Palacios, *Between Legitimacy and Violence*, 218.

20. Comacho Guizado and Gutiérrez, *Álvaro Camacho Guizado*, 268.

21. See Centro Nacional de Memoria Histórica, "Inicio."

22. Sánchez and Peñaranda, *Pasado y Presente*, 17.

23. Jaime Laurence Bonilla in González Santos, *Memorias del Primer Congreso Internacional*, 153.

24. Beltran Cely, *Microempresas Religiosas*, 190.

with possibilities of change."[25] As a result, many of these churches end up giving their unconditional and unquestioning support to the dominant political system.[26]

The Pew Research Center explains: "When asked what they think is the most important way for Christians to help the poor, Catholics in nearly every Latin American country point most often to charity work. By contrast, pluralities of Protestants in many countries say that 'bringing the poor and needy to Christ' is the most important way to help."[27] This understanding of the Church's role in relation to society results in delegating the Church's responsibility to charity agencies, spiritualizing that responsibility, and even supporting political parties without being aware that these political organizations may ignore or even contradict Christian values.

Given the above mentioned reality, Mennocostals in Colombia attempt to respond to their context inspired by the call they have received to be a reconciling people. From their point of view, this call is put into practice through social development ministry, peacebuilding, and restorative justice. With respect to social development, Mennocostals have clearly embraced a preferential option for the poor. Most congregations can be found in the midst of vulnerable populations located in low-income areas. Many have been displaced by the violence or have been directly affected by the civil war that has plagued Colombia for over five decades. Colombian Mennonites have founded church agencies that specialize in community development, but even so, the social responsibility of churches continues to be lived out via soup kitchens, free education, micro loans, cooperatives, and geriatric care. The gift of service is cultivated and social service seeks to involve the whole community, especially during times of natural disaster. Mennocostals understand that all social work is rooted in a personal relationship with God, guided by the Holy Spirit, with a goal to reach people regardless of whether they accept Christ or not, and without promotion of a specific church.

Mennocostals are also committed to peacebuilding. They depend on the Holy Spirit to inspire a new society characterized by forgiveness and reconciliation. Being peacebuilders in this context is not limited to, but does include, resolving political conflicts through the work of specialists and/or church agencies. The local congregation is a central pillar where

25. Moltmann, *Theology of Hope*, 25.

26. Cepeda van Houten, *Clientelismo y Fe*, 17.

27. Pew Research Center, "Religion in Latin America."

7

members learn to resolve conflict in their marriages, at school, at work, and in their neighborhood in a Christ-like way. When Mennocostals celebrate these attempts, they believe that peacebuilding in the footsteps of Jesus takes on certain dimensions that require being filled with the Holy Spirit:

Take the first step towards reconciliation. Whether the victim or the aggressor, the Holy Spirit inspires reconciliation with the other (Romans 12:18). Love the enemy. Jesus invites us to pray for those who persecute us (Matthew 5.44), seek the well-being of our enemies by serving them (Romans 12:20), and repay evil with good (Romans 12:17). Forgive those who offend us. This is a willingness to come to terms with the damage caused by an enemy without seeking revenge or retribution (Matthew 18:23–35). Embrace suffering. To renounce our own interests, well-being, or rights in order to act for the good of our enemies may result in our own loss (1 Pet 2:19–23).

Mennocostals in Colombia share C. Norman Kraus's position on restorative justice. He argues that Jesus regarded retributive justice as the same as revenge, and that he fully rejected retaliation as a valid motive or principle for justice.[28] This approach to justice is of vital importance in Colombia in so far as *impunity* is one of the roots and expressions of violence in the country.[29] This impunity is evidenced in the innumerable cases that wait to be defined in the courts and in the levels of corruption found in the judicial system. In addition, the norm in several previous peace processes has been to offer blanket amnesty to criminals as a way of obliterating their crimes.[30]

These amnesties, affirm Sánchez and Peñaranda, have not brought peace to Colombia. Instead, they have been converted into impunity for war criminals and human rights violators. This form of justice has left Colombians with a deep sense of injustice that in turn has fuelled new stages of violence.[31] The damage and pain produced by so much violence and suffering is not easily alleviated. Those who have suffered under the lack of opportunities and social inequality desire a *distributive justice* that asserts their rights. Many who have lost loved ones to the violence yearn for the impunity of the Colombian government to end, and for their aggressors to "get what's coming to them"—in other words, *retributive justice*. Much

28. Kraus, *Using Scripture in a Global Age*, 93.

29. See Sánchez and Peñaranda, *Pasado y Presente*, 390.

30. Chernick, *Acuerdo Posible*, 27.

31. Chernick, *Acuerdo Posible*, 208.

of this discourse and the many demands that accompany it are expressed and carried out in ways that exhibit and fuel resentment and bitterness. At times, the demand that others pay for what they have done along with the actual content of the discourse is in itself violent.

Mennocostals seek *distributive justice* among their members. They are people who have voluntarily decided to share their possessions with the most needy. They are local congregations that do not believe in retributive justice because they have experienced another type of justice amongst themselves—that of *compassion*. They are communities that follow Jesus because they have understood that Christ's teachings and ministry have shown us what justice looks like in every dimension of human life[32]. They are communities that have found new energy and hope for overcoming pain and violence as a result of their experience with God by responding with forgiveness and love.

Mennonites in Colombia seek justice in contexts characterized by violence and oppression. They exemplify the life of Jesus in the following manner; they choose to side with the most needy. From their inception, Anabaptists have maintained a close relationship with people in contexts of suffering and oppression, people crying out for justice and equity. This can be seen, for example, in the Twelve Articles of the German Peasant's War of 1525.[33] As Goldewijk says, "the need to unite the exercise of power among humans with norms about human dignity is as old as society itself."[34] To follow Jesus in the search for justice in Colombia means walking with those who are victims of inequity and the unequal distribution of wealth.

Practice mercy, love, and compassion. Jesus shows us that justice does not mean meting out what the other deserves. Justice has nothing to do with rewards and punishments, but rather means giving the other what they need: love, compassion, and mercy. "Justice and mercy are not opposites. On the contrary, it is only through mercy that justice can be achieved in people affected by criminal misconduct. Justice includes mercy, and mercy includes justice."[35]

Compassion applied in the context of justice is precisely what is known today as *restorative justice*. Christopher Marshall concludes that, from a Gospel perspective, "restorative justice can be catalogued as *compassionate*

---

32. Heltzel, "Holy Spirit of Justice," 44.

33. Driver, *La Fe en la Periferia de la Historia*, 162–63.

34. Goldewijk and Fortman, *Where Needs Meet Rights*, 3.

35. Marshall, *Compassionate Justice*, loc. 8205.

justice."[36] Mennocostals understand this justice is not to be limited to judicial courts, but practiced by parents, educators, employers, and employees to manifest justice in the church and society at large.

Peace and justice are the cornerstones of Mennocostals' reconciliation ministries as they respond to their Colombian context. This context also requires a change in the leadership style present in every sphere of our Latin American culture.

A LIFE GUIDED BY THE SPIRIT MEANS SERVING UNDER THE CROSS

One of the most disconcerting experiences for many pastors in Colombia is to be identified as an Evangelical Christian pastor. Someone once asked me, "Are you a pastor?" "That's right," I nervously responded. As I feared, the immediate response was, "Then you rob people of their money! You likely have a brand-new car, a very luxurious house and many bodyguards to protect you from everyone else, right? Tell me, what else do you do besides get rich and abuse others?" Ouch! How could I respond in the face of the overwhelming abundance of cases that support the validity of such claims? Unfortunately, too many Colombians have been cheated and hurt by *caudillo*-style leaders in Christian congregations. The *caudillo* is an important component of political and religious leadership in Latin America. It is a leadership style defined by authoritarianism and power concentration in one person only. It is in stark contrast to a participatory leadership style, where teamwork is valued over an individualistic approach.

This tendency among religious leaders in Colombia is reflected in the idea that pastors possess special, almost magical qualities that enable them to carry out their ministries in ways not available to congregants.[37] The concentration and abuse of power among Latin American Protestants and Evangelicals reflects this cultural characteristic.[38] For *caudillo*-style leaders, the laws and the Constitution of Colombia do not apply because the will of the *caudillo* is the real constitution. They do not follow democratic norms and limits.[39]

---

36. Marshall, *Compassionate Justice*, loc. 8270.
37. Gutiérrez de Pineda, *Familia y Cultura en Colombia*, 390–91.
38. Núñez, *Crisis and Hope*, 214.
39. Sáenz, *Caudillos*, 12, 23.

This is reinforced by the fact that Colombians typically default to leaders.[40] For example, the election history of the recent past reveals that some people vote according to how charismatic the candidate is, how they respond to the media, and what they look like. Programmatic questions and political ideology are not relevant for some Colombians when deciding which candidate to support.

Unfortunately, this cultural reality is sadly present among Latin American church leaders and raises the question as to how mennocostal leaders understand and carry out their ministries in Latin America. Following an Anabaptist heritage, Mennocostals understand that the Church must witness to societal models that demonstrate God's intent for human beings. Such models must offer leadership alternatives that counter the disastrous and ongoing Columbian story of abusive power.[41]

CONCLUSION

Colombian Mennocostals must frame ministry by a theology of the cross, where they depend on the presence of the Holy Spirit to refuse to adopt the dominant, consumptive worldview that surrounds them. Mennocostals must understand that God-given gifts must be relegated not only, or even primarily, for personal use and advantage, but for the well-being of the community. Once again, the simplicity of Jesus's life coupled with his teaching continues to be a relevant challenge in contexts marked by economic inequity, like Colombia.

Finally, in contexts of suffering and violence, of inequality and injustice, I suggest that the consummate mennocostal exemplifies the strengths of both Mennonites and pentecostals, and in so doing we preach and teach Jesus, the one who responds to violence and suffering with wholeness and hope. We need the Spirit given by Jesus to pray, worship, and live out our faith in the midst of our own weaknesses, limitations, and challenges. I am grateful for our shared experience of Jesus, and our mutual traditions. May God help us carry out a mennocostal mission!

40. Puyana, ¿Cómo Somos?, 32.
41. Bidegaín Greising and Demera Vargas, Globalización y Diversidad, 277.

BIBLIOGRAPHY

Beltran Cely, William Mauricio. *De Microempresas Religiosas a Multinacionales de la Fe: La Diversificación del Cristianismo en Bogotá*. Bogotá: Universidad de San Buenaventura, 2006.

Bidegaín Greising, Ana María, and Juan Diego Demera Vargas. *Globalización y Diversidad Religiosa en Colombia*. Bogotá: Universidad Nacional de Colombia, Facultad de Ciencias Humanas, 2005.

Camacho Guizado, Álvaro, and Alberto Valencia Gutiérrez. *Álvaro Camacho Guizado: Violencia y Conflicto en Colombia*. Bogotá: Universidad de los Andes, 2014.

Centro Nacional de Memoria Hisórica. "Inicio." http://www.centrodememoriahistorica.gov.co.

Cepeda van Houten, Alvaro. *Clientelismo y Fe: Dinámicas Políticas del Pentecostalismo en Colombia*. Bogotá: Universidad de San Buenaventura, 2007.

Chernick, Marc. *Acuerdo Posible: Solución Negociada Al Conflicto Armado Colombiano*. Translated from English. 3rd ed. Bogotá: Ediciones Aurora, 2015.

Driver, John. *La Fe En La Periferia De La Historia: Una Historia Del Pueblo Cristiano Desde La Perspectiva De Los Movimientos De Restauración Y Reforma Radical*. Colección Historia Abierta. Cd. Guatemala, Guatemala: Ediciones SEMILLA, 1997.

Goldewijk, Berma Klein, and Bastiaan de Gaay Fortman. *Where Needs Meet Rights: Economic, Social and Cultural Rights in a New Perspective*. Geneva: WCC, 1999.

González Santos, Andrés Eduardo. *Memorias Del Primer Congreso Internacional "Diversidad Y Dinámicas Del Cristianismo En América Latina."* Bogotá: Editorial Bonaventuriana, 2007.

Gutiérrez de Pineda, Virginia. *Familia y Cultura en Colombia: Tipologías, Funciones y Dinámica de la Familia: Manifestaciones Múltiples a Través del Mosaico Cultural y Sus Estructuras Sociales*. 4th ed. Medellín: Universidad de Antioquia, 1996.

Hall, Douglas John. *The Cross in Our Context: Jesus and the Suffering World*. Minneapolis: Fortress, 2003.

Heltzel, Peter Goodwin. "The Holy Spirit of Justice." In *The Justice Project*, edited by Brian McLaren, et al., 44–50. Grand Rapids: Baker, 2009.

Kanagy, Conrad, et al. *Global Anabaptist Profile: Belief and Practice in 24 Mennonite World Conference Churches*. Goshen, IN: Institute for the Study of Global Anabaptism Goshen College, 2017.

Kraus, C. Norman. *Using Scripture in a Global Age: Framing Biblical Issues*. Institute of Mennonite Studies Occasional Papers. Scottdale, PA: Herald, 2006.

Marshall, Christopher D. *Compassionate Justice: An Interdisciplinary Dialogue with Two Gospel Parables on Law, Crime, and Restorative Justice*. Theopolitical Visions. Eugene, OR: Cascade, 2012. Ebook.

Moltmann, Jürgen. *Theology of Hope: On the Ground and the Implications of a Christian Eschatology*. Minneapolis: Fortress, 1993.

Núñez C., Emilio Antonio. *Crisis and Hope in Latin America: An Evangelical Perspective*. Rev. ed. Pasadena, CA: William Carey, 1996.

Palacios, Marco. *Between Legitimacy and Violence: A History of Colombia, 1875–2002*. Durham: Duke University Press, 2006.

Pew Research Center. "Religion in Latin America." *Pew Research Center*, November 13, 2014. http://www.pewforum.org/2014/11/13/religion-in-latin-america.

Puyana, Germán. ¿Cómo Somos?: Los Colombianos: Reflexiones Sobre Nuestra Idiosincrasia Y Cultura. 3rd ed. Bogotá: Panamericana, 2005.

Roth, John D. Beliefs: Mennonite Faith and Practice. Scottdale, PA: Herald, 2005.

Sáenz, Mauricio. Caudillos: En América Latina Nada Ha Cambiado En Doscientos Años. Bogotá: Panamericana, 2010.

Sánchez, Gonzalo, and Ricardo Peñaranda. Pasado Y Presente De La Violencia En Colombia. 3rd ed. Medellín: La Carreta Editores EU, 2015.

Skidmore, Thomas E., and Peter H. Smith. Modern Latin America. 6th ed. New York: Oxford University Press, 2005.

Unamuno, Miguel de. La Agonía Del Cristianismo. Madrid: Espasa Calpe, SA, 1942.

Vanhoozer, Kevin J. The Cambridge Companion to Postmodern Theology. Cambridge Companions to Religion. Cambridge, UK: Cambridge University Press, 2003.

Volf, Miroslav. Captive to the Word of God: Engaging the Scriptures for Contemporary Theological Reflection. Grand Rapids: Eerdmans, 2010.

Yoder, John Howard, et al. A Pacifist Way of Knowing: John Howard Yoder's Nonviolent Epistemology. Eugene, OR: Cascade, 2010.

2

Reading Luke-Acts as a Mennocostal

Pentecostals, Mennonites, and the Prophethood
of All Believers

MARTIN W. MITTELSTADT

I AM A CRADLE pentecostal. As a young boy, I loved to read, hear, and experience biblical stories. Like many pentecostal children, I would picture myself standing in a crowd to listen to the parables of Jesus, climbing a tree like Zacchaeus, or singing hymns in prison with Paul and Silas. I learned early that these stories were somehow my stories, a continuation of the gospel. In this essay, I reflect upon my spiritual and academic formation from my years as a young college student, to a wannabe theologian, and to a mature scholar (at least in my own eyes). After decades of passion and energy given to biblical studies, I remain a pentecostal (not begrudgingly), but I also embrace the designation "mennocostal."[1] For this emerging identity, I must thank (or blame) Pastor Luke, possibly the most important voice in my formation. In the following narrative, I recount the impact of many years of reading, writing, and reflecting on Luke-Acts, particularly through the lens of various pentecostal and Mennonite scholars, who, unbeknownst to them, contributed to my ever-evolving mennocostal worldview.

1. Mittelstadt, "My Life as a Mennocostal."

Though much has changed from the day I enrolled in a small Canadian pentecostal college in 1982, I begin with a summary of the primary scholarly voices to shape my early years. My initial exposure to methodologies for biblical interpretation would both jumpstart and stunt my reading of scripture. Second, I choose to reject, if only for a moment, the advice I regularly give to my students; I succumb to an oversimplified use of Luke-Acts by applying oft-held stereotypes, namely the correlation of pentecostals to spirit and Mennonites to peace. I reflect upon two scholars, Roger Stronstad and John Howard Yoder, both of whom produced monumental contributions to their respective traditions (and beyond). Third, I turn to Luke Timothy Johnson, whose scholarship has helped me piece together the mennocostal puzzle. In his *Prophetic Jesus and Prophetic Church*, Johnson, a Catholic, captures well both the Stronstadian Jesus of the Spirit and the Yoderian Jesus of peace and justice. Fourth, I reflect upon my continuing formation by way of Mennonite and pentecostal contributions to Lukan scholarship. Along the way, I draw not only on pentecostal and Mennonite scholars, but on others who enlarged my mennocostal worldview. Finally, I conclude with an open invitation for ongoing pentecostal and Mennonite convergence.

TWENTIETH-CENTURY FISTICUFFS: MORE OR LESS HISTORY?

My introduction to biblical studies came at the height of historical criticism. As I entered college in the early 1980s, a full century of scholarship on the historical (un)reliability of the Gospels and Acts had surely fulfilled John's declaration "that the whole world does not have room for the books that would be written on the life of *historical* Jesus" (John 21:25, slightly modified). Dissertations, monographs, and textbooks filled libraries on topics such as source criticism (who used what?), form criticism (what's the raw form of any story?), synoptic studies (what might Mark and Q have to do with Luke and Matthew?), and redaction criticism (how did editors cut and paste their stories?). On the one hand, certain scholars called for increasing suspicion regarding the historical plausibility of the New Testament. Many of these same scholars worked tirelessly to undermine the credibility of scholars who chose to "err" on the side of historical reliability. On the other hand, twentieth-century "evangelical" scholars engaged in a spirited defense of early Christian historicity. It is here where I encountered my first predicament.

Initially, this debate proved overwhelming. My pentecostal pastors and Sunday school teachers never mentioned hermeneutical questions concerning historical reliability. Espousing the adage akin to "the Bible said it, I believe it, and that settles it for me," my pastors and teachers had either resolved the issue for themselves and felt no need to enlighten me, or they were not even familiar with the academic fisticuffs. Fortunately, at least as I understood things at that time, my professors steeped in evangelical hermeneutics walked me through this tumultuous period. Thus, the primary goal of my synoptic gospels course was to slither through A. T. Robertson's *Harmony of the Gospels* to properly reconstruct the life of Jesus.[2] In an Acts course, I tackled F. F. Bruce's *Acts*, the go-to commentary of evangelicals and pentecostals (sigh) primarily for his defense of Luke the historian.

Though my pentecostal professors (trained by evangelicals) saved me from the "evil liberals," I stumbled to the next quandary. This time I found myself standing before an insider, a pentecostal. Gordon Fee, a theological father to many academicians in the pentecostal tradition and a premier Pauline theologian, turned my world upside down. In his *How to Read the Bible For All Its Worth*, co-authored with Douglas Stuart, Fee "conceded" pentecostal methodology to the growing evangelical perspective. Though Fee continued to defend historical reliability, he expressed strong concerns over "normativity," that is, the idea that writers of biblical narrative would expect normative theologies and practices to be gleaned by readers. Fee wrestled with the "Question of Historical Precedent" and produced a controversial conclusion. At best, he would only acknowledge that "biblical precedents may sometimes be regarded as repeatable patterns—even if they are not understood to be normative." This chapter received not a little bit of attention among pentecostals.[3]

Before moving on, I must comment briefly on the contributions of two further "Evangelicals" (they're Anglican but cherished by Evangelicals), who published their inaugural monographs in 1970. James Dunn, in his *Baptism in the Spirit*, sounded like an earlier version of Fee. Dunn's resistance to the didactic value of biblical narrative pushed pentecostals to

2. See Robertson, *Harmony of the Gospels*.

3. Fee and Stuart, *How to Read the Bible*; Mittelstadt, *Reading Luke-Acts in the Pentecostal Tradition*.

the brink; since Luke comes off as a fanatic (Dunn's preferred term is "enthusiastic" and reminiscent of pentecostals), readers must turn to Paul the teacher for guidance on life of the Spirit. Luke's use of Spirit must agree or succumb to Paul's use of similar language. I. Howard Marshall, on the other hand, declared that Luke should be read as historian *and* theologian. Marshall maintained that "Luke has a theological interest [and] his narratives, though they are historical, are always more than . . . the record of brute facts."[4] Though Dunn and Fee run a different course than Marshall, these three men would impact the journey of many pentecostals and Mennonites.

By the mid-1980s, I had concluded (with the help of my professors) that the biblical narratives as recorded in the Scriptures proved to be historically accurate. I survived (sigh) and came to appreciate the historical accuracy, if not yet the literary artistry, of NT writers. As I look back, the efforts of my teachers and the extensive reading on defense of historicity may have dulled my ability to read, hear, and experience the stories of Jesus and the early church (I say these things not to slight them, for they were simply products of their methodological era).

TURNING THE CORNER: THANK GOD FOR ROGER STRONSTAD AND JOHN HOWARD YODER

I graduated college in 1985, the year Roger Stronstad published what became the go-to rebuttal against Dunn and Fee. I entered part-time pastoral ministry and discovered Stronstad's *Charismatic Theology of St. Luke* at a critical juncture in my journey. For many pentecostal students and pastors, Stronstad provided the methodological tools necessary not only to survive but thrive in our tradition. If adoption of the evangelicalized readings of biblical narratives (Dunn and Fee) would prevail, my pentecostals impulses on the Spirit-filled life, upheld by way of Luke and Acts, would be severely threatened. Stronstad took up this challenge and guided many pentecostals through this difficulty.[5] He provided me with timely answers. First, though Paul and Luke both employ the language of "baptized" and "filled" with the Spirit, Luke's decidedly greater use of the terms (3-to-1 and 9-to-1, respectively) must not be relegated to a Pauline meaning. Second, Luke employs Spirit in the life of Jesus and his followers in continuity with charismatic (think "prophetic") enablement of OT agents who fulfill God's

4. Stronstad, *Charismatic Theology of St. Luke*, 8.

5. Mittelstadt, *Reading Luke-Acts in the Pentecostal Tradition*.

purposes (e.g., Moses, David, Elijah). The same Spirit transferred from the likes of Moses to Joshua and Elijah to Elisha is transferred by Jesus to his disciples and beyond. And the same Spirit previously limited to OT leadership (e.g., prophets and kings) now become universally available for all believers. Finally, Luke's Jesus also functions as the consummate man of the Spirit, the model for future followers who will continue "all that Jesus began to do and teach" (Acts 1:1). In so doing, Stronstad amplified Luther's axiomatic "priesthood of all believers" to "prophethood of all believers," a new pentecostal and charismatic axiom.[6]

Shortly after discovering Stronstad, I began studies at Providence Seminary, a non-denominational institution with a predominance of Mennonite faculty, students, and constituents. At Providence, I first encountered the theologies of Mennonites. I owe my initial exposure to Mennonite scholarship to Edmund Neufeld (note the name), who introduced me to John Howard Yoder's *Politics of Jesus*. Deemed by many to be one of the most influential theological works of the twentieth century, I first detested Yoder's thesis, only to realize many years later that I had adopted his vision of the Lukan Jesus's radical worldview. If Stronstad's Jesus is the exemplary man of the Spirit, Yoder's Jesus is "a model of radical political action."[7] Yoder rejects any attempt to bypass the life of Jesus only to receive a heavenly-minded salvation. His Jesus is the preeminent model for radical discipleship and nonviolent resistance.[8]

It is no exaggeration for me to state that these scholars changed my life! First, Stronstad and Yoder refused to settle for the debate over historicity. Instead, they endeavored to give Luke voice not simply as historian, but as theologian and pastor. They reminded me that the biblical stories I embodied as a child remained critical to discipleship. Second, Stronstad and Yoder rescued me from a view of Jesus that made his life distant, unattainable, and irrelevant for everyday life. Instead, they strove to give Luke's Jesus precedent in our lives. Finally, their scholarship gave rise to a dawning convergence. The prophetic Jesus, filled with the Spirit and the model of nonviolent resistance to the powers, should produce a prophetic church. Enter Luke Timothy Johnson.

---

6. Stronstad, *Prophethood of All Believers*.

7. Yoder, *Politics of Jesus*, 2.

8. See Mittelstadt, "My Life as a Mennocostal."

LUKE TIMOTHY JOHNSON: A CATHOLIC GUIDE TO MENNOCOSTAL LIFE

If I had to choose the one biblical scholar who has most influenced my academic and spiritual formation, I would say, without hesitation, Luke Timothy Johnson. His emergence as the premier Lukan scholar of narrative criticism provided the technical language for biblical methods I had felt as a pentecostal. In his recent *Prophetic Jesus, Prophetic Church*, Johnson addresses *The Challenge of Luke-Acts to Contemporary Christians*:

> The pertinent question for believing readers is not, "Is Luke's rendering of Jesus historically accurate?" but rather, "How does Luke's imaginative construal challenge the values of the world?" The pertinent question is not, "Was the early church as Luke describes it?" but rather, "'How does Luke's portrayal of the early church challenge the church in every age?'"[9]

I read Johnson's dissertation during my seminary years and could not have imagined the role his lifework would have on my dissertation, future scholarship, and formation.[10] His use of narrative methodology set the bar for a generation of Lukan scholars, and his theological conclusions provided a new surge of meaning for the ecclesial import of Luke's story. For Johnson, if Luke's Jesus is the consummate prophet and the people of God continue Jesus's work, the church then and now embodies the prophetic life of Jesus. The Spirit of the living Jesus calls people to repent, demands their unmitigated allegiance and challenges all powers that usurp God's rule. The prophetic Jesus and all subsequent prophets commit to radical poverty signaled by shared possessions, prayerful dependence upon God, and dramatic itinerancy. Though classical pentecostals taught me about Acts as an open-ended narrative, how ironic that a Catholic scholar would hone my reading of Luke-Acts and further my development as a Mennocostal.

---

9. Johnson, *Prophetic Jesus, Prophetic Church,* 6. I would describe this particular work as a pastoral commentary on Luke-Acts. Johnson has spent a lifetime in Lukan studies, and produced numerous volumes on Luke-Acts. In this work, as I see it, he writes as a seasoned pastor-scholar and gives his reading of Luke based upon a life of meticulous study. See my reviews in Mittelstadt, "Prophetic Jesus, Prophetic Church."

10. Johnson, *Literary Function of Possessions.*

READING LUKE-ACTS AS A MENNOCOSTAL

With roughly two decades of Luke-Acts research on behind me, I'm occasionally asked why I don't just move on from Luke-Acts, only to respond that every time I'm ready to say "enough," Pastor Luke refuses to let me go. I say unequivocally that obsession with Luke-Acts does not primarily serve to advance my academic pursuits; instead, it results from the pervasive impact of Luke's story upon my life. In stating this, I owe much to the methodological advances made by pentecostal theologian Amos Yong, who calls upon pentecostals (and all Christians) to expand our collective "pneumatological imagination." For Yong, the many tongues of Pentecost serve metaphorically to enliven our contemporary Christian experience and praxis. If Pentecost launches the Spirit-filled life and if Pentecost is the domain not only of pentecostals, but of all Christians, including Mennonites, then Pentecost provides the impetus for continuous prophetic speech. Pentecost offers an early glimpse into Luke's many-tongued vision for the people of God.[11] For the final part of this essay, I describe my sojourn with Luke, a journey highlighted by seasons of pneumatological imagination.[12]

Spirit and Peace

In the fall of 2008, I was invited to deliver the Schrag Lecture Series at Messiah College (Mechanicsburg, PA), and I chose to share with my Anabaptist friends our common pacifistic impulses. Since many pentecostals remain unfamiliar with this heritage and those of us who maintain this impulse find the path difficult to tread, I sought fresh insight into Spirit-filled peacemaking from my newfound friends. For the first lecture, I mined scenes in Luke-Acts that brought together "Spirit and Peace."[13] I would not have launched into this paper without what I believe to be Mennonite New Testament scholar Willard Swartley's *magnum opus*. In his *Covenant of Peace*, Swartley cleverly seeks to discover *The Missing Peace in New Testament Theology and Ethics*. He surveys some twenty-five major studies of New Testament theology and laments that not a single study on Luke and Acts

11. Yong, *Spirit Poured Out*.

12. The following categories do not reflect a linear journey but rather lengthy and complex developments. The order seems fitting given the primacy of peace and justice for Mennonite theology and praxis.

13. Mittelstadt, "Spirit and Peace in Luke-Acts," 17–41.

paid attention to the peace motif (x). To counter this gaping hole, Swartley marches through Luke-Acts and opens my eyes yet again to a broken world inclined toward power, self-interest, and conflict. For Swartley, Luke's Jesus enters this world to announce the path/way of peace and to embody the gospel's radical hospitality; and if Jesus's vision for radically inclusive communities is to come to fruition, his disciples must follow his path. Not surprisingly, Luke first labels Jesus's followers as people of "The Way" (see section C!).[14]

As I examined Luke's use of the peace motif, I found that Luke revealed his agenda via Spirit-filled agents. The Lukan birth narrative includes three prophetic and programmatic announcements: Zechariah longs for "the way of peace" (Luke 1:67, 79); an angelic army (note the irony) sings to shepherds concerning "peace on those whom [God] favors" (Luke 2:14; cf. 19:38); and Simeon, an old priest, receives fulfillment of a promise that he would see God's Messiah before death—"now dismiss your servant in peace" (Luke 2:29). The adult Jesus filled with the spirit (Luke 3:22; 4:1, 14, 18) proclaims *shalom* for specific individuals (Luke 7:50; 8:48) and commissions his disciples to announce "Peace to this house" (Luke 9:51–10:24) in a world ill-prepared for "the things that make for peace" (Luke 18:35–19:44). At the Gentile Pentecost in Acts 10, a passage revered by pentecostals for Luke's emphasis on Spirit reception, Peter's declaration of the "good news of peace by Jesus Christ who is Lord of all" fulfills Luke's programmatic hopes announced at the beginning of the Third Gospel (Acts 10:36). Contrary to rule marked by heavy-handed propaganda that promotes an idyllic but corrupt *pax Romana* (not unlike *pax Americana*), the church counters with *pax Christi*. The ever-maturing Peter slowly but surely comes to understand that God is not impartial (see Acts 2:39). Peter pronounces Jesus as Lord and invites searching individuals and communities to experience the loving embrace of Jesus and his followers. The gospel provides a way for anyone looking to replace hatred and hostility with love and inclusion under the Lordship of Jesus Christ. I had a firm grip on Luke's pneumatology (detect sarcasm), yet I had failed to see the message of Spirit and peace without the help of my Mennonite friends.

---

14. See Luke 1:79; 2:14, 29; 7:50; 8:48; 10:5–6 (2); 11:21; 12:51; 14:32; 19:38, 42; 24:36; Acts 7:26; 9:31; 10:36; 12:20; 15:33; 16:36; 24:2.

Evangelism or Compassion

On May 22, 2011, an F5 tornado ripped through Joplin, MO, only seventy miles from my home in Springfield. A twenty-two mile tornadic track resulted in the death of 158 people, some 1,000 injuries, and the destruction of more than 7,000 homes and businesses. My family and I made several trips to Joplin to support with cleanup. We learned that the Mennonite Disaster Service (MDS) was the first volunteer-based relief service on the ground and later discovered they were the last to go.[15] On a trip to Joplin in the summer of 2012, I visited the MDS station, and my mind rushed to childhood memories of MCC and MDS in Winnipeg. I found myself reflecting upon the compartmentalization I had learned as a pentecostal, where relief and development via food, clothing, and shelter set up the gospel. On this day, I was reminded that Mennonites view such work as the gospel of the kingdom.

Until recently, the Assemblies of God (AG), my current denominational affiliation, cited three reasons for existence, namely, to evangelize the lost, worship God, and disciple believers. At the 2009 General Council of the AG, a resolution to add a fourth reason produced a hard-fought debate. The resolution was defeated but revisited due to the earnest plea of General Superintendent George O. Wood. The second vote passed narrowly, and the AG added compassion—not social justice—as a fourth purpose and emphasis. Not surprisingly, some cringed at the possibility that the AG that would mix evangelism and social justice and thereby slide down the slippery slope of Social Gospelers. Still, others decided not to vote for the addition of compassion since evangelism and compassion function as hand and glove. Whereas the AG resolution sought to heighten awareness and intentionality concerning compassion, some delegates wondered why the AG should distinguish between what's part and parcel of the gospel. Fortunately, some were swayed, and the AG announced a fourfold purpose with compassion alongside evangelism, worship, and discipleship.[16] Given the confusion over the inclusion of compassion, I am reminded that a Mennonite reading of Luke might help us better understand social justice (yes, I said it) as prophetic work.

Swartley states, "I would venture that Luke 4:18–19 has been used more often in pulpits and conference programs within Mennonite circles

---

15. Good, "MDS provides leadership in Joplin"; "MDS concludes Joplin project."
16. Miller and Yammamori, *Global Pentecostalism*.

than any other Scripture."[17] Like pentecostals, Mennonites place significant paradigmatic stock in Jesus's words both fulfilled and launched in his
hometown. Similarly, I cannot count the number of sermons and references to pentecostal appropriation of Jesus's exclamation that "the Spirit of
the Lord is on me because he has anointed me to proclaim the good news."
But what does this good news sound like? What does good news produce?
Luke's Jesus provides such a bridge. For Mennonites and pentecostal convergence, I cannot imagine a more passionate conversation concerning the
nature of Spirit-anointed preaching to the poor, restored vision and health,
the release of captives, and the announcement of Jubilee. More than buzz
words, pentecostals and Mennonites preach and practice the gospel. Both
traditions employ the word *euangelion* used in 4:18 with respective emphases, whether "good news" (think proclamation) or social justice (think
action). Concerning their order of importance, I would answer only "yes."
Surely, and through the Spirit, we have much to teach each other.

Nachfolge, (Im)migration, and Refugees

Given the evangelistic (think missionary) impulse of pentecostals, movement proves crucial to our identity. Pentecostalism has been described as
"a religion made to travel."[18] I picture preachers making use of John 3:16
and Acts 1:8 to implore Spirit-filled believers to leave their local Jerusalem
and take the message of God's love throughout the world. Though a cursory
reading of Luke-Acts delivers fulfillment of Jesus's words as the story moves
from "Jerusalem, Judea, Samaria, and to the end of the earth," Luke embeds
the often-unplanned circumstances for movement. In Jesus's inaugural
post-resurrection announcement, Jesus calls upon "witnesses" to fulfill this
task (Luke 24:48). Unfortunately, the English translation fails to capture the
Greek root "martyr." Such an oversight often causes readers to miss Luke's
twist on the movement of Jesus's witnesses. God's people often embark on
"The Way" not because of a strategic "Missions Conference." Instead, Philip
flees Jerusalem upon the death of his martyred friend Stephen, only to take
the Gospel to the Samaritans, and Paul consistently bolts from city to city
on account of persecution and finally travels to Jerusalem and Rome not as
a missionary, but as a prisoner for the gospel. Once again, these stories find

17. Swartley, "Smelting for Gold," 297.
18. Dempster et al., *Globalization of Pentecostalism.*

their beginning in Jesus's teaching, and I found that the Mennonite story offered sobering clarity.

In the mid-1990s, I pastored in Morden-Winkler, the heart of the Manitoba Mennonite belt (it is noteworthy that many in my congregation identified as ex-Mennonites). In 1994, Winkler Bible Institute hosted a summer-long exhibition of Thieleman Van Bragt's *Martyrs Mirror*, based upon a seventeenth-century commemoration of martyrological accounts from early Christianity to the Anabaptists of his day.[19] The exhibit displayed thirty of 104 recently discovered copper plates etched by the gifted Mennonite artist, Jan Luyken, for his 1685 edition.[20] In a new publication on the social history of *Martyrs Mirror*, David Weaver-Zercher, American Religious Historian at Messiah College, claims that no other book (and drawings) apart from the Bible has produced a greater impact on Mennonite identity. For me, I have been drawn to, and haunted by, the specific account and illustration of Dirk Willems. As Willems runs to safety across a frozen river, his pursuer falls through the ice, and Willems must make a split-second decision to continue his flight or save a life. In dramatic fashion, Luyken "captures" the moment Willems rescues his pursuer. Willems is subsequently returned to town and burned at the stake. Not unlike a pentecostal's testimony, Willems's story calls upon Mennonites to consider Jesus's hard teachings such as his exhortation to "love your enemies [and] do good to those who hate you" (Luke 6:27); his prediction "they will seize you and persecute you" and "hand you over to synagogues and put you in prison, and you will be brought before kings and governors, and all on account of my name" (Luke 21:12); and his promise that "those who want to save their life will lose it, and those who lose their life for my sake, and for the sake of the gospel, will save it" (Luke 9:24).[21]

Mennonites make much use of the German word *nachfolge*, their "way" to embody discipleship. Jesus's call to be a disciple can not be reduced to individual belief (i.e., theological assent); it demands that communities of believers literally "follow after" him. In short, the Mennonite story tells of people whose collective witness reads like a continuous migration narrative. If discipleship demands a daily walk in accordance with Jesus's radical teachings, the call to witness will include the kind of enemy love and possible martyrdom exhibited by Willems. And amid such difficulties,

19. Van Bragt, *Bloody Theatre, or Martyrs' Mirror*.

20. Kauffman Museum, "Mirror of the Martyrs."

21. Weaver-Zercher, *Martyrs Mirror*.

Mennonite history is replete with countless migration stories that resemble Acts; the Mennonites are a people ever-scattered because of witness and for witness. Nachfolge befits a life fraught with suffering, danger, and struggle. When they are pushed from "home," Mennonites must depend on the hospitality of others to reestablish their communities. Whether they flee persecution or go willingly to the ends of the earth, they are living examples of people given second and third chances. As these movements remain etched upon their contemporary memory, Mennonites preserve their identity and inspire contemporary witness.

As I look back upon my early pentecostal experience of Acts, I recall stories of Spirit-driven triumph. The classic invitation to participate in Acts-like reenactment typically began with Spirit-baptism, followed by a call to the world and the triumph of the gospel, something akin to "look out world, here comes Mittelstadt." My exploits failed to resemble anything like the sermonic rhetoric. In fact, my struggle with theological triumphalism nearly led to my departure from my pentecostals roots. Had it not been for about a three-year personal investigation of Luke-Acts during my pastorate in Morden, I might have gone another direction. As I lived among Mennonites and learned their stories, I completed my dissertation entitled "Spirit and Suffering in Luke-Acts." The dissertation proved autobiographical. I wrote to see if I could remain pentecostal. As I wrestled with the rhetoric of triumphalism versus my experience, I discovered that to be filled with the Spirit means living in the tension between acceptance and rejection, between the triumph and the tragedy of the gospel. God's agents from Jesus through the Twelve, Stephen, James, and Paul regularly witnessed under duress. Luke's Jesus not only modeled suffering for his followers, but he predicted opposition and persecution against future witnesses (Luke 12:1–12; 21:12–15). Far from a story of glory to glory, Luke strategizes a narrative of expansion driven by followers on the run.

Many Christians around the world live daily in such a climate. Life at home requires boldness and enemy love. Other Christians choose to leave their Jerusalem, enter volatile regions as agents of the gospel, and prepare, as much as they are able, for the difficulties ahead of them. But I must press further. My delineation of *nachfolge* thus far employs terms such as "the Way," journey motif, and migration, but what about a turn toward current language caught by the much-debated battle over immigration and refugees? *Nachfolge* compels me to perceive in Luke-Acts and among Mennonites, an immigration narrative, a story of refugees. Like Jesus's first followers and Mennonites of days gone by, other Christians leave home because of allegiance to the gospel. Severely persecuted and exhausted from ever-visible death, they finally flee for their lives. Like the Mennonites of old, many contemporary Christians receive gracious hospitality in new lands. I am deeply saddened when I listen to fellow pentecostals (and Christians in general) unwilling to follow Luke's barrier-breaking Pentecost, an event that launches welcome by and to all humans. For me, the Mennonite story, coupled with their radical obedience to the Gospels and Acts, makes Pentecost more plausible. Pentecostals with our emphasis on Spirit-led witness would do well to integrate the Spirit's call to provide a "way of peace," as thoughtful compassion toward the migrant embodied by our Mennonite friends.

DISCLAIMER AND INVITATION

First, I assume that readers will recognize limitations of this account. This is my story, a partial account of a life lived entirely in the church. This story is a testimony based on reading and rereading the Gospels and Acts among fellow academicians and believers. As I and others explore stories of pentecostal and Mennonite convergence, we assume that all Christians, with even a little history in the greater Christian community and the smallest amount of intentionality, find points of convergence with those of other traditions. I also want to make it clear that impulses described as emblematic of one tradition do not imply the other should be declared wanting. For example, if my discovery that "any gospel which is not social is not gospel" first found meaning among Mennonites, I do not suggest that pentecostals fail to teach and practice compassion.[22] Similarly, I am committed to nonviolence. I came to this position through Mennonites long before I discovered that my pentecostal history included a rich peace tradition. Having said this, I maintain that encounters with other traditions open our eyes to new understanding and practices not necessarily well articulated in every tradition. For me, early interaction with Mennonites not only gave birth to my formation of a social gospel and a life dedicated to non-violence, but encouraged me to reimagine and integrate these values with a pentecostal vision for life in the Spirit.

Finally, I propose that the most substantive dialogue partner for pentecostals should be Mennonites. Sadly, on more than one occasion, I

22. Kraybill, *Upside-Down Kingdom* 35.

have been told both by church officials and ecumenists that pentecostals/ Mennonite dialogue amounts to "small potatoes"; ecumenical investment with Mennonites, a tradition small in number and influence, seems futile compared to the large and powerful Catholic and Anglican traditions. To the contrary, I would suggest that such a dialogue might further enliven the vision of two traditions committed to radical apostolic Christianity. Both traditions work best as counter-cultural movements, yet struggle daily with the temptation to accommodate the gospel; on this matter, I fear a gospel message that ranges from one extreme that settles primarily for an introspective faith to a gospel defined by cultural domination, Christians bent on power. Both traditions derive their *raison d'être* from the Gospels and Acts and would do well to share their ongoing experience of these texts. Our shared approach to Scriptures that tell and envision the stories of God's people then and now should inspire common exposition, particularly among pastors and theologians. Both traditions would serve our larger Christian family well by modeling life together. Given our collective commitment to prophethood, I am hard pressed to imagine two traditions more in need of one another and more able to work together. I hope that Mennocostals scattered within our respective traditions will foster relationships that inspire Spirit-inspired life and witness.

BIBLIOGRAPHY

Dempster, Murray, Byron D. Klaus, and Douglas Petersen, eds. *The Globalization of Pentecostalism: A Religion Made to Travel*. Oxford: Regnum, 1999.

Fee, Gordon, and Douglas Stuart. *How to Read the Bible for all Its Worth*. Grand Rapids: Zondervan, 1981.

Good, Sheldon. "MDS provides leadership in ravaged Joplin." *Mennonite World Review*, June 6, 2011. http://www.mennoworld.org/archived/2011/6/6/mds-provides-leadership-joplin.

Johnson, Luke Timothy. *The Literary Function of Possessions in Luke-Acts*. Missoula, MT: Scholars for the Society of Biblical Literature, 1977.

———. *Prophetic Jesus, Prophetic Church: The Challenge of Luke-Acts to Contemporary Christians*. Grand Rapids: Eerdmans, 2011.

Kauffman Museum. "The Mirror of the Martyrs." https://kauffman.bethelks.edu/martyrs/index.html.

Kraybill, Donald. *The Upside-Down Kingdom*. Updated ed. Harrisonburg, VA: Herald, 2011.

"MDS concludes Joplin project." *Mennonite World Review*, April 29, 2013. http://www.mennoworld.org/archived/2013/4/29/mds-concludes-joplin-project.

Miller, Donald, and Tetsunao Yammamori. *Global Pentecostalism: The New Face of Christian Social Engagement*. Berkeley: University of California Press, 2007.

Mittelstadt, Martin W. "My Life as a Mennocostal: A Personal and Theological Narrative." In *Pentecostals and Nonviolence: Reclaiming a Heritage*, edited by Paul Alexander, 333–51. Eugene, OR: Pickwick, 2012.

———. "'Prophetic Jesus, Prophetic Church: The Challenge of Luke-Acts to Contemporary Christians,' by Luke Timothy Johnson. Grand Rapids: Eerdmans, 2011 & 'The Spirit and the 'Other': Social Identity, Ethnicity, and Intergroup Reconciliation in Luke-Acts' by Aaron J. Kuecker. Library of New Testament Studies (JSNTS), 444. London: T & T Clark, 2011." *Pneuma*, 35 (2013) 120–22.

———. *Reading Luke-Acts in the Pentecostal Tradition*. Cleveland, TN: Centre for Pentecostal Theology, 2010.

———. "Spirit and Peace in Luke-Acts: Possibilities for Pentecostal/Anabaptist Dialogue." *Didaskalia* 20 (2009) 17–41. Earlier version presented at Messiah College, Schrag Lectureship Series, April 9, 2008.

Robertson, A. T. *A Harmony of the Gospels for Students of the Life of Christ*. San Francisco: Harper & Row, 1922.

Stronstad, Roger. *The Charismatic Theology of St. Luke*. Rev. ed. Grand Rapids: Baker, 2012.

———. *Prophethood of All Believers*. Sheffield: Sheffield Academic Press, 1999.

Swartley, Willard M. *Covenant of Peace: The Missing Piece in New Testament Theology and Ethics*. Grand Rapids: Eerdmans, 2006.

———. "Smelting for Gold: Jesus and Jubilee in John H. Yoder's Politics of Jesus." In *A Mind Patient and Untamed: Assessing John Howard Yoder's Contributions to Theology, Ethics, and Peacemaking*, edited by Ben C. Ollenburger and Gayle Gerber Koontz, 297. Telford, PA: Cascadia, 2004.

Van Bragt, Thieleman J. *Bloody Theatre, or Martyrs' Mirror*. 1660. Reprint, Harrisonburg, VA: Herald, 1938.

Weaver-Zercher, David. *Martyrs Mirror: A Social History*. Baltimore: Johns Hopkins University Press, 2016.

Yoder, John Howard. *The Politics of Jesus*. Grand Rapids: Eerdmans, 1994.

Yong, Amos. *The Spirit Poured Out on All Flesh: Pentecostalism and the Possibility of Global Theology*. Grand Rapids: Baker Academic, 2005.

3

Explorations of a Methomennocostal

Wesleyan Theology as Grist
for Pentecostal-Anabaptist Conversation

MATTHEW PAUGH

MICHAEL J. CHRISTENSEN WRITES, "The Spirit blows where it wants to blow and leads us in wholly unexpected ways."[1] My spiritual journey supports Christensen's assertion. The wind of the Spirit has taken me from a born and bred pentecostal to a pentecostal with Anabaptist leanings. Subsequently, in a change I could not have predicted, the Spirit brought me to serve as a United Methodist pastor. In what follows, I reflect upon my journey from a theological and ecclesial perspective. This narrative testifies to my attempt to live as methomennocostal. From my perspective as a theological mongrel, I suggest that John Wesley, the progenitor of the Methodist movement, could serve as a link between Anabaptists and pentecostals. Out of many possible linkages, I explore soteriology as a promising topic for a Wesleyan contribution to Anabaptist-pentecostal dialogue, and, finally, I provide some implications derived from the soteriological discussion for both movements.

---

1. Christensen, foreword to *Henri Nouwen*, vii.

MY LIFE AS A METHOMENNOCOSTAL

The "costal" Foundation

Raised as a fourth-generation pentecostal, I could be found on the green-padded wooden pews of our small Assemblies of God (AG) church whenever the doors opened. I can remember gathering on Sunday morning, Sunday night, and Wednesday evening. I can still hear "Grandma Mills," one of the church matriarchs, singing sweetly "in the Spirit" during the extended times of "tarrying" at the altar. I can smell the sweet aroma of the slightly rancid olive oil our pastor, a Latvian immigrant, would use to anoint a church member facing surgery while the congregation gathered around with their arms outstretched praying fervently for healing. I can taste the weak cherry-flavored Kool-Aid provided to quench our thirst at vacation Bible school, one of summertime's highlights. I can see my mom with her hands uplifted in impassioned worship as "Spirit of the Living God" rang out on the upright piano. I can still feel the chill rising up my spine when someone—often a family member—would erupt in a "message" in tongues. We awaited the interpretation that would provide the word God had for us; depending on the tone, the interpretation would give rise to the congregation's audible response of praise or repentance.

Not only does that church bring back fond memories of my formative years, but it also boasts a storied heritage. Kitzmiller Assembly of God began in the throes of the pentecostal revival at the beginning of the twentieth century. In those years, Kitzmiller thrived as a coal mining town in rural western Maryland along the North Branch of the Potomac River. Due to its location on the Western Maryland railroad, early revivalists such as A. B. Cox and D. R. Moreland arrived in the early 1910s and conducted tent meetings in Kitzmiller and Blaine, WV, directly across the river.[2] The revivals resulted in several individuals receiving "the baptism in the Holy Spirit." According to oral history, the Spirit-baptized believers tried to return to the Methodist Episcopal Church, but when they become too exuberant the Methodists barred them from worship and even had some leaders of the new movement arrested for disturbing the peace. As a result, the pentecostal believers began meeting in the town's movie theater, and by 1917 they had built their own house of worship and affiliated with the burgeoning AG.

2. Gohr, "A. B. and Dora Cox," 10. As an aside, A. B. Cox was arrested after refusal to support the war fund during War World I. See Cox, "In Prison," 14.

I recall hearing the narrative of our pentecostal beginnings in Kitzmiller recounted frequently. Long after the coal mines closed and the town's population plummeted to 300 people, that story provided our identity. Along with that account, I recall sermons that cautioned us to "avoid the path of the Methodists." The warning, of course, centered around Methodism's promising origin in the Wesleyan revival and what our church saw as its decline into Protestant liberalism.

As a child, this story became my story. I "got saved" on numerous occasions. Sometimes I responded to the altar call in both the morning and the evening service; after all, I had probably committed some grievous sin during the afternoon. But eventually, one of my sinner's prayers must "have taken," and I became serious in my devotion to Christ. The Kitzmiller AG afforded me numerous avenues to participate in the life of the church. By the time I was a teenager, a visiting evangelist had come and preached on the baptism in the Holy Spirit. At the end of that week of revival services, I had my own pentecostal experience.

Encountering the "Menno"

Despite urgings from some folks in my home church to attend a pentecostal school, I decided to attend Messiah College in Grantham, PA. I knew nothing of the college's background other than that it claimed to be "rigorously academic" and "unapologetically Christian." At the convocation service, President Rodney Sawatsky spoke about the traditions that shaped the college. When he mentioned Anabaptism, I thought, "I'm going to have to figure out what that is."[3]

But understanding Anabaptism quickly faded from my mind as classes began. In a first-year seminar class on Dietrich Bonhoeffer, we received the assignment to work in pairs to debate a relevant topic. The professor assigned my partner and me to deliberate upon the question of war. I jockeyed to examine just war theory; after all, I knew it encompassed "the biblical position." In the research phase, I determined to explore some AG writers. They would provide insight I could trust.

3. Messiah College was founded by and continues to be in a covenant relationship with the Brethren in Christ Church. The school is "rooted in the Anabaptist, Pietist, and Wesleyan traditions." See Messiah College, "Three Traditions."

Imagine my surprise when the first article in my periodical search contained the words "pentecostal pacifism."[4] The phrase seemed like an oxymoron, but I read with curiosity. I learned that pacifism constituted "the predominant view" of the early Pentecostals.[5] My home church never taught me that, in the same year the church opened, the AG issued a resolution declaring participation in war "contrary to our view of the clear teaching of the inspired Word of God."[6] Despite this unexpected revelation, I did not linger long on the issue and continued my investigation to support the just war stance.

By my second semester, I enrolled in a theology class and learned about the Anabaptists. *Resident Aliens,* one of the assigned textbooks, spurred me to further inquiry into the Believers Church tradition. In the text, Stanley Hauerwas and William Willimon, who identify as Methodists, criticized the "Constantinian" religion that American Christianity had become. The church had embraced and supported the capitalism, materialism, and nationalism of the wider culture. The authors called the church to reject Constantinianism and to create a counterculture under Jesus's reign in which the priorities involve loving enemies, telling the truth, honoring the poor, suffering for righteousness, and testifying to "the amazing community-creating power of God."[7]

Hauerwas and Willimon based their project on Mennonite John Howard Yoder's concept of the "confessing church."[8] Thus, I plunged into Yoder's works, especially *The Politics of Jesus,* in which he argues that Jesus's teachings prove normative and indeed paradigmatic for a contemporary nonviolent social ethic.[9] Other classes in Bible and theology taught by Mennonite and Brethren in Christ scholars challenged me to take Jesus's life and teaching seriously. A course on the Synoptic Gospels and its analysis of the Sermon on the Mount proved particularly pertinent in this regard.

Practices from my pentecostal experience began to come into question, including our flag-waving patriotic service on the Fourth of July and the emphasis on spiritual experience over discipline and ethics. Our ethics focused on abortion and homosexuality; rarely did we discuss how we loved

4. Robins, "Forgotten Heritage," 3–5.
5. Robins, "Forgotten Heritage," 3.
6. Quoted in Robins, "Forgotten Heritage," 4.
7. Hauerwas and Willimon, *Resident Aliens,* 46.
8. Hauerwas and Willimon, *Resident Aliens,* 45.
9. Yoder, *Politics of Jesus.*

our neighbor or cared for the poor. Still, taking Jesus seriously seemed too ethereal; it sounded accurate in theory, but unfeasible in practice.

With that mindset, I determined I needed to take a break from the Anabaptists and receive some training in my pentecostal tradition. I enrolled at the Assemblies of God Theological Seminary in Springfield, MO. Two weeks into my seminary studies 9/11 happened. The shock of the coordinated terrorist attacks gave way to a deep sense of patriotism. Songs during baseball games and restaurant marquees invoked God's blessing on America. Citizens seemed to display the American flag everywhere; the Stars and Stripes appeared on houses, cars, and lapels.

To see the surge of patriotism in the wider culture meant one thing, but I became uneasy as loyalty to nation spilled over into the church. As a new seminary student seeking a place of worship, I visited AG congregations throughout Springfield in the weeks following September 11, 2001. I witnessed worshippers dutifully reciting the pledge of allegiance in the middle of a sermon. One sanctuary featured a cross draped by the American flag. When one soloist sang Lee Greenwood's "God Bless the USA," congregants stood with upraised hands in displays of reverence that did not occur earlier in the service when the order of worship contained hymns. Pastoral prayers called for revenge against our enemies.

In fairness, I also experienced heartfelt prayers for victims and their families, genuine calls for Christians to find hope in God, and sermons exhorting believers to love others, but the exhibitions of civil religion caused me to question adherence to my ecclesial tradition. As I scrutinized my convictions, however, I found pentecostals and other scholars who called for a reexamination of early pentecostalism and a revival of its prophetic voice against nationalism and violence.[10] I developed friendships with other pentecostals who shared my uneasiness about civil religion and my emerging sympathies for Anabaptist theology. I delved deeper into the works of Anabaptists such as Harold S. Bender, Donald B. Kraybill, and Paul M. Lederach.[11] These perspectives informed my expanding pentecostal theology as I journeyed through seminary, served as an associate pastor at an AG church, and taught as an adjunct instructor at Evangel University. I was becoming "mennocostal."

10. See, e.g., Beaman, *Pentecostal Pacifism;* Shuman, "Pentecost and the End of Patriotism," 70–96; Dempster, "Pacifism in Pentecostalism," 31–57; Alexander, "Spirit Empowered Peacemaking," 78–102.

11. Bender, *Anabaptist Vision;* Kraybill, *Upside-Down Kingdom;* Lederach, *Third Way.* Kraybill served as Provost at Messiah College when I attended there.

Adding the "Metho"

After a few years of appropriating and attempting to live out my menno-costal leanings, I moved home to rural western Maryland in the late 2000s. Not too long after my relocation, I experienced a distressing separation and divorce. I found myself in a crisis of faith. I preached a message of recon-ciliation and forgiveness, but bringing about restoration in my marriage proved impossible. I questioned myself. I questioned God.

In the midst of these questions, I found my way to Mount Bethel United Methodist Church (UMC). Somewhere along the way, I developed the conviction that believers should attend church in the community in which they live. Well, in Kitzmiller, that left two options: my home church or Mount Bethel. Due to my circumstances, I did not feel comfortable attending the AG church, but at Mount Bethel, a small church of about twenty-five worshippers, I encountered a congregation who welcomed me into their lives and demonstrated grace and love. Recognizing my spiritual gifts, the pastor encouraged me to continue in my ministry calling despite my brokenness. In fact, through telling her own story, she established that my woundedness could help minister healing to others. I began to lead worship, teach, and preach in that congregation, and in the process, I found hope.

Ironically, Mount Bethel was the congregation that allegedly rebuffed the pentecostals in the early twentieth century. Now, it became my church home. Fortunately, much had changed in the intervening 100 years, and the AG and UMC congregations joined together in ecumenical services and community ministries. Moreover, several Mount Bethel members claimed to have experienced Spirit baptism, and I felt at home in worship services in which I could hear individuals praying in tongues.

As I became more involved at Mount Bethel, I set out to learn more about the Methodist tradition. In John Wesley's theology, I discovered an emphasis on grace. His conception of grace includes not only forgiveness of sin, but also empowerment to live by God's will. This empowerment, which Wesley refers to as sanctification or holiness, means that the Holy Spirit enables believers to demonstrate their love for God and others not only in some future heavenly state, but in this world.

Along with the Wesleyan understanding of grace, I found myself drawn to what Paul Wesley Chilcote calls Wesley's "conjunctive approach" to theology.[12] In other words, Wesleyanism encompasses a "both/and"

---

12. Chilcote, *Recapturing the Wesleys' Vision*, 16.

instead of an "either/or" theological method. For example, rather than forcing a dichotomy between personal salvation and social action, Wesley presents a vision for the Christian life that embraces *both* the personal *and* the social dimension.[13] Within this conjunctive paradigm, I realized that both my pentecostal and my Anabaptist proclivities resonated with aspects of Wesleyan theology.

As a Pentecostal, for instance, I connected with Wesley's espousal of "heart religion."[14] For Wesley, faith entails more than intellectual assent; it means an experience in which believers *feel* God's love "shed abroad" in their hearts by the Holy Spirit (Rom 5:5).[15] Wesley, however, unites the "heart" and the "head." Knowledge devoid of genuine religious experience proved empty, but experience apart from learning amounted to nothing more than fanaticism. Thus, I saw a theology that allowed room for my pentecostal experience, but also provided a corrective to the excesses that frequently characterized pentecostalism.

At the same time, Wesley's contention that growth in holiness must take place in intentional community awakened my Anabaptist inclinations. Wesley declares, "'Holy solitaries' is a phrase no more consistent with the gospel than holy adulterers. The gospel of Christ knows of no religion but social; no holiness but social holiness."[16] Consistent with this outlook, Wesley established a system of societies, classes, and bands. These voluntary associations provided an avenue for edification, mutual support, accountability, and discipline.[17] Chilcote contends that "early Methodism was essentially a small group movement of empowered laypeople."[18] In contrast to the Anabaptist, Wesley did not withdraw from the established church, but the Methodist structure, which Wesley envisioned as renewing the whole

13. While I do not have space to flesh out the full nature of the Wesleys' conjunctive theology here, Chilcote, *Recapturing the Wesleys' Vision*, traces eight conjunctions that Wesley brings together, including Faith and Works, Word and Spirit, Personal and Social, Form and Power, Heart and Head, Pulpit and Table, Christ and Culture, and Piety and Mercy. Similarly, Snyder suggests that "Wesley's genius . . . lay in developing and maintaining a synthesis in doctrine and practice that kept biblical paradoxes paired and powerful" (Snyder, *Radical Wesley*, 143–52). Snyder points to Wesley's synthesis of divine sovereignty and human freedom, doctrine and experience, experience and structure, the charismatic and the institutional, and present and future salvation.

14. Sanders, *Wesley on the Christian Life*, 82.

15. Wesley, "Scripture Way of Salvation," §1.4, 373.

16. Wesley, "Preface to *Hymns and Sacred Poems*," 593.

17. See Thompson, "From Societies," 141–72; Watson, *Pursuing Social Holiness*.

18. Chilcote, *Recapturing the Wesleys' Vision*, 50.

church, parallels the Anabaptist ecclesiological emphasis on the church as a voluntary covenant community.[19]

With these links and many others, Wesleyanism helped me to integrate the various strands of my theological identity. On a practical level, circumstances also brought me to a moment of decision. My ministry training and experience came to the attention of the UMC district superintendent. He soon called me asking if I would consider becoming the pastor of a nearby two-point charge. After prayerful contemplation, I felt God's leading to accept this ministry appointment.

The decision, however, did not prove easy. In attending a UMC, I never intended to "leave" the AG or pentecostalism. Going down the road of ministry in the UMC would mean separating from my AG heritage. In the end, I felt that I could remain "pentecostal" in the UMC and help bring a renewal of Wesleyan, Spirit-filled living. Fortunately, as a UMC pastor for the past six years, I have remained connected to pentecostal friends in ecumenical and scholarly pursuits. I persist in my commitment to an exploration of both pentecostal and Anabaptist impulses, but I now follow Christ as a methomennocostal.

THE "METHO" BRIDGE BETWEEN THE "MENNO" AND THE "COSTAL"

As a methomennocostal, I possess a keen interest in the convergence of pentecostal, Anabaptist, and Wesleyan theology and practice. Studying these three traditions has enabled me to notice more and more overlapping emphases. An inquiry into Wesleyan theology could provide a venue for fruitful discussion and further exploration of commonalities between pentecostals and Anabaptists.

Early pentecostals suggested that the movement emerged "suddenly from heaven" and that it had no antecedents in church history because of a direct connection to the New Testament church.[20] Historians and theologians, however, have long held a connection between Wesley and the early pentecostal movement. Donald Dayton, for example, argues that Wesley's

---

19. For an explanation of how Wesley's ecclesiology fails to adhere to the criteria for a state church or sectarian church, see Runyon, *New Creation*, 102–7. For a survey of Anabaptist ecclesiology, see Unger, "Church," 33–47. Snyder, *Radical Wesley*, 117–19, also points to these connections.

20. Brumback, *Suddenly*; Lawrence, *Apostolic Faith Restored*, 12.

concern with restoring the corrupt church of his time to a more primitive one gave rise to pentecostalism's restorationist impulse.[21] From Wesley, pentecostals also inherited a "Christocentric" emphasis which became the foundation for the "full gospel" of Jesus as savior, baptizer in the Holy Spirit, healer, and coming king.[22] Along these lines, pentecostalism's Wesleyan heritage probably becomes most evident in its appropriation of sanctification. Wesley's contention that salvation entails pardon for not only sin but also the power to live as Christ leads.[23]

These connections, among others, cause Vinson Synan to declare Wesley "the spiritual and intellectual father" of the pentecostal movement.[24] But Wesley also provides a connection to the Anabaptists. In an essay exploring pentecostalism's roots, Matthew S. Clark suggests a line of continuity between the Anabaptist tradition and pentecostalism. Notably, Wesley mediates this link. Clark contends that Wesley's interactions with Anabaptist-influenced Moravians gave rise to his emphasis on the life of obedience, discipleship, class meetings, primitivism, and return to the pre-Constantinian church. Clark goes on to promote pentecostal research into Anabaptism.[25]

While I would echo Clark in endorsing pentecostal inquiries into Anabaptist theology and practice, I would also suggest that an exploration of Wesley by both pentecostals and Anabaptists could lead to a helpful discussion of convergences between the two movements. I believe Anabaptists would discover that Wesley, like their theological ancestors, emphasized the *way* of following Jesus as embodied in a life of obedience, service, and witness. At the same time, consideration of their Wesleyan roots could help pentecostals recapture these emphases as they live the life of the Spirit. An essay of this size and scope will not allow me to delve into every possible topic for consideration, but in what follows, I draw attention to soteriology

---

21. Dayton, *Theological Roots,* 41–45.

22. Dayton, *Theological Roots,* 43.

23. Dayton, *Theological Roots,* 48. The emphasis on sanctification was present in both the Wesleyan-Holiness and Keswickian steams of Pentecostalism. See Rice, "Pentecostal Triple Way," 163. See also Knight, "From Aldersgate to Azusa," 82–98, who argues that "*both* wings of the Holiness and Pentecostal movements are rooted in and indebted to the Wesleyan awakening of the eighteenth century."

24. Synan, *Holiness-Pentecostal Tradition,* 1.

25. Clark, "Pentecostalism's Anabaptist Roots," 194–211. For more on the Moravian-Anabaptist influence on Wesley, see Snyder "John Wesley," 13–38, who argues that Wesley represents "the Believers' Church tradition."

as but one potential area where Wesleyan theology could prove helpful for Anabaptist and pentecostal conversation.

SOTERIOLOGY AS A POTENTIAL "METHO-" INFLUENCE UPON "MENNO" AND "COSTAL" DIALOGUE

"Metho" Soteriology

In his sermon "The Scripture Way of Salvation," John Wesley summarized his soteriology. He began the sermon with the question "What is salvation?" and answered:

> The salvation which is here spoken of is not what is frequently understood by that word, the going to heaven, eternal happiness. . . . It is not a blessing which lies on the other side of death. . . . It is not something at a distance: it is a present thing, a blessing which . . . ye are now in possession of. . . . So that the salvation which is here spoken of might be extended to the entire work of God, from the first dawning of grace in the soul till it is consummated in glory.[26]

Salvation for Wesley entails more than a legal transaction that provides a future hope. Salvation encompasses a present reality in which God enables believers to live holy lives here and now. In other words, Wesley believed that, if God could save believers from the penalty of sin, God could also save them from the power of sin.[27]

As Albert Outler argues, Wesley's soteriology blended juridical and therapeutic elements.[28] Western theology highlights the juridical nature of salvation and sees grace as divine forgiveness. Eastern traditions focus on salvation as healing the corruption that results from sin; in such a conception, grace involves God's power renewing humankind's nature. Wesley amalgamated these traditions with an emphasis on justification as the pardon of sin and on sanctification as participating in the divine life and growing in the likeness of God. For Wesley, salvation implies the "restoration of the soul to its primitive health; a recovery of the divine nature; the renewal of our souls after the image of God."[29]

---

26. Wesley, "Scripture Way of Salvation," §1.1, 372.
27. Wesley, "Salvation By Faith," §2.2, 42.
28. Outler, "Place of Wesley," 29–30.
29. Wesley, "Farther Appeal," 219.

The concept of divinization lies behind Wesley's conception of the renewal of the image of God.[30] In this understanding, humans do not become gods, but they can reflect God's character and share in the divine life. 2 Peter 1:4 describes this participation as being "partakers of the divine nature" (KJV). Wesley's idea of sanctification involves growing and maturing in God's image.

In Wesley's view, God's free grace enables both receiving forgiveness and the living out of one's faith. Wesley proclaimed that "faith working by love" existed as the distinguishing mark of the true, or the "altogether," Christian.[31] This understanding held "faith" and "works" together. Faith without works of love and works arising from anything other than God's grace constitute equally incomplete visions of the Christian life. Wesley spoke of justification as a "relative change" in our status before God. But a "real" change also takes place as transformed believers grow in grace and become new creatures in Christ.[32]

"Metho-impacted" "costal" Soteriology

As mediated through the Holiness tradition, early Pentecostals embraced much of Wesley's soteriological outlook. For example, an emphasis on salvation as a real change and divinization becomes clear in early-twentieth-century pentecostal periodicals.[33] Influential British pentecostal Alexander A. Boddy conceived of salvation as accepting "a new nature from above, a New Life in Christ. . . . By trusting the Redemption through His precious blood, we become partakers of the Divine Nature." Boddy underscores that the Spirit "brings this about."[34]

30. Maddox, "John Wesley," 39–40; Christensen, "Theosis and Sanctification," 71–94.

31. Wesley, "Almost Christian," §2.6, 66–67.

32. Wesley, "Scripture Way of Salvation," §1.4, 373. I am able to provide only a brief synopsis of Wesley's soteriology. For fuller treatments of the subject, see Maddox, *Responsible Grace*; Collins, *Scripture Way*; Runyon, *New Creation*.

33. On the concept of divinization in pentecostalism, see Bundy, "Visions of Sanctification," 104–36; Kärkkäinen, *One with God*, 108–15. Rybarcyak identifies Wesley as "the historical sieve through which early Eastern Orthodoxy passed" to the Pentecostal movement (Rybarczyk, *Beyond Salvation*, 15).

34. Boddy, "Holy Ghost," 20. In a similar vein, Eldridge contends that the Holy Spirit's role involves imparting the divine nature to believers so that they take on the attributes of Christ including loving "the unlovely," patience, forbearance, and obedience (Eldridge, "Temple of the Living God," 3).

Similarly, Felix A. Hale, representing the Keswickian stream in the AG,[35] declares that "a new principle is born in the penitent sinner," which gives "understanding of God and passionate love for God and the ways of righteousness." Like Wesley, Hale suggests that this "new creature is fashioned after the image of God." This new nature derives from "a miraculous and supernatural impartation of the Divine nature." As a result of this impartation, believers can now "grow and mature to the stature of the fullness of Christ."[36]

John T. Boddy, the editor of *The Pentecostal Evangel,* underscores that salvation involves a real change. Challenging those who argue that believers do not "become real partakers of the divine nature," Boddy contends that salvation enables one to "identify with Christ through partaking of the divine nature." The divine nature, then, becomes "a vital feature of our humanity, transforming and renewing" believers and "permeating and saturating" them with new life. Boddy compares this reality to the flow of blood:

> In the natural the blood, which is the lifegiving principle, flows through our veins and arteries, carrying life to every part of our physical, so in the spiritual the life divine flowing, as it does, through our spiritual circulation, carries divine life to every part of our moral nature, going even farther in answer to faith, and quickening these mortal bodies by the Spirit which dwelleth in us.[37]

35. Yong, *In the Days of Caesar,* 169–70, uses the phrase "Keswickian stream" to denote classical pentecostals influenced by the Keswick "Higher Life" movement. These pentecostals rejected the Holiness notion of sanctification as a second work of grace and advocated progressive sanctification. Yong suggests, however, that the Keswickian stream did not minimize holiness in its first generation, but disconnecting sanctification from a separate work of grace led later generations to "unintentionally" subordinate "the emphasis on holiness to that of Spirit-baptism and the missionary task and mandate of the church." For his part, Wesley saw sanctification as both a crisis experience and a process. Ssee Snyder and Runyon, *Divided Flame,* 73.

36. Hale, "New Birth," 4. Along these lines, Holmes, "Beautiful Life," 4, traces the beauty of Jesus's life and poignantly declares that believers can share in his divine nature and imitate his example. See also Sawders, "Adjustment-Receiving," 4, who reproves the churches for being content with having sins forgiven and losing sight of the impartation of the divine nature.

37. Boddy, "Partakers of Christ," 4.

For pentecostals, salvation entails deliverance and victory over sin and evil.[38] According to Alexander Boddy, however, this victory is experienced through identification with Christ. As believers have faith, "we begin to understand . . . that we were on the Cross in Christ and in Him we buried self and sin in His grave, and with Him have already risen to 'Victory' in the Heavenlies." Again, the Holy Spirit makes this identification possible. Boddy exclaims that just "as Jesus of Nazareth was empowered by the Holy Ghost to live the 'Wonderful Life,' and to have constant victory over the Devil, so this same Holy Spirit is the power, and the only power, in which we may live out Christ's Life on Earth, and ever gain the victory over His enemy and ours."[39]

In seeing salvation as participation in the divine life and deliverance from sin and the devil, the early pentecostals thus followed Wesley in understanding soteriology therapeutically.[40] They, however, extend salvation to also encompass physical healing.[41] Alexander Boddy translates the term "saved" with the phrase "made whole." In his view, as "the representative human life," Jesus lives "without sin and *without disease*." As a result of sin and the fall, the "disease-stricken nature has been handed down to us," but Christ undoes "the Fall (and its consequences) in those who join themselves" to him.[42] Salvation understood as wholeness implies that the Holy Spirit enables believers to overcome sin and its impacts and to participate in the divine life.[43]

38. See, for example, Ward, "Some More Food," 1, who views salvation as "a work of grace which gives on power to live above sin" because the Holy Spirit imparts "a divine nature" that makes one "a new creature."

39. Boddy, "Holy Ghost," 19.

40. See Coulter, "Delivered," 447–67, who suggests "acquisition of God's life" and "deliverance" as "two dominant metaphors" for pentecostal soteriology.

41. Roots for this emphasis can also be located in Wesley. See, for example, John Wesley to Alexander Knox: "It will be a double blessing if you give yourself up to the Great Physician, that He may heal soul and body together. And unquestionably this is His design. He wants to give you . . . both inward and outward health" (Wesley, *Letters*, 327).

42. Boddy, "Health in Christ," 175.

43. For more on Pentecostal soteriology, see Studebaker, "Pentecostal Soteriology," 248–70, who proposes a "redemptive soteriology" in which "the Spirit recreates in the believer the redemption of humanity achieved in Christ's life, death, resurrection and ascension"; Yong, *Spirit Poured Out*, 81–120, who sketches a "pneumatological soteriology" in conversation with Wesley's "way of salvation"; Macchia, *Justified in the Spirit*, who upholds Spirit baptism as a "root metaphor" for understanding all aspects of salvation, particularly justification; and Alexander, "Baptism of Divine Love," 68–82, who argues

"Menno" Soteriology

Intriguingly, some Anabaptist soteriological understandings sound uncannily similar to Wesley. Alvin Beachy, for example, surveyed Anabaptist conceptions of grace and arrived at a definition of grace as "God's act whereby He renews the divine image in man through the Holy Spirit and makes the believer a participant in the divine nature."[44] According to Beachy, Anabaptist's behavioral expectations find their roots in this conception of grace whereby Christians must not only be *declared* righteous, but also *be* righteous.[45]

Like Wesley, Anabaptists do not see salvation as simply forensic. Salvation entails a real change of one's nature. Dirk Philips taught that "whoever has become a partaker of the divine character, the being of Jesus Christ and the power and character of the Holy Spirit, conforms himself to the image of Jesus Christ in all submission, obedience, and righteousness."[46] Partaking of the divine nature, however, does not imply that one finds themselves elevated to some otherworldly existence. Menno Simons made clear that becoming partakers of Christ's nature means to "understand and follow not according to his divine nature . . . but that we follow him and conform unto him in his life and work upon earth, as exemplified in his words and works."[47]

Thomas N. Finger characterizes the Anabaptist view of salvation as "christomorphic divinization." In this understanding, God's grace transforms believers so that they may participate in Christ's righteousness and live "in accord with his life and teachings, inwardly in intention and outwardly in action."[48] In other words, justification enables sinners to become Christlike disciples. Finger thus pushes for an organic understanding of justification. Just as a branch requires nourishment from a root to grow and

---

that a "Wesleyan-Pentecostal model of Spirit baptism places the experience on the *via salutis*, indicating that it is a salvific work, by grace, through faith."

44. Beachy, *Concept of Grace*, 5.

45. Beachy, *Concept of Grace*, 214.

46. Philips, "New Birth," 294.

47. Simons, "Spiritual Resurrection," 233.

48. Finger, *Contemporary Anabaptist Theology*, 142. Besides Philips and Simons, Finger finds this emphasis in Swiss (Balthasar Hubmaier), South German-Austrian (Hans Denck, Peter Riedemann, and Pilgram Marpeck), and other Dutch (Melchoir Hoffman) Anabaptists. For more on deification in Anabaptism, see Kärkkäinen, *One with God*, 67–72.

bear leaves, so divinization "originates from God and continually draws from and remains dependent on God's energies." At the same time, "anything planted is intended to bear fruit"; consequently, Christians should respond to grace by growing in Christlikeness.[49]

"Metho," "costal," and "Menno" Soteriological Convergences and Implications

This brief foray into the soteriological outlooks of Wesley, the early Pentecostals as Wesley's heirs, and Anabaptists has demonstrated key commonalities in their conceptions of salvation. At heart, all three movements emphasize that salvation implies transformation. God's grace enables believers to live differently. This conviction separates these movements from traditional Reformation perspectives that declare believers simultaneously sinners and saints. No, for Wesleyans, pentecostals, and Anabaptists, Christians can live as saints when rightly understood as "holy ones."

Their respective soteriologies underscore that pentecostalism denotes more than evangelicalism plus tongues, and that Anabaptism entails more than evangelicalism plus peace.[50] These movements focus on recapturing a New Testament vision that sees the Christian life as participation in the divine nature and following the pattern of Christ's earthly life. To put it another way, pentecostals and Anabaptists recognize that Christianity's essence involves being more than a believer who expresses belief in Jesus; it implies becoming transformed disciples who follow Jesus. Unfortunately, in my experience, both movements have capitulated to a larger American Christian ethos that understands salvation as "saying a prayer" so that believers can go to heaven when they die.

As a result of this capitulation, I encourage pentecostals to revisit their spiritual ancestor Wesley. Without denying the need for conversion, Wesley's practical theology will call pentecostal believers back to an emphasis on

---

49. Finger, *Contemporary Anabaptist Theology*, 151–52. For more on Anabaptist soteriology, see Hiebert, "Atonement in Anabaptist Theology," 122–38; Friedmann, *Theology of Anabaptism*, 78–100; Crell, *Cooperative Salvation*.

50. Defining evangelicalism has proven challenging. See Brown, "Introduction," 6–8. Here I follow Grimsrud, "Should Anabaptists Be Evangelicals," who suggests that evangelicals be understood as those who hold to a "doctrine-first" approach to faith, emphasize "the doctrine of scripture over the content of scripture," affirm a penal substitution view of the atonement and make it into "an explicit boundary marker," and often uncritically support conservative American politics.

holiness.[51] Furthermore, mining Wesley will enable pentecostals to rediscover that conversion does not consist of salvation's goal; the goal involves loving God and loving others or, to put it simply, becoming Christlike.[52]

A rekindling of Wesleyan emphases dovetails with emphases in the Anabaptist tradition. A dialogue along these lines might inspire a more cohesive soteriology in both traditions. Pentecostals can inspire a holistic view of salvation that encompasses deliverance from all forms of evil, including physical disease. Anabaptists can stimulate a stress on the christological contours of salvation as living out Jesus's teaching and following the pattern of Jesus's earthly life. Pentecostal triumphalism may be tempered by Wesleyan and Anabaptist focus on obedience and suffering. An overemphasis on individualism, a constant characteristic of a consumerist society, might be moderated by Wesley's contention that salvation entails an inherently social process that takes place in communities of accountable discipleship and impacts how believers treat others.[53] In this way, Wesleyan soteriology becomes the foundation for discussion of ecclesiology, ethics, and a host of other issues.

Donald Dayton argues that "neither Methodism nor pentecostalism can be fully understood without reference to the other. Historically, they are like 'Siamese twins' bound to each other while fighting for their own identities."[54] Along those lines, Howard Snyder and Daniel Runyon underscore that the Wesleyan and pentecostal movements need each other because of their respective emphases on holiness and power.[55] As a methomennocostal, I would take Snyder and Runyon one step further and say that both movements also need the Anabaptists. When sanctification, Spirit-empowerment, and Christlikeness merge, a holistic, transformational faith—and more importantly, transformed people—will follow.

---

51. Here I join others—such as Howard and Richie, *Pentecostal Explorations;* Alvarado, "Twenty-First Century Holiness," 237–50; Knight, "From Aldersgate to Azusa," 82–98—in summoning Pentecostals to reexamine their Wesleyan roots.

52. Wesley, "Scripture Way of Salvation," §1.4, 373.

53. From a Mennonite perspective, Kreider, *Social Holiness,* sets the stage for a discussion of the living out of holiness in community. Notably, the book's foreword is written by Howard A. Snyder, a Free Methodist, and the afterword is by Dale M. Coulter, a member of the Church of God (Cleveland, TN). See also Archer and Hamilton, "Anabaptism-Pietism and Pentecostalism," 185–202.

54. Dayton, "Methodism and Pentecostalism," 187.

55. Snyder and Runyon, *Divided Flame,* 88–93.

BIBLIOGRAPHY

Alexander, Kimberly Ervin. "A Baptism of Divine Love: The Pentecostal Experience of Spirit Baptism." In *The Continuing Relevance of Wesleyan Theology: Essays in Honor of Laurence W. Wood*, edited by Nathan Crawford, 68–82. Eugene, OR: Wipf & Stock, 2011.

Alexander, Paul. "Spirit Empowered Peacemaking: Toward a Pentecostal Charismatic Peace Fellowship." *Journal of the European Pentecostal Theological Association* 22 (2002) 78–102.

Alvarado, Johnathan E. "Twenty-First Century Holiness: Living at the Intersection of Wesleyan Theology & Contemporary Pentecostal Values." In *A Future for Holiness: Pentecostal Explorations*, edited by Lee Roy Martin, 237–50. Cleveland, TN: CPT, 2013.

Archer, Kenneth J., and Andrew S. Hamilton. "Anabaptism-Pietism and Pentecostalism: Scandalous Partners in Protest." *Scottish Journal of Theology* 63 (2010) 185–202.

Beachy, Alvin. *The Concept of Grace in the Radical Reformation.* Nieuwkoop, Netherlands: De Graf, 1977.

Beaman, Jay. *Pentecostal Pacifism: The Origin, Development, and Rejection of Pacific Belief Among the Pentecostals.* Hillsboro, KS: Center for Mennonite Brethren Studies, 1989.

Bender, Harold S. *The Anabaptist Vision.* Scottdale, PA: Herald, 1944.

Boddy, Alexander A. "Health in Christ." *Confidence* 3.8 (1910).

———. "The Holy Ghost for Us." *Confidence* 5.1 (1912).

Boddy, John T. "Partakers of Christ." *The Pentecostal Evangel*, May 1, 1920.

Brown, Candy Gunther. "Introduction." In *The Future of Evangelicalism in America*, edited by Candy Gunther Brown and Mark Silk, 1–17. New York: Columbia University Press, 2016.

Brumback, Carl. *Suddenly . . . From Heaven: A History of the Assemblies of God.* Springfield, MO: Gospel, 1960.

Bundy, David. "Visions of Sanctification: Themes of Orthodoxy in the Methodist, Holiness, and Pentecostal Traditions." *Wesleyan Theological Journal* 39 (2004) 104–36.

Chilcote, Paul Wesley. *Recapturing the Wesleys' Vision: An Introduction to the Faith of John and Charles Wesley.* Downers Grove, IL: InterVarsity Academic, 2004.

Christensen, Michael J. Foreword to *Henri Nouwen: A Spirituality of Imperfection*, by Wil Hernandez, vii–xi. Mahwah, NJ: Paulist, 2006.

———. "Theosis and Sanctification: John Wesley's Reformulation of a Patristic Doctrine." *Wesleyan Theological Journal* 31.2 (1996) 71–94.

Clark, Matthew S. "Pentecostalism's Anabaptist Roots: Hermeneutical Implications." In *The Spirit and Spirituality: Essays in Honor of Russell P. Spittler*, edited by Wonsuk Ma and Robert P. Menzies, 194–211. London: T & T Clark, 2004.

Collins, Kenneth J. *The Scripture Way of Salvation: The Heart of John Wesley's Theology.* Nashville: Abingdon, 1997.

Coulter, Dale. "'Delivered By the Power of God': Toward a Pentecostal Understanding of Salvation." *International Journal of Systematic Theology* 10 (2008) 447–67.

Cox, A. B. "In Prison and Out Again." *The Christian Evangel*, June 29, 1918.

Crell, Kate Eisenbise. *Cooperative Salvation: A Brethren View of Atonement.* Eugene, OR: Wipf & Stock, 2014.

Dayton, Donald W. "Methodism and Pentecostalism." In *The Oxford Handbook of Methodist Studies*, edited by James E. Kirby and William J. Abraham, 171–87. Oxford: Oxford University Press, 2009.

———. *Theological Roots of Pentecostalism*. Grand Rapids: Baker Academic, 1987.

Dempster, Murray W. "Pacifism in Pentecostalism: The Case of the Assemblies of God." In *Proclaim Peace: Voices of Christian Pacifism from Unexpected Sources*, edited by Theron F. Schlabach and Richard T. Hughes, 31–57. Champaign, IL: University of Illinois Press, 1997.

Eldridge, G. N. "The Temple of the Living God." *The Weekly Evangel*, November 13, 1915.

Finger, Thomas N. *A Contemporary Anabaptist Theology: Biblical, Historical, Constructive*. Downers Grove, IL: InterVarsity, 2004.

Friedmann, Robert. *The Theology of Anabaptism: An Interpretation*. Eugene, OR: Wipf & Stock, 1999.

Gohr, Glenn. "A. B. and Dora Cox." *Assemblies of God Heritage* 15.2 (1995) 9–11, 31.

Grimsrud, Ted. "Should Anabapists Be Evangelicals?" *Thinking Pacifism*, June 11, 2012. https://thinkingpacifism.net/2012/06/11/should-anabaptists-be-evangelicals.

Hale, Felix A. "The New Birth Is Supernatural." *Weekly Evangel*, January 26, 1918.

Hauerwas, Stanley, and William H. Willimon. *Resident Aliens: Life in the Christian Colony*. Nashville: Abingdon, 1989.

Hiebert, Frances F. "The Atonement in Anabaptist Theology." *Direction* 30 (2001) 122–38.

Holmes, N. J. "Beautiful Life." *The Bridegroom's Messenger*, February 15, 1911.

Howard, Randy, and Tony Richie. *Pentecostal Explorations for Holiness Today: Words from Wesley*. Cleveland, TN: Cherohala, 2017.

Kärkkäinen, Veli-Matti. *One with God: Salvation as Deification and Justification*. Collegeville, MN: Liturgical, 2004.

Knight, Henry H., III. "From Aldersgate to Azusa: Wesley and the Renewal of Pentecostal Spirituality." *Journal of Pentecostal Theology* 8 (1996) 82–98.

Kraybill, Donald B. *The Upside-Down Kingdom*. 25th anniversary ed. Scottdale, PA: Herald, 2003.

Kreider, Alan. *Social Holiness: A Way of Living for God's People*. Eugene, OR: Wipf & Stock, 2008.

Lawrence, Bennett F. *The Apostolic Faith Restored*. St. Louis: Gospel, 1916.

Lederach, Paul M. *A Third Way: Conversations About Anabaptist/Mennonite Faith*. Scottdale, PA: Herald, 1980.

Macchia, Frank D. *Justified in the Spirit: Creation, Redemption, and the Triune God*. Grand Rapids: Eerdmans, 2010.

Maddox, Randy L. "John Wesley and Eastern Orthodoxy: Influences, Convergences, and Differences." *Asbury Theological Journal* 43.2 (1990) 29–53.

———. *Responsible Grace: John Wesley's Practical Theology*. Nashville: Kingswood, 1994.

Messiah College. "The Three Traditions That Shape Our Mission and Why." *Messiah College*. http://www.messiah.edu/info/20265/the_three_traditions_that_shape_our_mission_and_why.

Outler, Albert C. "The Place of Wesley in the Christian Tradition." In *The Place of Wesley in the Christian Tradition: Essays Delivered at Drew University in Celebration of the Commencement of the Publication of the Oxford Edition of the Works of John Wesley*, edited by Kenneth E. Rowe, 11–38. Metuchen, NJ: Scarecrow, 1976.

Philips, Dirk. "The New Birth and the New Creature." In *The Writings of Dirk Philips, 1504–1568*, translated and edited by Cornelius J. Dyck, et al., 293–315. Scottdale, PA: Herald, 1992.

Rice, Monte Lee. "The Pentecostal Triple Way: An Ecumenical Model of the Pentecostal *Via Salutis* and Soteriological Experience." In *A Future for Holiness: Pentecostal Explorations*, edited by Lee Roy Martin, 145–69. Cleveland, TN: CPT, 2013.

Robins, Roger. "Our Forgotten Heritage: Pentecostal Pacifism." *Assemblies of God Heritage* 6.4 (1986–87) 3–5.

Runyon, Theodore. *The New Creation: John Wesley's Theology Today*. Nashville: Abingdon, 1998.

Rybarczyk, Edmund J. *Beyond Salvation: Eastern Orthodoxy and Classical Pentecostalism on Becoming Like Christ*. Eugene, OR: Wipf & Stock, 2006.

Sanders, Fred. *Wesley on the Christian Life: The Heart Renewed in Love*. Wheaton, IL: Crossway, 2013.

Sawders, J. E. "Adjustment-Receiving." *The Bridegroom's Messenger*, November 15, 1909.

Shuman, Joel. "Pentecost and the End of Patriotism: A Call for the Restoration of Pacifism Among Pentecostal Christians." *Journal of Pentecostal Theology* 9 (1996) 70–96.

Simons, Menno. "A Plain Instruction from the Word of God, Concerning the Spiritual Resurrection, and New or Heavenly Birth." In *The Complete Works of Menno Simons*, translated by I. Daniel Rupp, edited by John F. Funk, 230–37. Elkhart, IN: John F. Funk & Brother, 1871.

Snyder, Howard A. "John Wesley and the Radical Protestant Tradition." *Asbury Seminarian* 33.3 (1978) 13–38.

———. *The Radical Wesley: Patterns for Church Renewal*. Eugene, OR: Wipf & Stock, 1996.

Snyder, Howard A., and Daniel V. Runyon. *The Divided Flame: Wesleyans and the Charismatic Renewal*. Eugene, OR: Wipf & Stock, 2011.

Studebaker, Steven M. "Pentecostal Soteriology and Pneumatology." *Journal of Pentecostal Theology* 11 (2003) 248–70.

Synan, Vinson. *The Holiness-Pentecostal Tradition: Charismatic Movements in the Twentieth Century*. 2nd ed. Grand Rapids: Eerdmans, 1997.

Thompson, Andrew C. "From Societies to the Society: The Shift from Holiness to Justice in the Wesleyan Tradition." *Methodist Review* 3 (2011) 141–72.

Unger, Walter. "The Church 'Without Spot or Wrinkle': Testing the Tradition." *Direction* 33 (2004) 33–47.

Ward, A. G. "Some More Food for Hungry Saints." *The Pentecostal Evangel*, November 29, 1919.

Watson, Kevin M. *Pursuing Social Holiness: The Band Meeting in Wesley's Thought and Popular Methodist Practice*. Oxford: Oxford University Press, 2014.

Wesley, John. "The Almost Christian: Sermon 2 (1741)." In *John Wesley's Sermons: An Anthology*, edited by Albert C. Outler and Richard P. Heitzenrater, 61–68. Nashville: Abingdon, 1991.

———. "A Farther Appeal to Men of Reason and Religion." In *The Miscellaneous Works of the Rev. John Wesley in Three Volumes*, 218–374. Vol. 1. New York: J & J Harper, 1828.

———. *The Letters of the Rev. John Wesley, AM*. Edited by John Telford. Vol. 6. London: Epworth, 1931.

———. "Preface to *Hymns and Sacred Poems* (1739)." In *The Works of the Reverend John Wesley*, edited by John Emory, 591–93. Vol. 7. New York: J. Collord, 1831.

————. "Salvation By Faith: Sermon 1 (1738)." In *John Wesley's Sermons: An Anthology,* edited by Albert C. Outler and Richard P. Heitzenrater, 39–47. Nashville: Abingdon, 1991.

————. "The Scripture Way of Salvation: Sermon 43 (1765)." In *John Wesley's Sermons: An Anthology,* edited by Albert C. Outler and Richard P. Heitzenrater, 371–80. Nashville: Abingdon, 1991.

Yoder, John Howard. *The Politics of Jesus: Vicit Agnus Noster.* 2nd ed. Grand Rapids: Eerdmans, 1994.

Yong, Amos. *In the Days of Caesar: Pentecostalism and Political Theology.* Grand Rapids: Eerdmans, 2010.

————. *The Spirit Poured Out on All Flesh: Pentecostalism and the Possibility of Global Theology.* Grand Rapids: Baker Academic, 2005.

4

Mennocostal

Living in the Liminal

BRIAN K. PIPKIN

MARGINALITY, OUTSIDERHOOD, AND LIMINALITY

THE TERMS "LIMINAL," "MARGINAL," and "outsider" describe my faith journey. But before I share my mennocostal story, let me say a word or two about these terms. Margin denotes something on the "edge, brink, border, or margin." It literally means the edge of something—a lake, sea, or space between a block of text and the edge of a page.[1] Marginality is just that: to be on the margins of something. Victor Turner describes marginality as the state of simultaneously belonging to more than one cultural or social grouping. But marginality, as Turner says, should not be confused with "outsiderhood," that is someone outside the cultural, political, and social structure.[2] Marginality, unlike outsiderhood, excludes the free will of the individual. While some may choose outsiderhood as an act of social protest or lack of faith in a given system, outsiders often have a choice to operate "outside" the system. (Not all outsiders are outsiders by choice.) Marginality denotes people or groups being pushed toward inferiority *against their will*.

---

1. Online Etymology Dictionary, "Margin."
2. Turner, *Drama, Fields, and Metaphors*, 233.

The term "liminal" describes someone who occupies a position at, or on both sides of, a boundary or threshold.[3] The terms "liminal," "liminality," or "liminal state," as Turner says, denotes people or entities as "neither here nor there: they are betwixt and between the positions assigned and arrayed by law, custom, convention, and ceremony."[4] Liminality represents the "midpoint of transition between two positions."[5]

My story is one in which all three terms resonate. However, in my current stage of faith, liminal best represents my present reality as I feel like I have too much invested in two religious cultures to walk away from either. At times I feel suspended between both, holding both in tension, praise, and critique. My lack of experience (i.e., speaking in tongues) has marginalized me in the pentecostal church and my lack of culture and connection has impacted my life in the Mennonite church. While the Mennonite church has been accommodating to outsiders like me, I oftentimes feel like I will never truly assimilate. My "liminal" position in the Mennonite church began when I moved from Southern California to Pennsylvania and made the transition from a pentecostal to Mennonite community in 2008. While liminality provides me with freedom of movement and little constraint, it also fails to give any true sense of stability. Liminal living means you never fully feel like you belong anywhere and you are never fully committed to any one group. There are years of tradition and connection to history that I am not part of. I sometimes feel unintentionally left out in a church setting by my own ignorance of the songs, local Mennonite history, the names, foods, the jokes, the camps, the schools, and the vocabulary.

I admit some of my being an "outsider" is by choice. First, I have created some distancing by declining requests for church membership. My resistance to church membership predates my Mennonite days. I am opposed for reasons that have nothing to do with any particular religious orientation.

Second, during my teenage years in youth group at an Assemblies of God church in California, around the age of 15, I was a victim of sexual abuse by a trusted youth leader. As many victims of abuse have experienced, church leadership failed miserably at handling the situation and protecting the victims. My mother threatened a lawsuit against the church as the youth leader had criminal record which they failed to check, but at that

---

3. Oxford Living Dictionaries, "Liminal."

4. Turner, "Liminality and Communitas," 95.

5. Turner, "Liminality and Communitas," 261. See also La Shure, "What is Liminality?"

time, I was adamant that she could not do such a thing. It felt sacrilegious. Since the incident, I have developed a somewhat critical attitude (distancing) toward church polity and religious leadership as I have witnessed too many clergy obsess about self-advancement, promotion, careerism, and image maintenance. On one hand, I was a Jesus-loving, Bible-obsessed, God-and-country gullible teenager trying to make sense of what it means to follow Jesus while witnessing a pastoral staff that was falling one by one like dominos to some kind of sexual scandal. I had little but a small maroon Bible my dad gave me to keep me loosely anchored.

Third, by way of admission, I rarely attend music Sundays, though I do not have a deep philosophical reason why. (This is an example of how outsiderhood is also a choice.) For some reading this it may sound irreligious, offensive, or ignorant but for me, hymns and the assumption that everyone in the congregation knows how to interpret and harmonize music is a practice that needs another look, especially for outsiders. I once had one Mennonite colleague of mine criticize "evangelical" worship as "throw up music," referring to projecting the songs on a white screen instead of reading them out of a book. I also recall one presentation by Shane Hipps, then Mennonite pastor, which went out on a limb and told a group of Mennonites at Hesston College that hymns were a tribal in-group practice that discourages new growth from the outside. That was tough to hear, but there are elements of truth in what he said. Though I have been part of a Mennonite community since 2008, I feel that Mennonite worship (four-part harmony) is an in-group practice that can (not always) exclude non-cultured Mennonites like myself that come into the fold with few Mennonite connections and no Mennonite family tree. At the risk of blanket assumptions, singing hymns in a Baptist church in Philadelphia is very different than singing hymns in a Mennonite church in Pennsylvania. One is more casual and informal while the other is technical, sometimes requiring time to instruct the congregation, sort of like a choir. I have never been in a choir, nor have I taken any music classes, so when it comes to hymn singing in a Mennonite church, I oftentimes feel like an "idiot"—using Peter Rollin's term to describe people who do not understand a particular system of practice, the dos and don'ts of a ritual, tradition, or custom.[6] I find myself listening more than singing these days, and the theology of hymns remains inspiring.

Aside from this "narcissism of small differences," the descriptive term "mennocostal" remains appealing to me because it represents a liminal

6. Rollins, "How to be an Idiot."

state or faith practice—a betwixt and between state for those who identify with two different cultures and systems while remaining an "outsider" of sorts—by choice and sometimes not by choice.

There is more that needs to be said about the term "marginal." I acknowledge my reluctance in using the term "marginalization" because I am a white, abled-bodied, American, Christian, heterosexual male—all privileges that go unnoticed in the circles of my daily routine. I recognize this privilege came from a combination of luck, education, networks, gender, and ethnicity. I understand marginalities vary in definition, severity, and sacrifice. It means different things to different people and I respect the diversity of stories and struggles, recognizing that my use of the term is limited to my experience.

I acknowledge my participation in what Mary Fulkerson calls "white obliviousness to racialized habituations," in which white culture embodies racialized biases in the habits of faith. This "white habitus" of associations and networks strive unconsciously and synergistically to perpetuate the myth of white superiority through normalizing white culture.[7] Some, not all, of the pentecostal churches I attended had leaders that defined themselves by their oppositional stance towards enemies—not only "principalities and powers," but racial and anti-capitalist enemies. Sermons felt like pep talks about self-defense against threats posed by racial integration and cultural pollution.[8] The perceived existential threat to white racial survival was always subconsciously in the background. I also acknowledge my racial conditioning. Although I am conditioned by racism, I am antiracist by choice.[9] Challenging white assumptions, biases, judgements or "supremacy" requires cultivating a self-awareness of my assumptions as a white male in small town America.

Second, I realize my experience is just that—my personal experience which is contextually conditioned by the limitations of my worldview, sex, ethnicity, and economic status. While some experiences are good and bad—as I perceive "good and bad"—they do not define the movements I speak about. Exceptions exist, but there are exceptions with any group. What I interpret to be a negative in either pentecostal or Mennonite culture is perceived by others as a positive. Personal narratives are messy, complex, and anecdotal. The temptation is to project, generalize, exaggerate, judge,

7. Fulkerson and Mount Shoop, *Body Broken*, 10, 13, 18, 38.
8. Berry, *Blood and Faith*, 4.
9. Wise, "FAQs."

and superimpose my perspective as the norm for others. So I write with these cautions in mind. Because pentecostalism is so vast and diverse, my story does not speak for the movement at large. My experience is one of the 500-plus million experiences of those who walk inside the matrix of what we call the Pentecostal movement. Moreover, I am not writing as an academic. Instead, this is my personal story. Like all personal stories, my story is not neat and clean but messy, complex, and nuanced.

"Marginality" is the term my colleague, Jay Beaman, encouraged me to embrace after learning about my struggle with my pentecostal identity after graduating from Bible College. While I have experiences in both pentecostal and Mennonite traditions, I never fully assimilated into either group. I remain chunky and unblended. Though I have no official title within either denomination, I consider myself to be Menno-costal (in that order). I am more comfortable with the mennocostal label than with other religious labels—if I must label myself. I find myself connecting better intellectually with my pentecostal forbearers who championed gender equity, nonviolence, disarmament, racial equality, and forward-thinking politics. However, while my forebearers inspire me in my research, they are unable to provide the community support needed to follow Jesus today. This is where the Mennonite church comes into play by providing a community that expresses many convictions of early pentecostals that are now deemed insignificant by the movement. Holding pacifist convictions with an introverted disposition, I found it difficult to be faithful to my own peace convictions within an evangelical sub-culture that rewarded extroversion and provided religious rationalizations for state-sanctioned violence. In school, I made genuine connections with classmates, though many relationships have faded. I witnessed some who positioned themselves to take over existing churches while others were preoccupied with what Erving Goffman calls impression management—building your reputation, following, and brand at all costs.[10]

Experiencing cynicism and self-doubt, I never fully embraced the pentecostal ethos as presented in class and church. My understanding of Jesus as a non-white Amer-European, scripture as interpreted contextually from the margins, church tradition as radical rather than reformed, atonement as liberation, biblical nonconformity, and the church as countercultural, were unwelcomed themes in church. This is not to say that all pentecostals are in disagreement with these topics. I find pentecostals in academia more

10. Goffman, *Presentation of Self.*

intellectually open than local church or denominational leadership, making it difficult for new graduates to assimilate into local church ministry. Oftentimes what one perceives as a negative, others perceive as a positive. During my undergraduate studies, I followed the rules, completed my assignments, participated in church activities, developed friendships, but felt somewhat uneasy about the direction I was heading, though never publicly questioning this internal struggle for meaning and direction in fear of what others might think. At this point in my life, I was too financially and relationally committed to express doubt to my peers, especially with licensing on the horizon. On a subconscious level I emotionally withdrew, while intellectually I was determined to find answers to my growing curiosity.

After completing our studies in Bible College, my wife and I pursued a graduate degree in intercultural studies. We felt most comfortable in classes where professors drew sources from a non-western worldview as well as challenging status-quo understandings of God. We felt comfortable in classes on anthropology, contextual hermeneutics, communications, world religions, and ethics. We considered enrolling at Fuller Seminary but felt there was no better way to study missiology than to immerse ourselves in another culture. So in 2004, we moved to the Philippines to attend Asia Pacific Theological Seminary, an Assemblies of God school where we completed our master's degrees. Over 23 nationalities represented the student body. We were one of two couples from the United States. We were the minority, and it opened our eyes. It was a challenging but formative time as we began to deconstruct our faith in a non-American context. It was during this time in a pentecostal seminary that I had my first encounter with Anabaptism. This first encounter was truly accidental (or was it?) while studying a course in missiology with a Korean-American professor. After reviewing the course syllabus, I stumbled upon a book by Donald Kraybill, an Anabaptist expert on Old Order Amish, titled *The Upside Down Kingdom*.[11] Kraybill helped explain what I had been struggling with over the last four years of my theological education. His words felt like they were my own.

SPEAKING IN TONGUES

During my time in seminary, I had the opportunity to take a class with an official Assemblies of God historian, the late William Menzies and his son

11. Kraybill, *Upside Down Kingdom*.

Robert Menzies. The class was on the history and theology of the Pentecostal movement in which we spent substantial time on the doctrine of speaking in tongues (i.e., glossolalia). Sitting down after class I asked the question regarding tongues as normative doctrine (i.e., initial evidence) as necessary for Spirit baptism. After explaining my inability to speak in tongues—though I have prayed for others who have received this gift— their response to me was intriguing. Both William and Robert admitted that the argument they made for initial evidence in class was lacking. If Pentecostal groups relaxed their interpretation on initial evidence, they explained, what would separate pentecostals from charismatics? The Menzies explained that classical pentecostals are holding to initial evidence doctrine as a denominational distinctive despite it's weak pragmatic and theological basis and the severed relationships it produces. This was clearly a boundary issue—a form of self-preservation through boundary maintenance. It positions pentecostals apart from other competitors. This boundary marker is what Jay Beaman describes in this book as representing "difference." While difference can be prophetic, it often leads to doctrines of exclusion when elevated to essential expressions of belief and practice. Normative doctrine begins as a well-intentioned way of interpreting and capturing a mysterious work of the Spirit in a systematic way to encourage others to participate in the outpouring of the Spirit. Over time, however, another pattern begins to emerge. Good intentioned doctrine leads to difference, then difference leads to exceptionalism, then exceptionalism leads to boundary maintenance, then boundary maintenance leads to the exclusion and judgement of the Othered. When doctrines and denominations seek to form us in homogeneity, it is difficult for these systems to stretch into diversity. This "unruliness of difference" feels like chaos and loss of control.[12]

I felt good after my conversation with the Menzies. It was reassurance for me that maybe I should stop blaming myself for not speaking in tongues. Although I was open, believed in the gift, and tried to be as flexible and open-minded as possible—with advice by many pentecostal pastors and professors—to speak in tongues, I always fell short. I was told the problem is with me—it is my sin, my lack of faith—that prevented me from receiving this gift. The doctrine was never in question by the denomination; instead, my faith was interrogated. I was the problem, yet I could never identify the problem—if there was one. The Menzies' helped me to regain self-confidence and a deeper theological understanding as well as a healthy

12. Mount Shoop, *Let the Bones Dance*, loc. 206.

framework for questioning the structures and doctrines of religious organizations still operating within a Christendom mindset. It remains difficult to question doctrines that appeal to personal experience. How do you critique a hundred year old doctrine based on the subjectivity of the interpreter? I began to ask different questions—questions that would eventually take me on another path.

ODD DUCKS

After completing our studies in the Philippines, we moved back to Southern California where I continued my education in religious studies at Azusa Pacific University. During my studies, I began to test my pentecostal beliefs with my newly discovered Anabaptist values. My professors found my research interesting as I blended pentecostal spirituality with Anabaptist theology, but some of my classmates felt differently, especially regarding the pentecostal emphasis on gender equity and Anabaptist nonviolence. Males were threatened by the idea of a strong and independent (dare I say Spirit-empowered) female presence. Still others were offended at the thought of questioning loyalty to state power in matters of taking life. Because biblical nonconformity is more concerned with issues we typically associate with good citizenship and common sense—loyalty, obedience, respect, killing for the nation—I found it difficult to engage nonviolence at a deeper level with those in disagreement.[13] I learned that nationalism, which was never questioned in the pentecostal churches I attended, is a loyalty that supersedes all other obligations. As a Christian, it was permissible to believe in the "unreasonableness" of Christian nonviolence, but it had to remain subservient to loyalty to country.[14] Noncooperation with the State has historically brought the swift hand of the government down on pacifists during both World Wars. However, State punishment can also be nonviolent. Organizations and individuals can be punished by reduced status, friends, financial support, and opportunities. Conventional norms regulate behavior. People naturally have a strong tendency to imitate the successful. As cultural evolutionist Robert Boyd notes, cultural evolution creates "cooperative groups" that learn and internalize social norms, imitating the successful and avoiding punishment. Those that lack these instincts violate the prevailing norms and experience adverse reaction by the group.

13. Yoder, *Radical Christian Discipleship*, 54.
14. Watts, *Bowing Toward Babylon*, 8.

"People feel deep loyalty to their kin and friends, but they're also moved by larger loyalties to clan, tribe, class, and nation."[15]

It is hard to deconstruct Christian nationalism when it is couched in virtuous and obligatory rhetoric. It violates the norms of our tribe. Many congregations, while giving ascent to nonconformity, ultimately give priority to what is socially acceptable, even at the risk of violating core convictions like nonviolence. We naturally default to common sense, effectiveness, and acceptability over scripture, many times out of convenience.[16] Our rationalizations, as Stephen Mattson explains, are the subtle and invisible ways we routinely rebel against the Spirit.[17] We are rarely held accountable for being reasonable even if our "reason" violates the elementary principles of the gospel.

After graduating from a pentecostal college and seminary, I made myself available to take on any job that my denomination had within a local church, including making myself available for the risky venture of church planting. My wife and I arranged a meeting with a local district supervisor in Southern California to discuss ministry opportunities within the denomination. We shared our openness and availability. We were ready to do anything. After explaining our peace convictions, he said most local pastors would find us threatening. Since we were not the type to quietly follow someone without challenging the "why," he felt we would be frustrated by the restrictions of the denomination's vision and direction. We were "odd ducks," he said and "we have no pond for you to swim in." He suggested we look at other ministries or denominations that would better accommodate our convictions. I soon realized that being a non-tongues-talking pacifist narrowed my opportunities within the pentecostal movement.

Despite this set back, and being labeled "odd ducks," I pursued and received my ministerial license. My wife, however, chose not to pursue licensing following this conversation. Meanwhile, we both took on community outreach responsibilities at a Filipino pentecostal church in Norwalk, California. I soon learned the need to self-censor some of my peace convictions. As I began implementing my mennocostal convictions within a pentecostal church, as well as deconstructing my inherited worldview, I learned how much theology is pre-textual, especially related to issues of power and politics. Advances in moral psychology are helping us understand how biblical

---

15. Boyd and Richerson, "Culture," 17.

16. Yoder, *Politics of Jesus*; Niebuhr, *Social Sources of Denominationalism*, 4–5.

17. Mattson, "Christianity's Most Common Sin."

interpretation is more or less a rationalization of our pre-commitments to nation, sex, power, position, and money. We are all guilty of using the Bible to seek post-hoc justification of pre-determined positions. We feel first, then rationalize later. During the early months of ministry, I learned that many of my deeply defended beliefs were visceral, gut-level, instinctual re-actions. My rationalizations were a defense mechanism triggered by threats to my conservative, white, American, binary worldview.[18]

INTROVERSION AND PENTECOSTAL WORSHIP

Aside from the doctrinal tension I experienced trying to converge Anabap-tist convictions in a pentecostal culture, nothing proved more difficult than being an introvert navigating an extroverted pentecostal culture. I experi-enced a culture that was more concerned about charisma than character. Evangelical subculture, reflective of US culture, has an extroverted bias that is reflected in evangelism, preaching, worship, and in the choice of leader-ship in pentecostal churches. Most leadership positions require extroverted qualities. Those who are talkative, energetic, outgoing and assertive have the advantage over those who are caricatured as passive and antisocial be-cause they are thoughtful, quiet, and reflective. As Adam McHugh writes:

> Churches sometimes unintentionally equate faithfulness with extroversion; we draw up a composite sketch of the 'ideal' Chris-tian—gregarious, with an overt passion and enthusiasm, eager to participate in a wide variety of activities, shares their faith with strangers regularly, assumes leadership positions quickly, opens up their home to others often—and this ideal person starts sound-ing suspiciously like an extrovert.[19]

As an introvert, I was more at peace in a Mennonite congregation. Mennonite culture tends to be more introverted—or at least provides a worship context where introverts can reflect, think, and learn in a quiet and less noisy atmosphere. Worship in a Mennonite church is more con-servative and structured while pentecostal worship allows a type of flex-ibility and spontaneity rarely found in many white Mennonite churches. This worship style is both reflective of ethnicity and location. Non-white churches, whether Mennonite or Baptist, will generally be more energetic

18. Haidt, "Emotional Dog."

19. McHugh, *Introverts in the Church*; Weirick, "Why Introverts Would Rather Avoid Church."

with worship and movement than a white suburban church, regardless of affiliation or doctrine. Nevertheless, I tend to view the overall Mennonite worship culture as conservative, quiet, and more structured. Pentecostal worship—the level of noise, movement, emotion, and tone of the preacher, can be overstimulating for introverts. I remember one instance in a pentecostal church where the service was paused mid-way, someone went up front and began to prophecy. A small group broke out in spontaneous dance inside the sanctuary while about half the congregation watched (likely the introverts). One church leader ran up to me, grabbed my hand, and began tugging my arm to get me to join the dance around the sanctuary. I resisted and remained in my seat. After a few more instances like these, I looked for another church. While this situation happened to me, I will say the physical coercion I experienced is not commonplace in pentecostal settings. I do not wish to encourage stereotyping, as pentecostals have often been inaccurately portrayed by Hollywood. In my preaching practicum class, the professor told us that our last assignment would be an impromptu sermon—probably the worst fear of any introvert. If public speaking was not bad enough, being asked to speak on something you did not prepare for is a bad day for an introverted perfectionist. So, I did what most introverts would do; I skipped class. I also recall one of my first assignments in my Evangelism and Discipleship class where I was tasked to approach a stranger—preferably a homeless person—in a local park to share my faith. I reluctantly completed the assignment, but the approach made me feel sick. This confrontational approach did not reflect my personality or style. I am not questioning this form of confrontational evangelism, but it is not my preference. It may work for some, though I have my doubts about long-term effectiveness.

TOWARDS MENNOCOSTALISM

From 2006 to 2017 I served as an editor for *Pax Pneuma*, the journal of Pentecostals and Charismatics for Peace and Justice. During this period my Anabaptist values began to strengthen through interaction with like-minded friends and colleagues. I continued to hold on to my pentecostal tradition, though I discarded some beliefs while beginning to embrace Anabaptist practices. I was walking between two traditions while never occupying one entirely. I learned that walking in the margins is not binary. It does not mean you are all out or all in. Rather, you occupy the nonessential space of an organization. When I was turned away by one group, I was accepted by another. Some people never truly assimilate in either culture, as is my experience. And some leave altogether, never fully being accepted by any group.

After accepting a job in an Anabaptist para-church organization, my family moved from Southern California to Lancaster, Pennsylvania, where we immersed ourselves in Mennonite culture. Since living in Pennsylvania, I had the opportunity to work at Palmer Seminary of Eastern University, a Baptist-affiliated institution, and Ron Sider's Evangelicals for Social Action. During this period, my pentecostal license was suspended due to my admission to the licensing coordinator that I did not speak in tongues. I explained that I have prayed for people who have spoken in tongues, but I have never experienced that gift, no matter how hard I tried or how much faith I expressed. It was explained to me that there was a roadblock toward fulfillment or that something internal was hindering my release into this experience or I was not taking the necessary step of faith. The doctrine itself was never in question, but my faith was. Instead of being open that there are other "evidences" of God's spirit—if we must seek a material sign—I was automatically guilty of lack of faith, or sincerity, or not seeking enough, or having a sin in my life. I assured myself that many early pentecostals were relaxed on the necessity of speaking in tongues—many of whom did not make it a mandatory rule.[20] William Seymour, for example, rejected Charles Parham's initial evidence doctrine and was later rejected by white pentecostals who were unable to allow a sustained role for black leadership. What I feel is more in line with pentecostal spirit is the ability to break down gender and racial barriers.[21] When I think of the founder of my former pentecostal denomination, I see many Spirit-led "evidences" at work such as serving vulnerable populations through outreach. Evidence, for me, I explained, is more than personal experience—it is tangible Spirit-led justice-seeking, community-building activity. These are commonly repeated themes we see in the Bible that that receive much less attention and regulation than tongues. Though nonviolence has more biblical support than tongues, we continue to make tongues mandatory, while considering killing in warfare to be a matter of individual conscience.[22] Throughout the

20. Cartwright, "Everywhere Spoken Against."
21. Alexander, "Speaking in Tongues of Nonviolence," 1–19.
22. Alexander, Peace to War, 350.

conversation, I felt as though I was pentecostal enough for the founder of the movement, but not for the current organization.

I believe speaking in tongues is a legitimate working of the Spirit, however, I could not bring myself to advocate that it be mandatory (normative) for all followers of Jesus. In my last attempt to explain my position, I was quoted the book of Acts and that glossolalia followed Spirit baptism, almost mechanical in a way. This was the same conversation I had with William Menzies a few years earlier, who explained to me the weakness and exclusivity of normative belief. Pentecostals have creatively worked around this by linguistically separating gifts of the spirit versus signs of the Spirit—the former being speaking in tongues. I explained that Paul's desire for all to speak in tongues does not necessitate its universality. If Luke intended to communicate this normative doctrine in Acts, then why did he not consistently present tongues as the immediate result of Spirit baptism (Acts 8:17; 9:17–19)? As Gordon Fee writes, "if normativeness were Luke's concern in the matter of individual narratives, how does one explain his failure to narrate every instance of the same kind of experience?"[23] Speaking in tongues is a prominent accompanying sign, but by the same method, one can argue that prophecy functions in the same manner. Using the same systematizing approach to Acts, one can make the case that initial evidence is not tongues, but prophecy. By recording a multitude of responses to the Spirit, Luke shows that he was not concerned with any one phenomenon such as tongues. Signs included speaking the word of God boldly, speaking in tongues, prophecy, visions, dreams, or no physical evidence at all (Acts 2:4, 17; 4:31; 8:17; 19:6). Robert Menzies argued that the pentecostal gift is not tongues, but rather an empowering experience that enables Christians to participate effectively in the mission of God.[24] The need for initial evidence distracts from the biblical emphasis on what David Lim identifies as the "ultimate evidence" or the "primary evidence" of love.[25] Despite going through this unexpected situation, I continued to defend the gift of tongues to critics in my class. I tried to avoid two extremes: the cessationist who attempts to exclude the supernatural power of the Spirit in the church and those that limit the Spirit to a normative doctrine of tongues. Both seek to predict and control. I am reminded of what Richard Rohr says about the Spirit: "We are threatened by anything we cannot control, that part of God

23. Menzies and Menzies, *Spirit and Power*, 103.

24. Menzies and Menzies, *Spirit and Power*, 129.

25. Lim, "Evangelical Critique," 222.

'which blows where it will' (John 3:8) and which our theologies and church can never perfectly predict nor inhibit (Acts 10:44–48). We have a hard time measuring it, controlling it, predicting it, or inhibiting it. It sounds an awful lot like Spirit."[26] Although the licensing coordinator and I could not reach agreement on what I perceived to be a non-essential, we mutually respected each other's opinions. My license was eventually terminated.

I recall the first time I attended a Mennonite church. I was taken back, somewhat amazed and in disbelief, hearing themes of equity, poverty, justice, and peacemaking in the same sentence with Jesus. It was a new experience for me and my family. Today I find myself walking between two traditions while not fully placing myself completely in either camp. The term "mennocostal" remains the best label to describe the convergence of my convictions at this stage in my life. I embrace the democratic and gender inclusiveness of the pentecostal tradition while seeking to follow the Anabaptist emphasis on peacemaking. Although I am not a cultural Mennonite, I hope others realize that having a Mennonite last name does not guarantee having Anabaptist beliefs. There are many who do not carry a Mennonite last name or attend a Mennonite church that hold strongly to Anabaptist convictions. I am one of them.

FAILURE OF DIALECTIC

Reflecting on my dual pentecostal-Mennonite tradition, I wish to highlight an important observation. Within both traditions I experienced what Douglas John Hall calls the "failure of dialectic."[27] This failure of religious systems occurs when religious organizations overemphasize half of the Christian gospel at the expense of the whole. Progressive traditions, as represented in my branch of the Mennonite church, often give primacy to the collectivity of systemic concern (peace, poverty, war, injustice) while demoting concerns for the individual. Activism, then, fails to address of the loneliness, hopelessness, drama, and struggles in the lives of individuals. Speaking to the problems of the personal life, as Hall notes, generally requires a deeper commitment that is intellectually and spiritually more costly than addressing large-scale concerns "over there" or "across the street" that are less personal and more abstract. It takes a rigor and sympathy that is often lacking for the activist who is contextually removed from the perceived

26. Rohr, *Yes*, 96.

27. Hall, *Waiting for Gospel*, xxii.

social ill they fight. We become so "undialectically attentive" to social issues that the life of the person is neglected.[28] Pentecostals also struggle with imbalance. They, too, have participated in this unequal expression of faith by minimizing the collective. Some of these comparisons can be unfair. Pentecostals do seek "social justice" though not necessarily using a collectivistic framework. Pentecostals, as Donald Miller and Tetsunao Yamamori document, seek social change from the bottom up, one person at a time, in hopes of altering demonic systems that enslave.[29] I remain skeptical of this individual approach to social change. People rarely self-regulate their wants and desires for the greater good of their neighbor. In a capitalist market, economics wins out over religious loyalties, especially when profit depends on neglecting collective concerns. Survival is the game. Profit is the prize. And we as humans have mastered the art of denial and obfuscation. For me, it is not an either/or but both/and. I have seen glimpses of both/and in pentecostal and Mennonite churches. I also remain skeptical of a liberal framework that subordinates personal concern and transformation. It is common sense, though difficult to implement when leading people with contrasting political allegiances, to walk in a way that resists binary worldviews. A blending of these two traditions—the pentecostal emphasis on personal transformation and the Mennonite emphasis on collectivities—is a much needed combination for a new generation. I remain drawn to the Mennonite collectivism I hear each Sunday at church. I also find myself longing for worship that brings the gospel down to the personal realm—life, relationships, family, survival. Again, this is not suggesting Mennonites fail to relate the gospel to personal needs, but to suggest that it is an area for improvement.

OBLIGATIONS

The last few years I have spent a considerable amount of time with Jay Beaman documenting a plethora of primary sources giving evidence that the overwhelming majority of early pentecostals refused to kill.[30] It is imperative that peace churches do not dismiss the short-lived history of pentecostal pacifism, but pay attention to the particularities that led to its demise.

28. Hall, *Waiting for the Gospel*, xxiii.

29. Miller and Yamamori, *Global Pentecostalism*.

30. Pipkin and Beaman, *Early Pentecostals on Nonviolence*; Beaman and Pipkin, *Pentecostal and Holiness Statements*.

No group, no matter how strong their peace tradition, is immune from the same forces that led to the great reversal of pentecostalism. Pentecostals and Mennonites, like all movements, are in danger of proclaiming and creating statements that look better on paper than in practice. There's a temptation for some to brush aside the pentecostal peace narrative as haphazard, short-lived, an unusual exception. It could never happen to my group, we tell ourselves. The demise of pentecostal peace should serve as a cautionary reminder of the strong instinctual pull of cultural accommodation, conformity, and upward mobility. The relaxation of Christian pacifism is already underway in some Anabaptist groups.[31] This cautionary tale serves as a reminder that nationalism is a subtle force that narrows our commitments and concerns to a secular nation-state whose agenda is not God's kingdom.[32] The postmodern and entertainment culture we inhabit no longer lives by allegiances or obligations to denominations and their proclamations. Individual conscience has become the primary ethic by which we govern moral standards. Both conformity and individualization have roots in the fact that social ties and relationships are becoming slacker and less binding; therefore obedience to norms and personalities is intensified. As Jürgen Moltmann writes, "What is wanted by the dominant culture is precisely not a Christianity that that has 'become mature and wise.'" Instead, what is wanted is a "Christianity that can devote itself unquestioningly to the task of restoring the American Dream; the same Christianity that was wanted by Constantine, by Henry VIII, the German princes at the time of the reformation, and by Adolf Hitler—namely adolescent Christianity."[33]

The Anabaptist commitment to nonviolence is what ultimately stuck with me. I learned that gospel nonviolence is more than denying our natural impulse for retaliation and harm. It is offering strangers the unconditional, radical, and counterintuitive love that God has extended to us. We trust God with our souls in the next life—that is easy. But how much do we trust God with the outcomes of this life? Our human instinct is to predict, control, and commodify time, nature, and people. We shift allegiances as they are convenient and self-fulfilling. I remain intrigued as to why nonviolence remains so offensive to many Christians. Is it because nonviolence collapses the core pillars of evangelical theology and the core founding myths of American exceptionalism? If we reject all violence, how

---

31. Schrag, "Core Value at Risk"; Preheim, "Losing Peace, Leaving Identity."
32. Camp, *Mere Discipleship*, 158.
33. Moltmann, *Theology of Hope*, 13.

does that impact our understanding of atonement theory and the politics of the security state to which we depend? Are churches participating in subtle forms of symbolic idolatry during their worship services by co-mingling the Christian God with the American flag? What does God-and-country rhetoric tell us about the foundations of our trust and identity? Do we have the moral courage, even to the detriment of a career, relationships, and possibly ordination, to commit ourselves to the example of Jesus? "Authentic faith," writes Peter Rollins "is expressed not in the mere acceptance of a belief system, but in sacrificial, loving action."[34] Some pentecostals I know are familiar with the sacrifices of giving loyalty to the obligations of discipleship over citizenship. Mennonites know such consequences all too well. My hope is that whether by economic necessity or being pushed outside the fold, we remain faithful to our passions, purposefully making time to pursue our gifts in creative ways. For some, that might be identifying with a new term like "Mennocostal" to express their lived reality of converging traditions. Although "Mennocostal" is not an organized movement, it is a helpful term to identify a trend—a "bilingual identity"—for some who, like myself, no longer fit traditional categories.

CONCLUSION

I do not consider myself a prophet in the biblical sense, though I do see myself as pushing some boundaries. Prophets have always resided on the edge of the inside. Richard Rohr describes the prophet not as an outsider throwing rocks, or a comfortable insider who defends the status quo, but as someone who lives with two tensions held tightly—the faithful insider and the critical outsider. The prophet balances loyalty and critique. This, explains Rohr, leaves the prophet with "nowhere to lay his head" while meriting the "hatred of all." Prophets work within the establishment but are very critical of its shortcomings. People inside belonging systems are often threatened by those who are not within the in-group. The modern prophetic role allows individuals to critique the systems they work within. People like Martin Luther King, Jr., Dorothy Day, and Oscar Romero were marginalized, excluded, and persecuted because they exposed the systems they tried to reform. This, says Rohr, is always the fate of prophets. The point I take away from Rohr's analysis of prophetic ministry is that living on the edge means you are free from central seductions. You are free to speak your

34. Rollins, *Orthodox Heretic*, loc. 155.

convictions. You are less inclined to confuse essentials with non-essentials. You do not easily get tied down by loyalty tests, trivia, and job security. There is little room for truth when faced with insider restraints.[35]

I have made peace with occupying the margins. I am not an insider within either denomination. I embrace both traditions (with exceptions of course) and find hope knowing there are others like me who have similar stories of convergence. The Anabaptist faith has taught me the importance of following Jesus rather than drawing lines of who is in or out. Anabaptism is a tradition that remains suspicious of theological grids or traditions that undermine the radicalness of the Bible's message. My draw to Anabaptism is also rooted in the history of the movement. I do not wish to idealize the movement, but through my research, I found an appreciation for Anabaptist groups that were suspicious of the subjection of scripture to philosophy, reason, and theology. They did not produce systematic theology like their contemporaries. They functioned, a lot like early pentecostals, pragmatically and situationally, obeying scripture rather than analyzing or categorizing its doctrines.[36] Although I am not licensed with a pentecostal group, I continue to admire the freedom pentecostal culture provides in allowing God to move in diverse, unpredictable, and spontaneous ways. I may never know if my story is helpful to someone who might be struggling with the same identify crisis that I faced. However, I trust that God will be with those on the margins, those in a liminal state, those neither here nor there, but roaming the edges of the center, and finding the courage to express and follow their convictions outside the systems we inherit as children and inhabit as adults.

BIBLIOGRAPHY

Alexander, Paul. *Peace to War: Shifting Allegiances in the Assemblies of God.* Telford, PA: Cascadia, 2009.
———. "Speaking in Tongues of Nonviolence: American Pentecostals, Nationalism, and Pacifism." *Evangelical Review of Society and Politics* 1.2. (2007) 1–19.
Beaman, Jay, and Brian K. Pipkin. *Pentecostal and Holiness Statements on War and Peace.* Eugene, OR: Pickwick, 2013.

35. Rohr, "Life on the Edge."
36. Murray, *Biblical Interpretation.*

Berry, Damon T. *Blood and Faith: Christianity in American White Nationalism.* Syracuse, NY: Syracuse University Press, 2017.

Boyd, Rob, and P. J. Richerson. "Culture and the Evolution of the Human Social Instincts." University of California, Davis. Personal files of Brian Pipkin.

Camp, Lee. *Mere Discipleship.* Grand Rapids: Eerdmans, 2003.

Cartwright, Desmond. "Everywhere Spoken Against: Opposition to Pentecostalism 1907–1930." *Smith Wigglesworth.* http://www.smithwigglesworth.com/index.php/smith-wigglesworth-pensketches/miscellaneous/everywhere-spoken-against.

Fulkerson, Mary McClintock, and Maria W. Mount Shoop. *A Body Broken, A Body Betrayed: Race, Memory, and Eucharist in White-Dominated Churches.* Eugene, OR: Cascade, 2015.

Goffman, Erving. *The Presentation of Self in Everyday Life.* Anchor, 1959.

Haidt, Jonathan. "The Emotional Dog and Its Rational Tale: A Social Intuitionist Approach to Moral Judgement." *Psychological Review* 108 (2001) 814–34.

Hall, John Douglas. *Waiting for Gospel.* Eugene, OR: Wipf and Stock, 2012.

Kraybill, Donald. *Upside Down Kingdom.* Scottdale, PA: Herald,1994.

La Shure, Charles. "What is Liminality?" October 18, 2005. http://www.liminality.org/about/whatisliminality.

Lim, David. "An Evangelical Critique of Initial Evidence Doctrine." *Asian Journal of Pentecostal Studies* 1.2 (1998) 219–29.

Mattson, Stephen. "Christianity's Most Common and Subtle Sin." *Sojourners,* April 4, 2014. https://sojo.net/articles/christianitys-most-common-and-subtle-sin.

McHugh, Adam S. *Introverts in the Church: Finding Our Place in an Extroverted Culture.* Downers Grove, IL: InterVarsity, 2017.

Menzies, William W., and Robert P. Menzies. *Spirit and Power: Foundations of Pentecostal Experience.* Grand Rapids: Zondervan, 2000.

Miller, Donald, and Tetsunao Yamamori. *Global Pentecostalism: The New Face of Christian Social Engagement.* Berkeley, CA: University of California Press, 2007.

Moltmann, Jürgen. *Theology of Hope.* Fortress, 1993.

Mount Shoop, Marcia W. *Let the Bones Dance: Embodiment and the Body of Christ.* Louisville: John Knox, 2010. Kindle edition.

Murray, Stuart. *Biblical Interpretation in the Anabaptist Tradition.* Pandora, 2000.

Niebuhr, H. Richard. *The Social Sources of Denominationalism.* Henry Holt and Company, 1929.

Nugent, John C., et al., eds. *Radical Christian Discipleship by John Howard Yoder.* Harrisonburg, Virginia: Harold, 2012.

Online Etymology Dictionary. "Margin." *Online Etymology Dictionary.* https://www.etymonline.com/word/margin.

Oxford Living Dictionaries. "Liminal." *Oxford Living Dictionaries.* https://en.oxforddictionaries.com/definition/liminal.

Pipkin, Brian K., and Jay Beaman. *Early Pentecostals on Nonviolence and Social Justice: A Reader.* Eugene, OR: Pickwick, 2016.

Preheim, Rich. "Losing Peace, Leaving Identity." *Mennonite World Review,* July 23, 2014. http://mennoworld.org/2014/07/23/columns/losing-peace-leaving-identity.

Rohr, Richard. "Life on the Edge: Understanding the Prophetic Position." *Huffington Post,* May 25, 2011. https://www.huffingtonpost.com/fr-richard-rohr/on-the-edge-of-the-inside_b_829253.html.

———. *Yes, And . . . Daily Meditations.* Cincinnati, OH: Franciscan Media, 2013.

Rollins, Peter. *The Orthodox Heretic: And Other Impossible Tales*. Brewster, MA: Paraclete, 2016. Kindle edition.

———. "How to be an Idiot." Lecture at Central Avenue Church, March 15, 2014. Audio. 58:54. https://soundcloud.com/peter-rollins/how-to-be-an-idiot.

Schrag, Paul. "Core Value at Risk: Can a Peace Church Start Teaching Peace Again?" *Mennonite World Review*, December 23, 2013. http://www.mennoworld.org/archived/2013/12/23/core-value-risk.

Turner, Victor. *Drama, Fields, and Metaphors*. New York: Cornell University Press, 1974.

———. "Liminality and Communitas." In *The Ritual Process: Structure and Anti-Structure*, by Victor Turner, 94–130. New Jersey: Aldine Transaction, 1995.

———. Watts, Craig M. *Bowing Toward Babylon: The Nationalistic Subversion of Christian Worship in America*. Eugene, OR: Cascade, 2017.

Weirick, John. "Why Introverts Would Rather Avoid Church." *Huffington Post*, July 22, 2017. https://www.huffingtonpost.com/john-weirick/why-introverts-would-rath_b_11099954.html

Wise, Tim. "FAQs." http://www.timwise.org/f-a-q-s.

Yoder, John Howard. *The Politics of Jesus*. Grand Rapids: Eerdmans, 1994.

———. *Radical Christian Discipleship*. Harrisonburg, VA: Harold, 2012.

5

Lasting Impact of an Unforgotten Kindness

Overcoming Barriers and Building Bridges in Linking
Church of God and Mennonite Church USA Leadership

Tony Richie

OPENING REMARKS

MY PATH TO MENNOCOSTALISM began nearly fifty years ago. As a child in the family of a full-time pentecostal evangelist, I was forever impacted by the kindness of a local Mennonite community. Subsequently, my reflections on a journey of personal and denominational encounters between pentecostals and Mennonites led to theological observations on the shared history and distinctive identity of each, their complementary character, and a mutual need of intentional, sustained relationship. Therefore this chapter essentially evolves out of a personal testimony to the power of an amazing relationship issuing forth in an articulation of foundational theological priorities inherent in such an intentional bi-lateral partnership.

To establish significant relational contours for these occasionally contrasting but consistently complementing traditions, I propose that an insightful biblical precedent for Mennonite and pentecostal relationality may occur in the Holy Spirit's setting apart of kind Barnabas and bold Paul for a shared journey in divine service (Acts 13:1–3). Furthermore, I will suggest a symbiotic "mennocostal" reality stressing reciprocal appreciation, participatory theological stimulation, and cooperative partnership rather than organizational integration or ideological assimilation. I am persuaded that the respective missional emphases of pentecostals and Mennonites can call forth deliberate and dynamic reciprocating responses for potential spiritual enrichment and ecclesial effectiveness. Herein I will candidly acknowledge some possible barriers to the full development of this Mennonite and pentecostal critical relationship, along with offering concrete suggestions for building bridges essential for its continuing actualization. Ultimately, these two great traditions can embody and enact the "full gospel" more fully together than separately.

AN UNFORGOTTEN KINDNESS

As a child in the family of a fulltime pentecostal evangelist, I was forever impacted by the kindness of a local Mennonite community. Kentucky is one of the few southern states with a sizable population of Anabaptist groups, including Amish and Mennonites.[1] Growing up in southeastern Kentucky brought me into direct contact for the first time with Mennonite Christians.[2] This encounter was destined to have a lasting impact on my life.

For years my father conducted extended tent meetings or "revivals," a development of the camp meeting tradition rooted in the early America frontier.[3] The intent was to establish and/or promote spiritual life in various communities across the country. From a pentecostal perspective, revival aimed at people being converted to Christ, sanctified from sinful and worldly living, baptized in the Holy Spirit accompanied by speaking in tongues, physical healing—perhaps even exorcisms, and preparedness for the soon return of Jesus Christ. Tent preachers tended to travel extensively and be away from hearth and home for extended seasons. My dad was no exception. These revivals were unpredictable, and often stretched into several weeks, and, occasionally, even months.

1. Donnermeyer and Anderson, "Plain Anabaptists."

2. For an inspiring example of Mennonite presence in southeastern Kentucky, see Davis, *On Troublesome Creek*. Davis trained and served for a time with a Mennonite community near Hazard, KY, my boyhood home, with Mennonite Voluntary Service.

3. Often misunderstood, even maligned, the tent meeting tradition has a rich but complex history. Award-winning journalist Patsy Sims allows participants to speak for themselves in Sims, *Can Somebody Shout Amen!* Interestingly, although the tent revival phenomenon is most closely associated with pentecostals, some Mennonites were involved as well. See Lehman, *Mennonite Tent Revivals*.

Before leaving for a meeting Dad would always make arrangements for care of his family. Since my mother didn't drive, these arrangements necessarily included transportation. But we lived up in a hollow. Car access was not easy. When a meeting stretched out over longer seasons the arrangements could and did break down. Of course, email was unheard of. Even telephones were rare in that area in those days. Out of a desire not to distract Dad's mind from the work of ministry my mother frequently minimized the difficulties her family faced in the letters they exchanged regularly. Now in his eighties (and still preaching), my father recently admitted to me that he had no idea that the situation became as difficult as he now knows.

In any case, it was during one of my father's absences that I met the Mennonites. I was only eleven or twelve years old, and my mother had passed into the presence of the Lord, so I am not aware of all the details. I'm not sure how the Mennonite community became aware of our increasingly dire circumstances. I recall that they showed up and offered to give us a ride to town, to the grocery store, and wherever else Mom needed to go. And this offer continued to be extended when needed. In the days of large cars and no car seats for children, my mother would pile in five children and head off with a pleasant Mennonite couple to do our business. I also remember a bit of rebuke in my mother's voice when, after returning home on one such occasion, my younger brother and I remarked on their odd dress. We wondered at the ladies' bonnets and the men's "Abe Lincoln" beards.[4] My mother's firm comment was, "They may be a little different but they're good people!" Over the years I've come to agree wholeheartedly. I've never forgotten that long ago kindness. Furthermore, I've observed firsthand that kindness is not at all an exception for many contemporary Mennonites.

JOURNEYING TOGETHER

Subsequently, reflections on a journey of personal and denominational encounters between pentecostals and Mennonites have led me to theological observations on the shared history and the distinctive identity of each, on their complementary character, and on a mutual need of intentional,

---

4. I doubt my mother understood, and certainly it was years before I understood, that the distinctive appearance of Mennonites and other "plain people" entails spiritual commitment to a life of simplicity and expresses Christian identity in a visible language. See Scott, *Why Do They Dress That Way?*

sustained relationship. For me, this remarkable journey began in 2004 at an annual Society for Pentecostal Studies (SPS) meeting.[5] Mennonite Church USA (MC USA) theologian Tom Finger; Church of God (CG) missionary Rick Waldrop, who had extensive experience with Mennonites in Latin America; and I collaborated on a joint dialogue.[6] A little later, scholar and activist Cheryl Bridges Johns joined the group, and she subsequently became the first chair to represent the CG. Waldrop followed up as chair subsequent to Johns. Both served for one year, along with their counterpart, Virgil Vogt, a Chicago area pastor and leader in the MC USA. I served as CG chair (mostly with Vogt) from 2007–2016. At various stages Andre Gingrich Stoner and Gerald Shenk (both MC USA) were directly involved in the organizing process. Shenk in particular has been a frequent dialogue partner. Christopher "Crip" Stephenson is currently CG chair.[7]

Early efforts were characterized by organized dialogue between the two traditions. However, consultations between the two movements indicated the prime importance of connecting leadership at the highest levels in a more formal manner to facilitate an enduring and sustainable relationship. Thus began a series of top tier leadership meetings. Erin Stutzman, (executive director, MC USA), Vogt, and I visited the CG International Offices (Cleveland, TN) for fellowship, conversation, and prayer with CG then general overseer Raymond Culpepper and the entire executive committee.[8] Stutzman, Vogt, Stoner, and Shenk have also attended several CG International Assemblies as special fraternal guests.[9] In addition, then CG general overseer Mark Williams and I were hosted by the MC USA General Convention (Phoenix, AR).[10] These leadership meetings were characterized by mutual respect and deepening appreciation. I often felt a sense of divine providence at work in bringing us together.

It seems fitting, as the initiative for the CG/MC USA relationship was originally launched at SPS, that we have been able to conduct formal and

---

5. For more information on SPS, see Society for Pentecostal Studies, "Home."

6. Tom Finger is author of *Contemporary Anabaptist Theology*, among other texts.

7. Stoner narrates the background to these developments as well as noting the current process of the partnership in Stoner, "MC USA." Crip Stephenson is Assistant Professor of Systematic Theology at Lee University, a Church of God institution (Cleveland, TN).

8. Richie, "Leaders Meet."

9. Richie, "Mennonites, Church of God"; "Church of God Hosts Director."

10. Richie, "Williams Represents."

informal dialogues within the SPS framework between the two traditions.[11] In this venue, others, including MC USA scholar Alan Kreider and Assemblies of God scholar Martin Mittelstadt, were more involved. I hope SPS will continue to be a place where a broader application of mennocostal identity can occur. The respective movements are now moving forward in a collaborative partnership of formal and specific ecumenical and theological dialogue.[12] There is every reason to be optimistic that the relationship between the CG and MC USA will continue to grow and be fruitful. I am certainly honored to be part of a process bringing these great movements together in Christian unity.

A BIBLICAL PRECEDENT

An insightful biblical precedent, if not outright paradigm, for the Mennonite/pentecostal relationship may be inferred in the Holy Spirit's setting apart of Barnabas and Paul, out of a larger group of prophets and teachers, for a shared journey in divine service (Acts 13:1–3). As French Arrington observes, "The work of Barnabas and Saul [Paul] originates with God— not with plans devised by humans—and is undertaken in obedience to the voice of the Spirit."[13] Doubtless, the complex missionary partnership thus forged has immensely influenced Christianity, and Christian ministry, through the ages. Arguably, neither Paul nor Barnabas is well understood in isolation. An accurate appreciation for both of these men arises only in their relation to one another.[14]

Barnabas was presumably an older, seasoned, and highly regarded Christian leader who took the younger and more charismatic but notorious, and perhaps somewhat tempestuous, Saul under his wing (Acts 4:36; 9:27; 11:22–26). Barnabas and Paul worked well together for years in spite of Paul quickly becoming much more prominent in the early Christian community (Acts 11:30; 12:25; 13:1–15:35). Eventually they parted ways due to a sharp dispute over John Mark, Barnabas's cousin, as a member of their missionary team, because Mark had apparently abandoned them on a previous journey (Acts 15:36–41). Further, an uncompromising Paul

11. See, e.g., Richie, "2016 Society for Pentecostal Studies."

12. See Stoner, "Inside the Church of God"; "Ecumenical Dialogue"; "Mennonite Church USA and Church of God."

13. Arrington, "Acts," 598.

14. Robertson, Barnabas vs. Paul.

reports he and Barnabas did not always agree on the egalitarian status of Gentile Christianity (Gal 2:13). Nevertheless, Paul later speaks of both Mark and Barnabas in amicable terms as valued co-workers in Christ (Col 4:10–11; Phil 24). During his last days in Rome Paul specifically requested that Mark be brought to him because he considered Mark helpful in the ministry (2 Tim 4:11). R. R. Melick is quite probably correct that "Most likely, Barnabas, who had discipled Paul in his early Christian years, discipled Mark from that point and saw him develop into an effective Christian minister."[15] If so, Barnabas's reputed disposition toward consolation and encouragement served well in affirmation of two important early Christian leaders (Acts 4:36).

For illustrative purposes, this apostolic pair may serve to portray in simple relief some relational contours between the radical discipleship, peace church, and community-oriented tradition of Mennonites and the fiery pneumatology, bold evangelism, and apocalyptic eschatology of classical pentecostals. The kind and the bold dispositions are both necessary for Christian discipleship and service. Admittedly, the bold tends to get more "press" but the kind generally makes its own genuine impact. Relationships can be complex, but the kind and the bold do better together than apart.

A SYMBIOTIC REALITY

Christian theology today is increasingly cognizant of the importance of relationships for the development and nourishment of all human life and especially of life in Christ.[16] The interpersonal relations of the Trinity suggest a robustly relational paradigm for humanity and, again, especially for life in Christ. In a word, no person can be all that she is created by God to be, that is, to be fully human, in solitary existence. Centuries ago John Wesley famously noted that there is no such thing as a solitary Christian, and that Christianity is essentially a "social religion."[17] Even so the Church is not an isolated entity either; rather, it reflects and represents God's being and presence in a world with others by the infilling with and outflow of the Holy Spirit.

---

15. Melick, *Philippians, Colossians, Philemon*, 328–29.
16. See, e.g., Haroutian, *God with Us*; Zizioulas, *Being in Communion*.
17. Wesley, "Our Lord's Sermon."

Jürgen Moltmann speaks of "symbiosis" as a model for Christianity's involvement in the processes of economic life.[18] In his explicit pneumatology Moltmann earlier applied the concept of symbiosis to all the living.[19] However, he makes clear that a legitimate understanding of symbiosis does not entail the loss or diminishment of individuality.[20] Herein I employ symbiosis as a metaphor for ecumenical interaction.

Etymologically, the term symbiosis means that which "lives together." In biology symbiosis signifies a close and prolonged association or interaction between organisms of different species. Symbiosis may exist as mutualism (benefit for both), commensalism (benefit for one neutral for the other), and parasitism (benefit for one, costly for the other).[21] Clearly, Moltmann appropriates the concept for affirmation of positive interdependence. In a similar vein, I suggest a symbiotic "mennocostal" reality stressing reciprocal appreciation, participatory theological stimulation, and cooperative partnership rather than organizational integration or ideological assimilation. In other words, the life of God is nourished within the souls of Mennonites and pentecostals and becomes more flourishing, for God's glory, as our living together moves beyond proximity and appreciation into partnership and interpenetration. This depiction does not point to assimilation, or loss of individuality, but it does suggest cooperation, or intentional mutuality.

Conversely, isolationism inevitably leads to spiritual and theological "inbreeding." A homozygous state, to borrow another term from biology, in which the perceptual gene pool is limited to one's own movement, is unethical and unhealthy—especially for future generations. The deficiency becomes increasingly more pronounced or worse over the course of time. To a certain extent this description should inspire renewed commitment to the overall ecumenical movement.[22] And there is good reason to be hopeful regarding increasing attention by pentecostals to ecumenism.[23] However, I here address my firm conviction that Mennonites and pentecostals need each other in order to live and grow healthily, and to bear good fruit for Christ's sake. I prefer symbiosis over zygosity.

18. Moltmann, *Church in the Power*, 168, 174–76.

19. Moltmann, *Spirit of Life*, 219.

20. Moltmann, *Spirit of Life*, 226.

21. Biology Online, "Symbiosis."

22. Kinnamon, *Can a Renewal Movement Be Renewed?*, is helpful here.

23. See, e.g., Hocken, et al., *Christian Unity and Pentecostal Faith*.

RESPECTIVE MISSIONAL EMPHASES

Mennonites are part of the historical stream of "Anabaptists" (*anabaptizein*, "to rebaptize"), a label given to the movement by opponents in the sixteenth century for denunciation of infant baptism—a feature of a vision to restore the early church. Anabaptism is a wing of the Radical Reformation stressing pacifism, separation of church and state, church membership consisting of believing adults, and a consistent conviction that ethics are essential to the gospel of Jesus Christ. Mennonites are named after Menno Simons (c. 1496–1561), a Dutch Anabaptist leader. Mennonites believe that the state, ordained by God to maintain order in the world, has no authority in the realm of faith. Christians are disciples who follow the way of Jesus as revealed in Scripture, including commands to reject violence and the oath, and to serve humanity in humility and love. In the modern era Mennonite refusal of military service has at times replaced rebaptism as a touchstone of identity and conflict with the world. Today many North American Mennonites display characteristics of conservative evangelical Protestant denominationalism. However, progressive leaders and thinkers present their tradition as a viable alternative to fundamentalist/modernist polarities.[24] Interestingly, Anabaptists have some history of charismatic manifestations similar to modern day pentecostals.[25]

The Pentecostal movement most noticeably emerged in 1901 during the Azusa Street Mission and Revival (Los Angeles, California). Classical pentecostals have in common a conviction that conversion to Christ should be followed by an experience of Spirit baptism (Acts 1:8; 2:1–4) typically evidenced by tongues speech. Pentecostals further affirm manifestations of gifts of the Spirit (*charismata*) (1 Corinthians 12; 14). Older pentecostal denominations generally affirm divine healing and premillennial eschatology.[26] Many early pentecostals embraced pacifism. Most every major pentecostal body adopted a pacifist resolution at some point in its history. Most of these resolutions, however, have been abandoned by subsequent generations. Early pentecostalism was a preeminently participatory religion, marked by strong egalitarian tendencies. Testimony, song, sermon, prophecy, prayer, divine healing, and glossolalic utterance were potentially open to everyone, not just the restricted privilege of a designated few from

---

24. Juhnke, "Mennonite Churches."
25. Murray, "Anabaptism as a Charismatic Movement"; "Anabaptist Network."
26. Blumhofer, "Pentecostal Churches."

a certain class or race or gender. In ethical matters, pentecostals generally adopted the rigorous asceticism of their holiness heritage. Contemporary pentecostalism is an especially diverse phenomenon. Although few generalizations apply, threads of continuity are evident in frank openness to supernatural gifts, in an intimate experience with God, and in straightforward biblicism.[27]

I suggest that the respective missional emphases of pentecostals and Mennonites call forth deliberate and dynamic reciprocating responses for potential spiritual enrichment and ecclesial effectiveness.[28] For example, perhaps pentecostals can learn much from Mennonites about existing in commitment to Christian community and radical discipleship in a countercultural mode of selfless service in Christ's love. Perhaps Mennonites may learn from pentecostals regarding the in-breaking of God's Kingdom in the power of Christ's Spirit in the last days. Might not pentecostals be enriched by exemplary Mennonite discipleship? Might not Mennonites be enriched by exemplary pentecostal evangelism? Might not our respective emphases in such areas, as well as others, be mutually informative and enriching? I do think so![29]

POSSIBLE BARRIERS

Here I acknowledge candidly a few possible barriers to the full development of this critical relationship, and offer concrete suggestions for building bridges essential for its continuing actualization. As noted above, Anabaptist and Mennonite opposition to militant nationalism through pacifism has been increasingly a hallmark characteristic of the movement. Although pentecostals share an early heritage of pacifism, contemporary pentecostals tend to reject pacifism.[30] The CG in recent decades has passed assertive

27. Robins, "Pentecostal Movement."

28. For more information on the MC USA, see Mennonite Church, "Home." For more information on the Church of God (Cleveland, TN), see Church of God, "Home."

29. My holistic ambition coincides with the multidimensional missional and soteriological approaches of MC USA theologian Thomas N. Finger and pentecostal (Assemblies of God) theologian Amos Yong. See Finger, *Contemporary Anabaptist Theology*, esp. 109–324; Yong, *Spirit Poured Out on All Flesh*, esp. 81–120.

30. Pentecostalism has never been universally pacifist, and it's generally pacifist position has seriously declined over the years. Early pentecostal pacifism was not of an active variety (working to promote world peace) but was deliberately passive in nature (prohibiting Christian participation in war). Even early pacifist pentecostal leaders had

resolutions such as "9/11, The War on Terror, & Support for the President of the United States and Other World Leaders" (2010). The CG decries the catastrophic consequences of war and acclaims the aims of peace, although frequently set in contexts of regional and/or religious alliances and nationalistic contexts: "Global Crises (1992), "Peace of Jerusalem" (2002), and "Pledge of Allegiance to the Flag of the United States of America" (2002). However, it also expresses a transcendent and undiluted desire for a greater global peace in "Prayer for Peace" (1982). Sometimes these conflicting values result in mixed or ambiguous messages as in "International Terrorism" (1980).[31]

I argue that, whether or not one supports pacifist principles, making it the core basis of pentecostal/Mennonite dialogue and cooperation may well result in sidelining the entire process. Impact on the pentecostal side will be minimized, and the dialogue itself marginalized. Of course pentecostals and Mennonites ought to explore together the immense implications of their shared pacifist heritage. However, exploiting the budding pentecostal/Mennonite relationship as a means of promoting pacifism among pentecostals (I fear) will not only be ineffective in that regard but likely derail any potential for the relationship to become a vital, and revitalizing, influence for either movement.

Some years ago I was present at a CG International Assembly when a pacifist friend attempted to propose an egalitarian resolution on peace in the Middle East in a General Council session. I had read it in advance. It was in my opinion essentially sound. It advocated peaceful overtures and actions among both Israelis and Palestinians. But the resolution did not pass. During his speech, my friend appealed to Mennonite brethren present within easy hearing (in an area just off the General Council floor) as a model for pentecostal emulation. But the debate became heated, and the effort failed. Afterwards I was approached by irate bishops who knew me to be a friend of the speaker and closely involved with Mennonites. They

---

an indefinable impact on rank-and-file members. Today it has been said that "while some pentecostals retained residues of the general pacifism of an earlier era, others had even gone beyond nonpacifism and had hardened into an antipacifist position," although with a rueful "continuing to reflect, rather than to instruct, public opinion" (Wilson, "Pacifism," 953–55). For another perspective, see Beaman and Yoder, *Pentecostal Pacifism*. *Pentecostal Pacifism* asks, "Have pentecostals altered their pacifistic views as a result of new biblical insights or cultural accommodation?"

31. See Church of God, "Resolutions," for those resolutions adopted in the General Council of Bishops.

expressed agitation at his appeal to Mennonites in the CG General Council. One took time to explain pacifism as an example of over-realized eschatology.[32] He cleverly referenced pentecostal notoriety for extremes regarding divine healing as a comparable example. Yes, he continued, divine healing and pacifism are part of pentecostal history, but extreme forms have not stood the test of time. Divine healing and peacemaking are laudable values but shouldn't be conflated with perfect health and absolute pacifism. I suggest exploring a shared pacifist heritage is expected and essential; pushing a pacifist agenda is ill advised—and ill-fated.

Briefly, the MC USA is currently struggling with navigating unresolved same-sex marriage issues (as are many others).[33] The CG, like other pentecostal organizations, staunchly supports monogamous heterosexual marriage, and adamantly and unequivocally opposes homosexual marriage.[34] Same-sex marriage is an ethical/theological litmus test for many pentecostals, who walk away from anyone viewed as compromising the purity of the biblical marriage covenant. When I attended the 2015 Kansas City MC USA General Convention, I observed the painstaking care dedicated to discussing this controversial topic—which went ultimately unresolved. In deep and long conversations with Gerald Shenk I heard the hearts of those who struggle to integrate twin commitments to compassion and purity.

Compassion without compromise is a lofty, but at times difficult, goal.[35] However, I have little to no doubt that a choice to embrace same-sex marriage within the MC USA would effectively sound the death knell for serious, sustained dialogue and cooperation with the CG and with other pentecostals in any formal or official capacity. Though I pray that does not happen. I concur that ecumenical movements must prioritize the spiritual vitality of the churches.[36]

---

32. Land, *Pentecostal Spirituality*, argues that the paradoxical tension of promise-fulfillment, already-not yet (inaugurated) eschatology is most conducive for pentecostals. See Land, *Pentecostal Spirituality*, 3, 44, 46–47, 92, 94, 105, 114–15.

33. Mennonite Church, "Biblical and Theological Resources."

34. Church of God, "Marriage and Family"; "Sanctity of Biblical Marriage"; "Transgender Restrooms."

35. See Barr and Citlau, *Compassion without Compromise*.

36. Williams, *Renewal Theology*, 3:47.

A FULLER FULL GOSPEL

Pentecostals tend to self-define the core essentials of their movement in terms of "the full gospel," including various versions of a Christocentric commitment to Jesus Christ as Savior, Sanctifier, Spirit Baptizer, Healer, and Soon Coming King. Frank Macchia affirms the importance and limitations of the established theological loci, adding that "no theology can claim to fully capture the essence of the living Christ without promoting an arrogance that borders on blasphemy."[37] The full gospel model actually "encourages a theological reflection that is potentially pluralistic and ecumenical since no single cultural or ecclesiastical perspective can capture Christ in his fullness."[38] In short, the full gospel is fuller than anyone has realized or can describe.

Accordingly, when I encounter the distinctive Mennonite heritage regarding "the standard of full gospel reform" I find it both affirming and stimulating.[39] It is affirming because I recognize and identify with the concept of a commitment refusing to settle for partial or incomplete interpretations of Christian experience, understanding, and action. It is stimulating because I am challenged to expand my theological and ethical horizons if I am to be consistently faithful to that core commitment.

My friend Tom Finger notes that "the most basic convictions" have always guided Anabaptist/Mennonite belief and practice:

1. The church is a close-knit, participatory, nonhierarchical community.

2. Practical Christian living is patterned after Jesus's life and teachings, including his way of peace, servanthood, and critique of wealth and social privilege.[40]

Finger adds that "these convictions have often distanced Anabaptists from ordinary society and politics, sometimes because forced to be separate, sometimes by choice."[41]

I am fully persuaded that as a pentecostal I need to hear this Mennonite message. Surely I need to apply it to my life within the context of my faith community. Ultimately, I contend, the "full gospel" may be thus

---

37. Macchia, "Theology," 1124.
38. Macchia, "Theology," 1124.
39. Bender, "Mennonite Origins."
40. Finger, "Anabaptist Theology," 23–27.
41. Finger, "Anabaptist Theology," 23.

embodied and better enacted. In sum, an authentic full gospel moves me toward this expansive mennocostal ethos.

CLOSING REMARKS

I have testified about, explained, argued for, critiqued, and defended my firm conviction that Mennonites and pentecostals can be a great blessing and benefit to each other. I highly prize this mutual relationship for my own life, as well as our respective movements. I am convinced that we are better together than apart. I close with an account of a conversation that, for me, sums up this conviction.

When Mennonite Pastor Virgil Vogt was visiting me in Knoxville, I inquired concerning what he most desired to accomplish in the MC USA dialogue with the CG. He answered without hesitation, "For us to be more pentecostal!" He then turned the question on me. Profoundly inspired by his words, I replied that I desired "for us to be more Mennonite!" In other words, I think it safe to say that we both wished, not only for ourselves but for our respective movements, to be "mennocostal." I still feel the same.

BIBLIOGRAPHY

Arrington, French L. "Acts." In *Full Life Biblical Commentary to the New Testament: An International Commentary for Spirit-Filled Christians*, edited by French L. Arrington and Roger Stronstad, 535–692. Grand Rapids: Zondervan, 1999.

Barr, Adam T., and Ron Citlau. *Compassion without Compromise: How the Gospel Frees Us to Love Our Gay Friends Without Losing the Truth*. Bloomington, MN: Bethany House, 2014.

Beaman, Jay, and John Howard Yoder. *Pentecostal Pacifism: The Origin, Development, and Rejection of Pacific Belief among the Pentecostals*. Pentecostals, Peacemaking, and Social Justice. 1989. Reprint, Eugene, OR: Wipf and Stock, 2009.

Bender, Harold S. "Mennonite Origins and the Mennonites of Europe." In *Mennonites and Their Heritage*, by Harold S. Bender and C. Henry Smith, 1–39. Rev. ed. Scottdale, PA: Herald, 1964. http://www.bibleviews.com/menno-heritage.html.

Biology Online. "Symbiosis." *Biology Online Dictionary*. http://www.biology-online.org/dictionary/Symbiosis.

Blumhofer, E. L. "Pentecostal Churches." In *Dictionary of Christianity in America*, edited by D. G. Reid, et al., 882–85. Downers Grove, IL: InterVarsity, 1990.

Church of God. "Home." *Church of God*. http://www.churchofgod.org.

————. "Marriage and Family." *Church of God*. 2012. http://www.churchofgod.org/resolutions/marriage-and-family-2012.

————. "Resolutions." *Church of God*. http://www.churchofgod.org/resolutions.

————. "Sanctity of Biblical Marriage." *Church of God*. 2016. http://www.churchofgod.org/resolutions/sanctity-of-biblical-marriage-2016.

————. "Transgender Restrooms." *Church of God*. 2016. http://www.churchofgod.org/resolutions/transgender-restrooms-2016.

Davis, Melodie M. *On Troublesome Creek: A True Story About Christian Service in the Mountains of Kentucky*. Harrisonburg, VA: Herald, 1983.

Donnermeyer, Joseph, and Corey Anderson. "The Growth of Amish and Plain Anabaptists in Kentucky." *Journal of Amish and Plain Anabaptist Studies* 2.2 (2014) 215–44. https://kb.osu.edu/dspace/bitstream/handle/1811/63996/JAPAS_Donnermeyer-Anderson_vol2-issue2_pp215–244.pdf?sequence=1.

Finger, Thomas N. "Anabaptist Theology." In *Global Dictionary of Theology: A Resource for the Worldwide Church*, edited by William A. Dryness and Veli-Matti Kärkkäinen, 23–27. Downers Grove, IL: InterVarsity, 2008.

————. *A Contemporary Anabaptist Theology: Biblical, Historical, Constructive*. Downers Grove, IL: InterVarsity, 2004.

Haroutian, Joseph. *God with Us: A Theology of Transpersonal Life*. Princeton Theological Monograph Series. Eugene, OR: Pickwick, 1991.

Hocken, Peter, et al., eds. *Christian Unity and Pentecostal Faith*. Boston: Brill, forthcoming.

Juhnke, J. C. "Mennonite Churches." In *Dictionary of Christianity in America*, edited by D. G. Reid, et al., 725–29. Downers Grove, IL: InterVarsity, 1990.

Kinnamon, Michael. *Can a Renewal Movement Be Renewed? Questions for the Future of Ecumenism*. Grand Rapids: Eerdmans, 2014.

Land, Stephen Jack. *Pentecostal Spirituality: A Passion for he Kingdom*. 1993. Reprint, Cleveland, TN: CPT, 2010.

Lehman, James O. *Mennonite Tent Revivals: Howard Hammer and Myron Augsburger, 1952–1962*. Kitchener, Ontario, Canada: Pandora, 2002.

Macchia, Frank D. "Theology, Pentecostal." In *New International Dictionary of Pentecostal and Charismatic Movements*, edited by Stanley M. Burgess and Eduard M. Van Der Maas, 1120–41. Grand Rapids: Zondervan, 2002.

Melick, R. R. *Philippians, Colossians, Philemon*. Nashville: Broadman & Holman, 1991.

Mennonite Church USA. "Biblical and Theological Resources on Sexual and Gender Identity." February 1, 2015. http://mennoniteusa.org/wp-content/uploads/2015/02/Biblical_TheologicalResources.pdf.

————. "Home." *Mennonite Church USA*. http://www.mennoniteusa.org.

Moltmann, Jürgen. *The Church in the Power of the Spirit: A Contribution to Messianic Ecclesiology*. Minneapolis, MN: Fortress, 1993.

————. *The Spirit of Life: A Universal Affirmation*. Minneapolis, MN: First Fortress, 1992, 2001.

Murray, Stuart. "Anabaptism as a Charismatic Movement: Diverse Phenomena in Early Decades." *Anabaptism Today*, February 8, 1995.

Richie, Tony. "2016 Society for Pentecostal Studies: A Personal Reflection and General Report." *Pneuma Review*, March 30, 2016: http://pneumareview.com/2016-society-for-pentecostal-studies-a-personal-reflection-and-general-report.

————. "Church of God Hosts Director of Mennonite Church USA." *Faith News Network*, August 10, 2012. http://www.faithnews.cc/?p=12664.

————. "Church of God and Mennonite Church USA Leaders Meet." *Faith News Network,* August 19, 2011. http://www.faithnews.cc/?p=23567.

————. "Mennonites, Church of God continue to build relationship." *Mennonite Church USA,* September 11, 2012: http://mennoniteusa.org/news/mennonites-church-of-god-continue-to-build-relationship.

————. "Williams Represents Church of God at Mennonite Church USA General Convention." *Faith News Network,* August 14, 2013. http://www.faithnews. cc/?p=15366.

Robertson, C. K. *Barnabas vs. Paul: To Encourage or Confront?* Nashville: Abingdon, 2015.

Robins, R. G. "The Pentecostal Movement." In *Dictionary of Christianity in America,* edited by D. G. Reid, et al., 885–91. Downers Grove, IL: InterVarsity, 1990.

Scott, Stephen. *Why Do They Dress That Way?* People's Place Book 7. Intercourse, PA: Good Books, 2008.

Sims, Patsy. *Can Somebody Shout Amen!: Inside the Tents and Tabernacles of American Revivalists.* Religion in the South. Lexington, KY: University Press of Kentucky, 1996.

Society for Pentecostal Studies. "Home." *Society for Pentecostal Studies.* http://www.sps-usa.org.

Stoner, Andre Gingrich. "Ecumenical dialogue explores Mennonite Church USA—Church of God Connections. *Mennonite Church USA,* November 11, 2016. http://mennoniteusa.org/news/ecumenical-dialogue-explores-connections.

————. "Inside the Church of God (Tennessee)—Mennonite Church USA Dialogue." *Mennonite Church USA,* November 2, 2016. http://mennoniteusa.org/church-to-church-relations/inside-church-god-tennessee-mennonite-church-usa-dialogue.

————. "MC USA explores connections with the Church of God." *The Mennonite World Review,* n.d.

————. "Mennonite Church USA and Church of God Begin Ecumenical Dialogue." *Faith News Network,* October 25, 2016. http://www.faithnews.cc/?p=23567.

Wesley, John. "Our Lord's Sermon on the Mount: Discourse Four." Wesley Center Online. http://wesley.nnu.edu/john-wesley/the-sermons-of-john-wesley-1872-edition/sermon-24-upon-our-lords-sermon-on-the-mount-discourse-four.

Williams, J. Rodman. *Renewal Theology: Systematic Theology from a Charismatic Perspective.* 3 vols. Grand Rapids: Zondervan, 1996.

Wilson, D. J. "Pacifism." In *New International Dictionary of Pentecostal and Charismatic Movements,* edited by Stanley M. Burgess and Eduard M. Van Der Maas, 953–55. Grand Rapids: Zondervan, 2002.

Yong, Amos. *The Spirit Poured Out on All Flesh: Pentecostalism and the Possibility of Global Theology.* Grand Rapids: Baker, 2005.

Zizioulas, John D. *Being in Communion.* New York: St. Vladimir's Seminary, 1997.

6

My Journey to Anabaptist Progressive Pentecostalism through Experience of a Liberating Latin American Mission

Rick Waldrop

EARLY PENTECOSTAL PACIFIST INFLUENCES

Growing up in the Deep South of the United States and, by that time in the development of North American pentecostalism, in a traditional, classical church affiliated with the Church of God (Cleveland, TN), my life, understandably, was very limited in terms of perspective on the "outside world." In the 1950s and 1960s, my Euro-American church and parents, although having begun the spiral of upward mobility toward the "respectable" world of middle class existence, was still oddly entrenched in the contradicting spaces amid pentecostal spiritual practices with fundamentalist and dispensational impulses.

I was the first son of my parents, William Durwood Waldrop and Thelma Virginia (Durr) Waldrop, who had grown up poor as migrant cotton sharecroppers and woodcutters in the nearby Mississippi Delta (referred to by one sociologist as the most Southern place on earth[1]) and the surrounding hill country. Upon marriage, they were determined to find a better way of life for themselves and their new family and moved to several

---

1. Cobb, *Most Southern Place on Earth.*

places before settling across the Mississippi River in the nearest city of Monroe, Louisiana, where my father found work as a house painter and my mother settled into her traditional role as homemaker and seamstress.

During my childhood and youth, I experienced the strange mixture of the "counter-cultural" ethos of a church trying to maintain its distance from—but slow embrace of—the encroaching influences of the post-World War II economic boom and the modernizing influences of consumer capitalism juxtaposed with the legalistic imposition of a written and unwritten "holiness code" related to dress, entertainment, and sexuality.

A critical component of my immediate context was the imposition of Jim Crow laws which enforced racial discrimination and strict segregation, and provoked the rise of the Civil Rights Movement. Although the issue of race was seldom mentioned in my home or church, we grew up with the clear understanding that Blacks and Whites were to remain separate and that African-Americans were inferior to us White folks.

My life revolved primarily between home, church, and school. From an early age I was always in tune to spiritual matters and took my faith and church life very seriously, participating in all facets of church life. My parents were also faithful and active members in the life of our small congregation. By age 10, through a series of pentecostal spiritual encounters,[2] I had accepted a call from God to serve as a missionary to some unknown foreign land. But as I grew into adolescence and matured in my faith, I also began to question the de facto position of the church on the issue of race, even as I continued to participate in racist attitudes and activity. My attitudes toward violence and war were also beginning to take shape during this period. Although my father had taught us the "art" of boxing and had encouraged us to defend ourselves against any aggression, my deeper spiritual instinct was to question and resist the inclination to both violence and racism. The burning question of my soul on these matters would repeatedly come to mind in these terms: "How can I use violence against another person or harbor prejudice in my heart against a black person and pretend to be called by God to be a missionary? Does not God love all people and want to save them?"

By this time in my adolescent years I had not yet heard of the Mennonites, but I understood from simple Sunday School lessons, sermons, and Bible reading that Jesus was a man of peace and love for all people. Although I could not yet articulate it, Jesus's teaching related to peacemaking

2. Waldrop, "Youth Camp," 22.

and nonviolence in the Sermon on the Mount and elsewhere was taking root deep in my being. Being the conscientious, but sometimes conflicted, young Christian I was, I continued to struggle with the deeper meaning of these teachings for my life and calling.

As a teenager, while reading through the *Minutes of the 50th General Assembly of the Church of God*, I came across a statement that struck a chord in my soul and helped to set the trajectory for what would inspire and soon define my life and work:

COMBATANT MILITARY SERVICE

The Church of God believes that nations can and should settle their difference without going to war; however, in the event of war, if a member engages in combatant service, it will not affect his status with the Church. In case a member is called into military service who has conscientious objections to combatant service, the Church will support him in his constitutional rights.[3]

After I read and meditated on the words of this church teaching and on the words and teaching of Jesus, I soon decided that I would register for the draft in 1968 as a Conscientious Objector. Although I did not yet understand the early radical pacifist inclinations of the Church of God and other pentecostal groups, I began to realize that my denomination had something of pacifism built into its spiritual DNA and that my pacifist sympathies were indeed valid and even protected, at least at that time.

Upon registering for the draft as a CO in 1968, I was required to appear before a draft board shortly thereafter. I remember going into the meeting with my Bible and my copy of the *Church of God Minutes*. When asked about the reason for my conscientious objection I responded briefly but clearly, giving my understanding of the nature of my convictions based upon both sources.

---

3. Church of God, *Minutes 50th General Assembly,* 10. The exact same statement has been published in the biennial *Minutes* of the Church of God from 1964 to the present. Earlier in the history of the Church of God more definitive positions had been taken against participation in war but by the 1960s they had been scaled back to the one reference mentioned above, allowing for conscientious objection to military service.

LOSING MY FIRST NAÏVETÉ[4]

Within a year of registering as a CO, I began to make plans for post-secondary ministerial education and decided to study Christian Education at Northwest Bible College in Minot, North Dakota. From the deep, warm and sunny southland, I began the process of, not only geographical relocation to the Northern Plains, but cultural adaptation and critical theological inquiry related to my own pentecostal tradition and Southern enculturation. Although it was a small Bible college, I soon became acquainted and friends with fellow students from Mexico, Palestine, Canada, Jamaica, Japan, and from other parts of the United States.

Through these relationships and the open learning environment, slowly but surely I came to a greater understanding of my own racism, rooted in my own cultural context and family of origin, and continued to push ahead with my own understanding of pacifism. It was also during that formational period that I first encountered the people who were called Mennonites and took the opportunity to visit some of their churches, although I still did not fully capture the significance of their theology for my own pilgrimage. The impact upon me of the "counter-cultural" peace movement and folk artist Bob Dylan became much more evident during this period, and while in college, I began to play guitar and perform Dylan's "Blowin' in the Wind" and similar tunes for various audiences.

Upon my college graduation in 1972 and marriage shortly thereafter, my wife Janice and I relocated to Cleveland, Tennessee, near her hometown, where she finalized her education at Lee University and where I continued studies until we moved to Minneapolis, Minnesota the following year. In Minneapolis I served a local church as Associate Pastor and enrolled in Bethel Theological Seminary in order to be better prepared for future missionary work. At seminary, I became more aware of the Anabaptist movement through courses in church history and ethics but with the rigors of study, family, and ministry was not able to make any further connections with my Mennonite counterparts.

---

4. See Ricoeur, *Symbolism of Evil,* 351.

LATIN AMERICA AND THE CONSOLIDATION OF MY "MENNOCOSTAL" IDENTITY

Within a year of seminary graduation in 1975, we made plans to move to Central America for Spanish language study, and afterwards we were assigned to serve at the Church of God Bible Institute in Quetzaltenango, Guatemala. There we embarked upon a long journey of having our own consciousness raised and began direct contact with Anabaptist thought through a series of events, relationships, and study opportunities. This journey eventually took us to the two additional Central American nations of Costa Rica and Honduras, and back to Guatemala, and to studies at Fuller Theological Seminary, all spanning eighteen years.

We arrived in Guatemala in 1977, at the height of a long-standing civil war, and we were immediately thrust into a situation which came to require, in my mind, a clear commitment to the poor and peacemaking. It became clear to me that my earlier inclinations toward pacifism would hold me in good stead, as I would soon find to be true. As I experienced firsthand the horrors of the violence perpetrated by the US-backed military dictatorship at the time, I became "radicalized" through my own reading, writing, interaction with other missionaries and, above all, through the relationships developed with pastors and leaders of the Church of God in the region and of other churches, not least, the Mennonites.[5]

Through this early period of ministry and study, I read widely in the areas of integral mission, liberation theology, and Latin American history, politics, and culture. Along with the everyday life and ministry of

5. For a recounting of my own "radicalization" and development of social consciousness, see Coeller, *Beyond the Borders*. Other works to have a particular impact upon my developing theology and social consciousness at that early stage were Galeano, *Open Veins of Latin America*; Gutiérrez, *Theology of Liberation*; Bonino, *Doing Theology*; Maslow, *Bird of Life*. Although a nearby settlement of Old Order Mennonites drew my attention and occasional visit, my closest associates at that early period were Presbyterian fraternal workers Dennis and Rachel Smith, David and Sarah Scotchmer, and Donald Sibley, who were living near us in the city of Quetzaltenango, Guatemala. We met regularly and clandestinely with them and other church leaders to talk about the deteriorating political and human rights situation in Guatemala and issued an anonymous letter to the Guatemalan government denouncing their violence and demanding a cease of the repression against the poor and indigenous populations. These secret meetings were part of the larger efforts of the Comité Pro-Justicia y Paz de Guatemala (Guatemalan Pro Justice and Peace Committee) which later begin publishing annual reports on the human rights situation in Guatemala with the support of the World Council of Churches (see Comisión Interamericana, *Situación*).

involvement in theological education by extension and social ministry with hundreds of students and church leaders, I came to suffer the traumatic experiences of death threats, assault and abduction by a para-military group, Guatemalan military accusations and surveillance, and arrest and false accusations by the Guatemalan government related to our work with children-at-risk. During this time (1976–1994), over forty pastors of the Church of God in Guatemala were assassinated, as well as smaller numbers in El Salvador and Nicaragua.

During our first furlough in 1981, after experiencing the trauma of the civil war in Guatemala during our first term of service, we relocated to Fresno, California and began therapy at Link Care, the missionary service agency. I was granted the opportunity to teach at West Coast Christian College, a small Church of God Bible college. One of my assigned courses was "Christian Ethics." On the issue of war and peace, I sought out the services of Dr. A. J. Klassen, at the nearby Mennonite Brethren Biblical Seminary, whom I invited to class as a guest lecturer. Through my contact with the Mennonite seminary I came to participate in my first event of direct non-violent action, a March for Jobs and Peace at Fresno City College, and made additional visits to the seminary and to the Mennonite Brethren Church in Fresno.

Back in Central America after the furlough, I turned increasingly toward the Mennonites as friends and allies. I was already sensing through my relationships and conversations with my pentecostal colleagues and friends at the Church of God School of Theology (now Pentecostal Theological Seminary) such as Cheryl Bridges Johns, Steven J. Land, and Harold D. Hunter,[6] that a different understanding of pentecostalism was possible. This coincided with my association with the Society for Pentecostal Studies and my reading of the works of Walter J. Hollenweger, Gabriel Vaccaro, and Carmelo Álvarez[7] with whom I took a formal course on pentecostalism at the Seminario Bíblico Latinoamericano during our time of service in San José, Costa Rica in 1983. In Costa Rica I also developed close association with other socially progressive missionaries,[8] church leaders, and organizations such as the Centro Evangélico Latinoamericano de Estudios

6. Bridges Johns, *Pentecostal Formation*; Land, *Pentecostal Spirituality*; Hunter and Hocken, *All Together in One Place*.

7. Hollenweger, *Charismatic Movement*; Vaccaro, *Identidad Pentecostal*; Álvarez, *Pentecostalismo y Liberación*.

8. Consider, for example, the case of our friends John and Doris Stam (see Coeller, *Beyond the Borders*).

Pastorales (CELEP) and the Fraternidad Teológica Latinoamericana (FTL). These agencies were both Evangelical and Latin American, with a much more holistic understanding of the life and mission of the church than the other, more traditional, evangelical and pentecostal groups. I have continued as a member of the FTL and believe they proved to be a third major influence in my life, along with my pentecostal upbringing and association with Mennonite theology.

Reassigned to La Ceiba, Honduras in 1984, I was drawn to cultivate close relationships with Christian Brethren and Mennonite pastors and missionaries, such as Janet Brenneman, with whom we set up periodic meetings for dialogue, unity, and theological reflection. By the time we returned to Guatemala in 1986, I begin to earnestly seek out more intentional relationships with Mennonite leaders in that country. By that time, I was seeing myself clearly as an Anabaptist-pentecostal, or "mennocostal."

As director of a pentecostal seminary in Guatemala City, I sought to become friends and colleagues with Amzie Yoder and Juan Martínez, the directors of Seminario Menonita-Anabautista Latinoamericano. We exchanged professors on occasions and enjoyed wonderful fellowship and camaraderie in meetings and in personal relationships. During this time, through publications available at the Mennonite seminary and the Ediciones SEMILLA-CLARA publisher, I became acquainted with and impacted by the writing and theology of Anabaptist luminaries such as John Driver, Daniel Schipani, John Howard Yoder and David Shenk.[9] Little did I realize then how strong their influence would become. I personally met them all and even had John Howard Yoder as a roommate during a conference sponsored by the Fraternidad Teológica Latinoamericana in Quito, Ecuador during that period. I intentionally began to incorporate the writings of this group into my course syllabi and teaching in the US, Latin America, and eventually in other parts of the world where I was invited as a visiting professor.

During our second term in Guatemala, one of the Mennonite pastors and professors who had the most significant role in my embracing my identity as an Anabaptist-pentecostal was Gilberto Flores, whom I had met earlier in San Pedro Sula, Honduras.[10] In addition to teaching courses at the Mennonite seminary, and at our own pentecostal seminary, the Facultad

9. These works included Schipani, *Freedom and Simplicity*; Driver, *Images of the Church*.

10. See Robinson, "Gilberto Flores."

Teológica Pentecostal, Gilberto was a church planter and pastor of a newly forming Mennonite congregation in Guatemala City, Iglesia Menonita Shalom. Gilberto and his wife, Rosa, became good friends with us during a critical and difficult time with our relationship with Church of God World Missions. Because of my developing associations with more progressive Evangelical and ecumencial groups, and my perceived sympathies with Latin American liberation theology,[11] my work was called into question by my mission agency supervisors who sanctioned me and curtailed my teaching ministry for a year. It was during that difficult time that I turned to Gilberto for counsel and began to regularly attend the Iglesia Menonita Shalom with Janice and our four children.

Ironically, Gilberto and Rosa had spent their early years in pentecostal churches in El Salvador and Guatemala respectively, but later "converted" to an Anabaptist understanding of faith and ministry. We had regular conversations about the similarities and differences between the pentecostal and Anabaptist history, theology, and praxis and I became convinced that the two movements belonged together. Never did Gilberto try to convince me to join with the Mennonites, even though I at times seriously entertained the idea. He was always respectful and affirming of my call to pentecostal missionary service and helped me fulfill my mission with the pentecostal tradition, even as a committed and faithful critic.

Thankfully, we were able to work through the most difficult time of our relationship with Church of God World Missions and in 1994 I transitioned to our next stage of ministry when I was invited to teach mission studies at our denominational seminary, Pentecostal Theological Seminary, in Cleveland, Tennessee, being seconded to the seminary by Church of God World Missions.

11. I had already come under the scrutiny of Church of God World Missions officials earlier and had been threatened with being barred from returning to Central America after my participation as a panelist in a taped forum in Chattanooga, Tennessee, that was critical of US foreign policy in Central America under president Ronald Reagan. For a more nuanced account of my position on Latin American liberation theology, see Waldrop, "Teología de la Liberación," a paper first presented for the Simposio Internacional Jürgen Moltmann, at the Universidad Evangélica Nicaragüense in Managua, Nicaragua in October 2006, and later revised and published in English with Kenneth J. Archer (see Archer and Waldrop, "Liberating Hermeneutics").

EXTENDED RELATIONSHIPS WITH MENNONITES ON SEVERAL FRONTS

While at our seminary in the heart of the Bible Belt in the Deep South, I continued to think about and explore possibilities of developing closer relationships with Mennonites. With the earlier rise of the Religious Right, into which so many Euro-American pentecostals had been drawn, I was fully convinced that we needed, more than ever, to reconnect with our pacifist roots. What better dialog partners would we need than our Mennonite friends? The president of the seminary at the time, Steven J. Land, and I talked about some possibilities and he gave me his blessing to forge ahead. I found opportunities during this time to become involved as a pentecostal in the work of direct social action in support of human rights, immigration reform, the protest against the Y2K nuclear bomb factory in Oak Ridge, TN, the School of the Americas at Fort Benning, GA, the struggle against US aggression and militarism in Vieques, Puerto Rico, and the invasions of Iraq.[12]

After a meeting with Steve Land, I began informal and preliminary conversations with Mennonite Church USA representatives Jim Schrag and Virgil Vogt, followed by my unofficial attendance at the Mennonite Church USA conference in Atlanta in July, 2003.While there we reconnected with our friends Gilberto and Rosa Flores. We continued our correspondence with Mennonite leaders through 2004, and at the March 2005 meeting of the Society for Pentecostal Studies in Virginia Beach, Tony Richie and I met with Mennonite theologian Dr. Thomas Finger to work on details for a follow-up Mennonite Church USA visit to Cleveland, TN in the following year. On May 26–28, 2005, a small contingent of Mennonites, including then Executive Director Jim Schrag, Tom Finger, and Gilberto Flores, visited the Church of God Theological Seminary (now Pentecostal Theological Seminary) and met with a small group of Church of God pastors and scholars including myself, Cheryl Bridges Johns, and Tony Richie, for what would begin as a movement and lead to increasingly formal discussion. Since then laity, clergy, and scholars from the two movements have met on a number of occasions for dialogue and interaction. In that context, Tom

12. These included the "Rally Against Hate Crimes" in Chattanooga, TN, April 10, 2000; "Acto Ecuménico por la paz en Viequez" in Carolina, Puerto Rico, April 19, 2000; "Service of Prayer and Discernment and March to the White House" in Washington, DC, January 19, 2003; and a "School of the Americas Protest Rally" at the gates of Fort Benning, GA, November 18–19, 1990, resulting in my arrest and brief detention.

Finger and I organized the first official Church of God/Mennonite Church USA meeting under the banner "A Consultation on Mission" at Reba Place Mennonite Fellowship in Evanston, IL, from September 8–10, 2006, with the participation of ten Mennonite representatives and nine from the Church of God. Since that time several official meetings between leaders of the two denominations have been conducted.

In the meantime, I and several pentecostal friends began to organize and work on our own peace initiatives and launched an organization named "Pentecostals and Charismatics for Peace and Justice" (PCPJ). While serving as an organizer and founding board member for PCPJ, along with Paul Alexander and others, I continued to take every opportunity to attend conferences and meetings with Mennonites. One of those experiences was to participate in "Seeking Peace: The Courage to be Nonviolent," a peacemaking conference sponsored by the Plowshares Initiative, held in Indianapolis, IN, from September 8–11, 2005. There I met many Anabaptist peace activists and was able to represent our own budding pentecostal peace organization in a meeting of peace fellowship leaders. Another opportunity came later, in January 2009, when again I was with Paul Alexander, Gilberto Flores, and James Kraybill in Philadelphia for "A Gathering on Peace" held at the historic Arch Street Friends Meeting House.[13]

I should note that some pentecostals and charismatics were becoming more and more active in peace and justice initiatives during this time, with active collaboration with Mennonites. Several annual PCPJ "Shalom" conferences were held in various locations between 2003 and 2008 with the participation of notable figures such as Mennonite theologian Ronald J. Sider and Baptist ethicist Glen Stassen. We participated in pentecostal peace delegations to Palestine during this period. I assisted in leading, along with John Harris, one of the delegations in 2009 with orientation given us by Dr. Bishara Awad, then president of Bethlehem Bible College, and fraternal visits to several pentecostal congregations in Aboud, Bethlehem, and Ramallah. We also stayed at the Christian Peacemaker Teams apartment in Hebron and spent one night with a Muslim family whose home had been demolished on two occasions by the Israeli security forces. Our delegation also visited the offices of various peace, human rights, and development organizations such as The Holy Land Trust, Israeli Committee Against House

13. Kraybill serves as Director of the Mennonite Mission Network and editor of *Missio Dei: Exploring God's Work in the World*. I have benefited from this work published both in English and Spanish.

Demolitions (ICAHD), The Hebron Fund, Land Defense General Committee, the Sabeel Center, Musalaha Reconciliation Center, and the Council of Evangelical Churches of the West Bank. During this time, pentecostals became deeply involved with issues of Palestinian solidarity and participated in the annual "Christ at the Checkpoint" conferences sponsored by Bethlehem Bible College.[14]

In the meantime, I traveled extensively as a visiting professor of mission studies in Church of God-related schools back in Latin America. When my travels would take me to Colombia, I regularly visited the offices, bookstore, and seminary of the Colombian Mennonite Church, where I eventually met Mennonite leaders such as Peter Stucky, Alix Lozano, and César and Patricia Moya. I was particularly drawn to Colombia because of the long-standing civil war that persisted and the consistent peace witness I had heard and read about from the Mennonite Church there. I also wanted to learn more about pentecostal peace efforts in that country. In December 2007, through the agency of the Mennonite JustaPaz office in Bogotá, I was able to participate with Christian Peacemaker Teams in an official delegation to Barrancabermeja, a region hit hard by institutionalized violence. In the city we were able to meet, converse with, and offer solidarity with several groups targeted by paramilitary violence such as the Coca Cola Syndicate, the Consejo Regional para la Defensa de los Derechos Humanos (Regional Council for the Defense of Human Rights), the Organización Popular Feminina (the Popular Women's Organization), and others. From Barrancabermeja we embarked on a special pilgrimage of solidarity to be physically present in one of the hardest hit outlying rural areas, the village of Tiquisio in Bolivar Province. For three days we slept in the Catholic Church and heard testimonies from various victims of the para-military violence. Back in Barrancabermeja, we finalized our activities with a direct action Christmas rally in the central park to protest the ongoing violence.

My experience with Christian Peacemaker Teams gave me the opportunity to become acquainted with pentecostal pastors and members who were engaged in the struggle against the para-military violence. Two years later, in May 2010, I returned to Colombia to assist with the selection, interviewing, translation and research process for the Templeton Foundation-sponsored Flame of Love project. The purpose of this research was to document the work of pentecostal and charismatic leaders in high-risk ministry situations in the service of peace and justice with their

14. Alexander, *Christ at the Checkpoint*.

communities. One high profile leader was Salvador Alcántara, pastor of the Iglesia del Evangelio Quadrangular (Foursquare Gospel Church) in the small town of Garzal, where he had successfully lead a citizens' nonviolent movement to protect the population from the violence of the drug lords and para-military forces.[15] Later that month, the "Flame of Love" project also took us to Guatemala where we interviewed several at-risk pentecostal and charismatic leaders as well.

LOOKING AHEAD

Finally, in this most recent stage of my journey, I see, more than ever, the great possibility of the emergence of the mighty streams of dynamic pentecostal spirituality and counter-cultural Anabaptist peace witness moving together as a great river flowing with justice for the oppressed. Admittedly this is a minority movement among North American pentecostals, but signs of this emerging river can be seen on at least three fronts. First, as the conversations and partnerships continue among Mennonites and pentecostals in the Global North, we will discover that we belong together and are stronger together, giving us strength for the journey. Second, the consolidation of many of the pentecostal churches in the Global South, especially in Latin America, bode well for the future of Christian faith and social transformation as long as the connections are maintained with our Anabaptist roots and in dialog with our Mennonite partners in mission. Many of these pentecostal churches and their leaders understand all too well the cultural captivity of their counterparts in the North and are making headway toward the articulation of a pentecostal praxis of holistic liberation nourished by their understanding of Anabaptist piety and ethics.[16] Finally, there is a small but growing global community of pentecostal peacemakers, including scholars (a number of them have contributed to this series), pastors, and millennials who are also discovering and recognizing Anabaptists as "scandalous partners in protest"[17] and are moving beyond denominational labels and rigid fundamentalist dogmas. This last movement reflects the continuing efforts to organize pentecostals and charismatics into a

---

15. For a report on pastor Alcántara's peace work, see "Bearing Witness: Stories Project," sponsored by the Institute for the Study of Global Anabaptism at Goshen College (Miller, "Salvador Alcántara").

16. For example, see López Rodríguez, *Liberating Mission of Jesus*.

17. See Hamilton and Archer, "Scandalous Partners in Protest."

confessional peace fellowship, with the participation of many Mennonites who see themselves also as pentecostals. We welcome these developments and pray that God will use us mightily together as instruments of peace, justice, reconciliation, and healing—salvation for all creation and all people.

BIBLIOGRAPHY

Alexander, Paul N., ed. *Christ at the Checkpoint: Theology in the Service of Justice and Peace.* Pentecostals, Peacemaking, and Social Justice 4. Eugene, OR: Pickwick, 2012.

Álvarez, Carmelo, ed. *Pentecostalismo y Liberación: Una Experiencia Latinoamericana.* San Jose, Costa Rica: Editorial DEI, 1992.

Archer, Kenneth J., and Richard E. Waldrop. "Liberating Hermeneutics: The Intersections of Pentecostal Mission and Latin American Liberation Theology in the Margins." In *The Gospel Revisited: Toward a Pentecostal Theology of Worship and Witness,* 138–51. Eugene, OR: Pickwick, 2011.

Beaman, Jay. *Pentecostal Pacifism: The Origin, Development and Rejection of Pacifist Belief among the Pentecostals.* Pentecostals, Peacemaking, and Social Justice 1. Eugene, OR: Pickwick, 2009.

Beaman, Jay, and Brian K. Pipkin, eds. *Pentecostal and Holiness Statements on War and Peace.* Pentecostals, Peacemaking, and Social Justice 6. Eugene, OR: Pickwick, 2013.

Bonino, José Míguez. *Doing Theology in a Revolutionary Situation.* Philadelphia: Fortress, 1975.

Bridges Johns, Cheryl. *Pentecostal Formation: A Pedagogy Among the Oppressed.* Sheffield: Sheffield Academic Press, 1993.

Church of God. *Minutes of the 50th General Assembly.* Cleveland, TN: Church of God, 1964.

Cobb, James C. *The Most Southern Place on Earth: The Mississippi Delta and the Roots of Regional Identity.* New York: Oxford University Press, 1992.

Coeller, Rodney A. "Beyond the Borders: Radicalized Evangelical Missionaries in Central America from the 1950s through the 1980s." PhD diss., American University, 2012.

Comisión Interamericana de Derechos Humanos. *Situación de los derechos humanos en Guatemala: Diversidad, desigualdad y exclusión.* https://reliefweb.int/sites/reliefweb.int/files/resources/Guatemala2016.pdf. Geneva: Consejo Mundial de Iglesias, 1985.

Driver, John. *Images of the Church in Mission.* Scottdale, PA: Herald, 1997.

Galeano, Eduardo. *Open Veins of Latin America: Five Centuries of the Pillage of a Continent.* Translated by Cedric Belfrage. New York: Monthly Review, 1973.

Gutiérrez, Gustavo. *A Theology of Liberation.* Translated by Sister Caridad Inda and John Eagleson. Maryknoll, NY: Orbis, 1973.

Hamilton, Andrew S., and Kenneth J. Archer. "Scandalous Partners in Protest: A Continuing Dialogue." In *Pentecostals and Nonviolence: Reclaiming a Heritage,* edited by Paul Nathan Alexander, 313–15. Pentecostals, Peacemaking, and Social Justice 5. Eugene, OR: Pickwick, 2012.

Hollenweger, Walter. *El Pentecostalismo: Historia y Doctrina.* Translated by Ana S. de Veghazi. Buenos Aires: Editorial La Aurora, 1976.

———. *The Pentecostals: The Charismatic Movement in the Churches.* Translated by R. A. Wilson. London: SCM, 1972.

Hunter, Harold D., and Peter D. Hocken, eds. *All Together in One Place: Theological Papers from the Brighton Conference on World Evangelization.* Sheffield: Sheffield Academic Press, 1993.

Land, Steven J. *Pentecostal Spirituality: A Passion for the Kingdom.* Sheffield: Sheffield Academic Press, 1993.

López Rodríguez, Darío. *La Propuesta Política del Reino de Dios: Estudios Bíblicos Sobre la Iglesia, Sociedad y Estado.* Lima: Ediciones Puma, 2009.

———. *The Liberating Mission of Jesus: The Message of the Gospel of Luke.* Translated by Stephanie Israel and Richard Waldrop. Pentecostals, Peacemaking, and Social Justice 4. Eugene, OR: Pickwick, 2016.

Maslow, Jonathan Evan. *Bird of Life, Bird of Death: A Political Ornithology of Central America.* New York: Dell, 1986.

Miller, Elizabeth. "Salvador Alcántara." *Bearing Witness: Stories Project,* February 12, 2014. http://www.martyrstories.org/salvador-alcantara.

Pipkin, Brian K., and Jay Beaman, eds. *Early Pentecostals on Nonviolence: A Reader.* Pentecostals, Peacemaking, and Social Justice 7. Eugene, OR: Pickwick, 2016.

Ricoeur, Paul. *The Symbolism of Evil.* Boston: Beacon, 1967.

Robinson, Laurie Oswald. "Gilberto Flores: A Man of Peace." *The Mennonite,* November 10, 2013. https://themennonite.org/feature/man-peace.

Schipani, Daniel, ed. *Freedom and Discipleship: Liberation Theology in an Anabaptist Perspective.* Maryknoll, NY: Obris, 1989.

Vaccaro, Gabriel. *Identidad Pentecostal.* Quito: Consejo Latinoamericano de Iglesias, 1990.

Waldrop, Richard E. "La teología de la liberación: un enfoque crítico." *Pastoralia* 7.15 (1986) 44–58.

———. "Youth Camp '60—An Experience Unforgettable." *Church of God Evangel* 67.5 (1976) 22.

7

Deconstructing My Life as a Mennocostal

What Has Los Angeles to Do with Kansas?

JAY BEAMAN

WHAT HAS LOS ANGELES to do with Kansas? I grew up pentecostal. Two competing narratives, one centered on Kansas and one in Los Angeles, have been told as the origin myth of pentecostals. The Kansas one has the advantage of being first at the turning of the twentieth century, a sort of apocalyptic century. Today others have asked disparagingly, "What's the matter with Kansas?"[1] The Los Angeles narrative is more compelling, as I was born in Southern Oregon in the early 1950s when we were experiencing migrations from Los Angeles. By the time I graduated high school in 1971, Oregon's governor was saying to Californians, "I urge them to come and come many, many times to enjoy the beauty of Oregon. But I also ask them, for heaven's sake, don't move here to live."[2] But it was too late. Being left coast means I gravitated to the Los Angeles narrative. But something happened in Kansas, no doubt. In fact, my parents converted to the pentecostal faith in Oregon in 1953; recent transplants from the prairies.

In my childhood, all of life was interpreted through a specific religious-cultural lens. I remember the Cuban missile crises. My mother came into

1. Frank, *What's the Matter With Kansas?*
2. Cain, "Former Governor."

our room after dark and told us that the Russians had a plan to take over our country within 24 hours, so it was important that I be ready to meet God. You bet I prayed with her! When I was a child I spoke in tongues. I was still expected to complete math problems at school, but several times a week I would gather with the called-out ones to experience deep subterranean differences from the larger society. My people represented difference. When we were hopeful, we spoke of our difference representing the future. We saw in the spirit what others could not yet see. In worship, we were reconciled to our creator and to each other. As a youth, I was greeted as Brother Beaman. I greeted others in the same fashion. We were healed and we could heal. How can one tell outsiders to the holy community about the deep rites of passage through which one moved into the holy common life?

On some deep level, we knew "the difference" was our brand. Without difference, we had no purpose and no message worth hearing. Any difference could remind us of "the difference" and drive us to reflect, "Why do they not like us?" or "Why do they mock us?" or "Why do they persecute us?" As a child, I could not distinguish why neighbors avoided us or painted on the walls of our house, "tar paper shack," from the fact that my parents sent me to school with a note saying I could not participate in square dance in class because it was against my religion. It was all an experience of difference. Full participation in the larger society was not possible. Religious faith gave meaning to difference. We were poorer, but we were purer. To this day, I cannot dance to save my life—just ask my wife! Still, we were not the purest. Just down the street another family moved to the suburbs and was more purer than us. The girls wore old-fashioned dresses and they did not allow a television in their house. The obvious fact that they could not afford a television had been sanctified. They were separate and holy, and we were too, mostly.

My friend, Mark Molinski, was our grade-school's resident Jehovah's Witness. We were both different, but we still fought bitterly with each other over the right differences. And the differences had a political edge. In the fifth grade at school, by some accident, I was in the principal's office, on a fateful day. She was listening to the radio and crying. I could hear Walter Cronkite on the radio. President Kennedy had been shot. Principal Fink waved me back to class and announced over the loud speaker that the President of the United States had been shot. Mark Molinski looked at me and said, "I guess we know where Kennedy is right now." We both had a secret moment in common over the Catholic president getting his eternal reward.

Still, Mark and I were both pretty sure the other was headed straight for hell, he the Jehovah's Witness and I the pentecostal. Mark would sit out during the flag salute every morning like I sat out during the dances in physical education class. We were both conscientious objectors. At home I told my dad that that president Kennedy was now in hell. My pentecostal father, uneasy with the logic of my political faith, nudged me back from the edge. Little did I know that Mark and I had other differences from the larger society, some of which took us back together to WWI. Molinski's were Russian immigrants. Many Russians were Mennonites, Jehovah's Witnesses, and pentecostals—all resisted WWI. All three groups were different from the rest of society, and in that difference they were persecuted, even imprisoned.

As a teen, I began to choose faith for myself. Far too early, I was a youth leader at church and led youth group on a Sunday night. Often running out of ideas, we repeated a worship event that I now see as a ritual to celebrate difference. This ritual helped build a wall between our religious group and the larger society, clarifying reasons the larger society rejected and persecuted us. Only through difference could we entice others to join our movement and save the world. Only through difference could we be saved from the world. Our differences were prophetic and served the symbolic purpose of making us a beloved community and a light to the world.

What was this ritual event? We reenacted a persecuted religious cell hiding from an evil dictatorial government. That government was variously Communist or Nazi, set on stamping out religious belief. All that was needed for the ritual was a few candles, matches, and a very dark room. We gathered and were instructed to sit in a circle and remain very silent. The leader would enter the room in silence and the lights would be turned out. The leader announced that it was a time when the government had been taken over by secular forces that identified religious belief as a problem to be stamped out. Some of our members had been taken away to prison. Some of our families had lost loved ones. Then we were asked to take a lit candle and speak of our faith and affirm that we would be willing to die for our faith. We read words of Jesus that his followers would be persecuted for their faith. We were earnestly imagining life and death persecution, suspicion of political systems, and suffering more than being embarrassed for sitting out a dance. Then the leader would ask us, "What if this had been real? What if the authorities came for you? Would there be enough evidence to convict you?" We wept in the darkened room. We felt fear of persecution and guilt for being conformist and compromising. Then we turned on the lights and asked our parents if we could go out for a burger and fries before coming home. Later, as an adult and professor at a Mennonite college in Kansas, I learned that Mennonites in Russia used to keep a packed suitcase by the door at all times, so when the secret police came, they would be ready to leave and have more moments to spend assuring family they loved them before being taken away.

No doubt we were reenacting Cold War fear, channeled through the emerging religious right. But somewhere in this reenacted ritual was a marker from the history of pentecostals persecuted by a secular government demanding allegiance they could not give. What was it in my brief pentecosal history that made them deeply wary of persecution by the state? What if we turned the question back on the early pentecostal adherents, "Would there be enough evidence to convict them of being followers of Jesus?" Whence the question? When is difference threatening to power structures? Is it the level of difference or the kind of difference? Some difference is prophetic. Pentecostal religion has prided itself in being prophetic to a secular age, in finding the numinous and providing evidence.

At college, I seldom watched the news or read a paper. We were not allowed TV sets in our dorm rooms. We all gathered in a common room one evening to watch the lottery being drawn for the Selective Service draft. I was in complete denial. Somehow we knew we might get ministerial deferments if we were drafted. We had a discussion about the war in a dorm room. Other things were obviously changing. Several of us had recently lobbied for permission from the college to attend the movie "The Ten Commandments" with Charlton Heston. That did not go well. Pentecostals were not consumers of entertainment.

I graduated from college and applied for my ministerial license. On the form I filled out they asked if there were any of the 16 Fundamentals of the Faith that I disagreed with. I noted that I did not find complete support for the fundamental that stated, "Speaking in tongues is the initial physical evidence of the Baptism in the Holy Spirit." It had come to mean that everyone who is baptized in the Spirit will give evidence by speaking in tongues. Neither my experience, nor my reading of the New Testament led me to that conclusion. I spoke in tongues, but wasn't convinced everyone else would do so. When I met with the elders, I was reminded that this belief was the thing that distinguishes pentecostal denominations from others. *This* was our difference. The elders told me I needed to go back and study the Bible and return to them. They also suggested I might want to become a Baptist. I supposed they were right on both counts. Before becoming a Baptist, I had begun to call myself an Anabaptist. Anabaptists were the third branch of the Protestant Reformation in Europe called re-baptizers because they did not accept the efficacy of their infant baptism.

Right after graduating college, a friend gave me a copy of the *Post-American*, later called *Sojourners*. As I read, I experienced something of a conversion. I began to see my religious experience up to that point as complete justification of my middle-class and racist pretentions, and that my life was embedded in a culture predicated on violence and greed. The Vietnam War was the unholy ghost in the background. In *Sojourners* contemporary events were interpreted prophetically. I believed Jesus was calling me to care for those on the edges of society, whom the church seemed to be forgetting. Some of the voices in *Sojourners* were Mennonites. I wanted to find out more about them. Unable to be ordained, I was working in a factory in Central California. I met a clerk at a department store and she wore a bonnet. I asked her if she was a Mennonite. "I sure am," she said in her surprising Oklahoma accent. She invited me to a revival meeting that night. I dragged my wife Rockie and our baby Heather to that meeting. We arrived late at the large barn-like building out in the country. Upon entry a bearded usher greeted us. The service was well underway. Bearded men in black and white were sitting on one side; traditionally-dressed and "bonneted" women and children were on the other side. Rockie said "Let's just go. Let's go." The usher allowed us to be seated together with the women. The biblical preaching was very familiar to me. The heavy German accent, pietism, and Russian spiritual sensibility drew me in. Later, upon reflection, I realized we could not go back there again. It was a cultural bridge too far.

We did become members at a Mennonite Brethren church in Madera, California. I read the official history of that church, their sojourn in Russia, and their communitarian and pacifist roots, and was deeply impressed. After seminary I pastored a rural Baptist congregation in Iowa for four years and immediately pursued a doctorate at Iowa State University and was contacted by Tabor College, a Mennonite Brethren school in Kansas, to teach sociology. We were in Kansas five years before I returned to Iowa to finish my degree. In Kansas, the cultural tension was quite in play. I did not overplay the pentecostal part, and by and large, the Mennonite Brethren seemed more evangelical than Anabaptist. It was while I was at Tabor College that the Mennonites graciously published my seminary thesis on pentecostal pacifism. I had tried to get a pentecostal press to publish it. They said it was solid work, but they saw no market. The title of the book, *Pentecostal Pacifism*, must have cried neither fish nor fowl.[3] Most pentecostals at the time couldn't be troubled. They had moved on. It wasn't that they didn't like pacifism, they couldn't imagine it. Telling pentecostals that their recent forbears were pacifists wasn't remotely interesting. Worse, it was implausible.

During seminary I worked as a Christian education director at Faith Temple. While in Seminary I was regularly visiting a young Mennonite pastor in Sioux Falls, Melvin Janzen, who helped me clarify and formulate my thinking. What I did not know then was that the founding pastor of Faith Temple and earlier founder of the Church of the Bible, Rev. William Dirks, had grown up as a Mennonite. Although being born to Russian Mennonites in Howard, South Dakota, his family moved to Saskatchewan for WWI, perhaps to keep their son out of war. Some of that same Russian Mennonite sensibility and religious cultural difference was passed into pentecostal worship and life in my wife's family through Rev. Dirks. When Rev. Dirks left The Church of the Bible he was replaced with evangelist Charles R. Imler of Indiana. Rev. Imler was a graduate of Fort Wayne Bible College in Indiana and had experience as a Superintendent in the Missionary Church Association. The Missionary Church was a Mennonite denomination in the Holiness Movement. While Rev. Imler was at Church of the Bible in Sioux Falls, Faith Temple was part of the Open Bible Standard denomination, which was officially against members going to war, and the denomination Rev. Imler left to come to Church of the Bible, the Missionary Church, would reiterate their strong position against going to war again in 1960. While allowing that some members would choose to serve in the military, the statement stressed that "the historic position of the Missionary Church Association is to oppose the bearing of arms in warfare and gendering of strife between nations, classes, groups or individuals." Their official position stressed, "Pastors are advised to instruct their churches and particularly their youths on the teaching of the Scriptures regarding war and its evils and to seek to give guidance in the Word to those subject to call in the service to their country."[4]

I have had to revisit my own childhood and adult years through the lens of my current research to see that even it was not without connections

---

3. See Beaman, *Pentecostal Pacifism*.

4. Beaman and Pipkin, *Pentecostal and Holiness Statements*, 116–18.

to pentecostal pacifists. Even as pentecostalism was becoming the religious right, there were remaining vestiges of its pacifist past in living pentecostals who had survived that earlier time. I couldn't see them, but they were right there in front of me. Many Mennonites also came to be pentecostals and today, in the Portland Mennonite church where I am a member, some number are former pentecostals and others are pentecostalized Mennonites. My Mennonite pastor grew up in the Open Bible Standard. One man in our congregation grew up as the son of an Assemblies of God pastor. Another man grew up the son of a Vineyard Fellowship pastor. One woman on our elder board is highly pentecostalized. Others are charismatic Mennonites. One young leader came to faith among the Salvation Army (Holiness). One retired missionary trained at a Holiness college in Portland before marrying a Holiness-Mennonite. Let me share briefly some other examples. For years I have been collecting a database of war-resisters. One of my goals is to show what part of past war-resisters were pentecostal and closely related holiness groups. So, I have been gathering names of war-resisters from the past wars, into a list, mostly of those who were conscientious objectors to those wars.

One example is emblematic of my researching WWI history of pacifism using Ancestry.com and finding my own roots. After years of finding WWI draft cards with conscientious objectors listing their pentecostal denomination—"Church of God" or "Assemblies of God"—as the reason they could not go to war, I decided to take the opposite approach. Instead of searching lists of pentecostal names to see if they had WWI draft cards requesting conscientious objector status, which I could find all the time, I would take a different tack. Would those records give a witness? If I looked in locales where pentecostals had early success, would I find them there in the government record before finding them in pentecostal sources? Would they give a witness? Would they raise their hands and stand out from the other conscientious objectors and shout "here, take me, I'm a pentecostal!" Would they give a witness? I started looking at draft cards, pouring over every draft card from a locale. What about the churches I grew up in? Could I get a witness there? Was it completely lost?

Similarly, I searched for "conscientious objector" on Ancestry.com. I found thousands of men whose family tree had listed a conscientious objector. I catalogued them all. In many cases, they did not tell the denomination. I had to research their genealogy looking for a denomination, or write to their family genealogist and ask for the denomination of their relative.

One ancestry source had listed their relative as Benjamin E. A. Hoffman, a CO to WWI.[5] I found his draft card. Benjamin Hoffman gave his reason for religious objection to WWI as "religious creed." Which creed was that, I wondered? In the 1930 census, Benjamin Hoffman was listed as "clergy," and specifically as "Full Gospel Church." Full Gospel was short-hand for the faith of the original apostles, complete with powerful miracles or signs of the Spirit of God. Benjamin Hoffman was a pentecostal draft resister in WWI, a farmer by trade, and in the 1930s a preacher. The Assemblies of God archives listed him in a file called the deceased ministers record.[6] He was from my own denomination of origin, the Assemblies of God. But, this was still not part of my biography. He was ordained in 1924, six years after the end of WWI, and died in Grants Pass, Oregon in 1967. But wait, I was a teenager in 1967, and a member of that very congregation in Grants Pass, at that time. I didn't know any Benjamin E. A. Hoffman. How could that be? Why didn't I know him? As I reflected, I would only know him as "Brother" Hoffman. We addressed each other as brother and sister. I was Brother Beaman. Brother Hoffman was very old when I knew him. He had been the pastor of that very congregation some years before, but now had Parkinson's disease and sat in the back in a wheelchair. Of course I knew him. I worshipped with a pentecostal pacifist, who had asked for and received conscientious objector status because his religious creed, my religious creed, which prohibited killing in war. That creed was being modified in 1967 as he died. The Vietnam draft was upon us, and no one in my church bothered to tell me that Spirit-filled Christians don't kill in war. Brother Hoffman was dead, his passing unnoticed by me.

My pastor for most of my youth was L. D. Krause. His manner and style were gentle and warm, and during the Vietnam War he would be concerned to see young men join the military. He would be vigilant in warning them of the perils of military service, even if such service was necessary. They would have a great opportunity there to be heroic and even to give witness to godless men about a personal savior in Jesus Christ and the fullness of the spirit. But they would also be tempted to drink and smoke and curse, which could grieve the Holy Spirit, and to generally be coarse and rough in ways that would damage their testimony. They might even begin playing cards, with face cards. L. D. Krause, the pastor who baptized me into the faith, and prayed with me often to receive the spirit, had himself

5. "US World War I Draft."
6. "Deceased Ministers—Hoffman."

been a coarse and crude and godless young man. What I didn't know was that he had become godless and crude among his forbears, the Mennonites. I have fifteen Krause men in my database so far who were Mennonites and religious objectors to war. Two of them, Jacob (or Jack) Krause and his brother Harvey Harry Krause, were religious objectors to WWI. Jacob was father and Harry was uncle to my pastor, L. D. Krause. My pastor came from Bakersfield, California to Medford, Oregon, where I lived. But years later, when I became a Mennonite professor at Tabor College in Kansas, I lived in the community of Mennonites in Kansas where my pastor, L. D. Krause's father and Uncle had been born. In retracing my faith lineage back to work among Mennonites for a peace-church tradition, I had worked in the very community of Mennonites that Pastor Krause's relatives had come to from Russia in the 1800s. One could say that I came to the Mennonites in order to find peacemaking. Some of them had left Kansas and in leaving that community had lost contact with God and found faith again among the pentecostals. I asked my mother about it, and she always knew our pastor had come from Mennonites. He said the Mennonites he came from had lost spiritual focus and he needed to find it among the pentecostals.

So, Jacob F. Krause, father of L. D. Krause, might be considered my spiritual grandfather among the Mennonites. And my sojourn in Hillsboro, Kansas, among the Mennonites was in some sense, full circle. Call me Mennocostal.

But L. D. Krause was not the only one related to WWI conscientious objectors; some of the pentecostals in our congregation, Bethel Church in Medford, Oregon, were close relatives of WWI conscientious objectors. Gene Quiring's father, Jacob Herman Quiring, was born in 1878 and was too old to be drafted in WWI. However, Jacob Quiring was an older brother to Henry, John, Cornelius, George, and David; all from near Hillsboro, Kansas; all registered as religious objectors to WWI as Mennonites. When I informed my mother recently that the Quirings at Bethel church were close relatives of WWI Mennonites from Kansas she answered that she knew they were close relatives of Brother Krause. Gene Quiring's grandparents had come from Russia to Kansas as Mennonites in the late 1800s.[7]

---

7. See "Quiring, David"; "Quiring, George"; "Quiring, Jacob Henry"; "Quiring, John Cornelius."

Some cases of conversion of Mennonites to pentecostal were quite spectacular, as in the case of Canadian Mennonite leader, Soloman Eby. Soloman Eby (1834–1931) moved by stages from Mennonite to revivalist or holiness-styled Mennonite and finally to pentecostal. For much of his adult ministry, he was the founder and leading light with Daniel Brenneman of the Reforming Mennonites and the Mennonite Brethren in Christ. After retiring, he became a pentecostal for years. Still, his relationships with the Mennonites were strong enough that he was buried in the Mennonite Cemetery in Kitchener, Ontario.[8] It is significant that a large Holiness denomination in the US and Canada was quite literally Mennonite. However, quite a number of Mennonites continued along a path that led them to become pentecostals. Canadian Pentecostals have known all along that a significant group of Mennonites, no doubt influenced by Solomon Eby, followed him into pentecostal churches.

Canadian censuses in the late 1800s and early 1900s collected data on religious affiliation along with other demographic data. In Kitchener and

8. Storms and Thiessen, "Eby, Solomon." See also Erdel, "United Missionary Church," 257–59.

Winnipeg alone I was able to identify 48 family units comprising about 200 individuals that were counted as pentecostals in the 1921 Canadian census.[9] By following the same individuals from these 48 pentecostal family units back to earlier censuses, I found their previous denomination. Certainly, the majority were previously either the Methodist or Evangelical Association. However, 17 family units came from former Mennonites who became pentecostals. Thus, over a third (37.5 percent) of the pentecostal family units in the Kitchener area were former Mennonites. A number of the Mennonites in Kitchener who became pentecostal were later buried along with their larger kinship group in First Mennonite Cemetery in Kitchener. Call them Mennocostal.

In Kansas, Mennonites as a group were greatly influenced by the Holiness movement. I recently asked Jeanie Zook, an elderly woman at Portland Mennonite Church where I am a member, if she had always been a Mennonite. She told me she was raised in the Holiness Movement and went to a Holiness College in Portland, then married a Mennonite, John Zook, and they became Mennonite missionaries to the Congo. I was surprised. I told her that I believed I had records on Zooks from Iowa who were early leaders of the Hepzibah Faith Missionary Association and school, a Holiness group in Tabor, Iowa during the 1920s.[10] Jeanie told me that this was her husband's family. The group was highly influential among Brethren and Mennonites in the Midwest. Jeanie helped me get a set of privately published diaries, *The Diaries of Ezra W King: from 1907–1933*. Ezra King (1887–1934) was a Mennonite from Hesston, Kansas. He worked as a concrete contractor, and was essentially a bridge builder. As such, he would be known for building many of the first concrete bridges and culverts in south central Kansas, and the first buildings for Hesston College, a Mennonite College. Ezra King was also an advocate of the Holiness Movement and a proponent of sanctification as a second work of grace while being a deeply devoted Mennonite. King was a modestly educated layman, with only months of college at Hesston College, and worked a physically grueling and time consuming occupation, yet he participated in a host of religious activities for the purpose of renewing his church and the surrounding churches of Kansas and beyond. His diaries give us some glimpses of the passions of many Mennonites in Kansas in the early 1900s. The diaries also document the role of the Zook family in promoting the Holiness Movement

9. "1921 Census of Canada Results."

10. Koslevy, "Hephzibah Faith Missionary Association," 128.

in Kansas. One of the earliest entries, from February 1907, reads, "Papa and I cut hedge until C. Molzen's came over. Emma, Mama, and I went to prayer meeting at Mr. Shertz's. Bro. Zook leader. Realizing I have not been living as close to my Savior as I should have, I made a confession & my sins were pardoned. Praise the Lord!" The next day, he drove a horse-drawn "omnibus" some 35 miles with a group of Mennonites to the Holiness Bible College in Hutchinson for special meetings.

> [March 3] Rev. Zook preached today. . . . [March 6] I cleaned the stables and finished the garden fence. This eve to prayer meeting at C. Ruff's. Thank God tonight after earnest seeking, and full consecration to God I received the Holy Ghost. 'Hallelujah.'[11]

A diary entry for January 1, 1910, summarized, "Fourfold gospel; . . . my blessed Savior, whom I have accepted as my Savior, Sanctifier, Healer, and Coming King."[12] I have to say, Ezra King, in citing the fourfold gospel, could have been quoting directly from my upbringing in Medford, Oregon.

But Holiness Mennonites in Kansas were not new in 1907. As early as 1879, near Peabody, Kansas, not far from Hillsboro, Daniel Brenneman's group of Reforming Mennonites, connected to the group around Kitchener, Ontario, were making inroads. A. H. Kaufman was already in the Holiness camp and wished to be a local Mennonite leader. When the casting of lots, the traditional way of choosing a Mennonite preacher, failed to identify him, he believed that his experience of the baptism in the Holy Ghost was evidence he should lead. He "had a friend rebaptize him and ordain him to the ministry . . . set up a tent a half mile north of Catlin [Mennonite] Church and held a series of meetings." It wasn't long before Kauffman, "moved to Michigan, and started a group which he called the Apostolic Church."[13]

But what might be considered an aberration in 1879 had thoroughly leavened the lump by 1910. As early as 1890 a group of laymen were holding prayer meetings. Historian Paul Erb notes, "Kansas Mennonites were greatly influenced both by the Great Awakening in the entire Mennonite Church and by the holiness revival which had swept the country with Wesleyan emphasis. . . . The Kansas-Nebraska Conference in 1899 adopted a position that 'the baptism with the Holy Ghost is as necessary to

11. King, *Diaries*, 6.

12. King, *Diaries*, 41.

13. Erb, *South Central Frontiers*, 188.

be obtained as conversion and that it becomes the duty of every believer to seek and tarry until they have it definitely experienced.' The next year the conference resolved that bishops should pray at baptisms that applicants who 'have not yet received the Holy Ghost' might receive Him. Some leaders both in the conference and in other parts of the church were concerned about this language."[14]

Ezra King's diary:

> [May 28, 1911] D. D. Zook preached on Sanctification.[15] . . . [February 5, 1912] D. D. Zook gave a good talk, but the majority of ministers were against him, but he gave plenty of scripture and cleared his soul. . . . [February 6] Number of ministers still questioning Zook, God give him grace to stand true. [June 23: J. B. Smith questioned King] considerably, which made much confession, hope and pray the Lord will overrule all so we may just know what to do. . . . [By the end of the year] D. D. Zook left church; Bro Bender preached this a.m., then made the statement about D. D. Zook, not to preach etc. . . . John Brunk preached this a.m. John Weaver withdrew from church. Wonder what will be the result of this, afraid many more will go.[16] . . . [January 1913] Days of real darkness in many ways, quite a few are leaving the church, and have started up new cottage meetings. Don't think however they should have left, but hope it will work out to God's glory. . . . [January 19] Those who have withdrawn from church are going to put up a new building for services.

The Emmet church, a Holiness-styled Mennonite church near Hesston, was started.

In 1917, the US entered the Great War in Europe, and Holiness Mennonites in Kansas, like other Mennonites, faced a crisis. Much of the preaching had turned to the second coming of Christ:

> [February 25] Bro Zook preached a good sermon on the thought of being ready for Christ's return. . . . [April 3] Very windy days, sure signs all around us of the last days, a great war seems certainly upon us, but I'm sure the Lord is going to take us through. Hallelujah. . . . [April 5] Sure seems more blessed to meet together as we near the end. . . . [April 6] Surprisingly wonderful[17] how

---

14. Erb, *South Central Frontiers*, 242–43.

15. King, *Diaries*, 54–56.

16. King, *Diaries*, 63, 67, 71.

17. Obviously using "wonderful" in an ironic sense. "It makes you wonder . . ."

people in the US have the war spirit.... [April 7] War declared on Germany. Sure we are nearing the end, don't know what's ahead or what we may have to pass through, but thank God for victory through blood. Getting anxious for Christ's return.... [April 9] This country is surely getting into war, but God will see those through who really trust him I'm sure. Our prayer and cry is even so come Lord Jesus and come quickly.... [April 14] War is all the talk (for worldlings).

The National Selective Service was being constructed. On June 5, 1917, all men ages 21–29 were required to register for the draft. Patriotism ran high. "What the world calls a great day, Registration day, what it may mean for me the future alone will reveal, but surely God will take care of his own." We know from his draft card that Ezra King asked for exemption as a religious objector.

[July 24] Quite a few names out in paper, but mine has not appeared yet, thank God.... [July 25] My name seems to be toward the last in county, something to be thankful for indeed.... [August 13] Tests are coming on the people of God, but there's a bright side, in the thought that Christ may come any day. Even so come Lord Jesus.... [August 15] Had a special prayer meeting 15th at JGLs in behalf of some of the men who are drafted. The Local Board seemed to accept by Huby Overholt and that is such a surprise to us.... [August 30] Huby Oberholt is exempt from going to war. Thank God for it.... [September 16] Sermon on holiness in a.m., missionary talk in p.m.... [September 26] At Zooks; heard from Fannie that Irvin had to leave for camp; this awful war, but God's hand in upon this wicked world for their disobedience. May God use Irvin in the salvation of many souls is our prayer. Believe Fannie will have grace sufficient for this test.... [October 11] Irvin received exemption certificate from the district board. Thank God for that.... [October 20] Got form back in good shape and filled. ... Another week nearer to Christ's return, sure believe this age will soon close.... [December 31] Well, praise the Lord for his presence, see more and more what I have been delivered from, to God be all the glory ... Jesus may come before another year. God help me to live true and ready all the time is my prayer. Amen.[18]

18. King, *Diaries*, 112–17.

The year 1918 was a trying year.

[January 1, 1918] By the help of my Lord, I expect to live so as to be ready when the last trumpet sounds to then go out and meet Jesus. Even so come Lord Jesus, come quickly. . . . [January 2] Elmer not getting satisfaction from Local Board. The Lord only knows the tests and things just a little way ahead of us, but he knows how to take us through. . . . [January 8] Hesston ME [Methodist Episcopal] Church, some good but some quite shallow preaching. . . . [January 9] Received my questionnaire[19] this eve; feel I need God's help in answering it correctly. . . . [January 14] Getting my questionnaire ready to hand in. . . . [January 15] Had questionnaire filled out and handed in to local board, with a prayer that God shall have his way and work things out to his glory, I am his and know he can undertake. . . . [February 10] Newton; Praise God for such men who are preaching the full gospel. Praise the Lord for victory. . . . [February 19] Found out today that Elmer is in class 1-E.[20] . . . [February 20] To Newton found out that we

19. King is referring to his draft questionnaire, asking rationale for exemption request.

20. Class 1 is fully available for call-up.

could not make an appeal for Elmer. Surely the testing times are coming fast, and God more than anything else. . . . [February 21] This world sure is in a sad condition war and bloodshed, strikes and all kind of troubles, but bless God, our redemption is drawing nigh. Lord Jesus, come quickly. . . . [February 24] Elmer, also John Kennell came this morning trying to get some help out of Class 1, hope and pray the Lord will somehow overrule things to his glory. . . . [April 12] Meeting up with tests on line of Liberty Loan, but feel that God wants me to stay out and put all money I can spare into Mission work, trusting God for results. . . . [May 10] Victory even though this world is all in a tumult and war seems to be all you hear. . . . [May 11] Another week passed into eternity, a feeling of carefulness comes over me in these last days, knowing the end is near. Praise God for his keeping power over sin. . . . [June 5] Registration day for those who have become 21 since last June 5. Final card, put in Class 4,[21] thank God. . . . [June 11] Found out I could not get Phil. W. to work as he is called for the Army, wonder if Elmer is not called also. . . . [June 28] Did not go to school house for the meeting in regard to stamps.[22] . . . [September 13] World war is sure a sad affair these days. Oh Lord, hasten the day when men shall learn war no more. . . . [November 11] Heard the good news this morning that the awful war with Germany has closed. Thank God all this is another mark in prophecy. Sure surprising how the people holler and tare around, If Christians would shout and go on like that they sure would be locked up. . . . [January 5, 1919] Had a great searching message from Bro. Roy Hare today on 1 John 1:7. Many things came to my mind that have been done the last few years, and while Bro. Hare did not mention Liberty Bond's yet I feel I would have been better off if I had not bought any, according to my first conviction. . . . [March 2] A good day in Zion. Bro. Eshleman gave us a very good talk on Prophecy. To see Eli Overholts this p.m. Good Bible reading tonight: Sub "Signs of Christs Second Coming." 1 Thess 4:18. . . . [March 23] Irvin preached in the power of the Spirit this a.m. and eve. Text this a.m. Heb 12:14.[23] . . . [June 4] I have been feeling a lack and need for some time and especially during the last week of meetings I asked the Saints to pray for me that I might be sanctified, for I sure feel that is my need.[24]

21. King is in class 4, least likely to be called up in draft.

22. In other words, King refused to purchase war stamps.

23. "Follow peace with all men and holiness, without which no man shall see the Lord" (Heb 12:14).

24. King, *Diaries*, 119–27.

Ezra King's family would move on to become members of the Nazarene church, and his son would be a soldier in WWII. Ezra King was a bridge-builder.

Historian William Kostlevy, in a paper originally presented at Tabor College in Hillsboro, Kansas, where he taught for years, made the following astounding claim: "In terms of theological and ethical substance, the Anabaptists of the sixteenth century are not really the major spiritual ancestors of Goshen College alumni. It could be effectively argued that modern American Mennonites have about them more that has been derived from John Wesley or Dwight L. Moody than from Conrad Grebel, Pilgram Marpeck, or Menno."[25]

Mennocostal is a bridge. It is a bridge that connects two cultures. If by design or not, when we connect two cultures, people move back and forth across the bridge. Some Mennonite people are moving towards becoming pentecostal (or something else) and some pentecostal people are moving towards becoming Mennonite (or something else). Many people do not so much set down permanent roots as move, and to be Mennocostal is to be moving one way or other on that bridge. So, to trace my Mennocostal connections is to see someone moving one way or the other.

In my own state, the Apostolic Faith denomination is headquartered in Portland, Oregon. One of the early members of the Apostolic Faith at Azusa Street was Florence Crawford. She came to Portland in 1907 and founded the Apostolic Faith. Of 991 WWI pentecostal religious objectors I have identified, 60 (6 percent) of them were Apostolic Faith, Portland. By systematically searching the WWI Selective Service Draft Cards in rural Willamette Valley in Oregon, I found 187 religious objectors to WWI, of which I was able to identify the denomination of 147. Of those identified by denomination, 60 of these (41 percent) were Mennonite or Brethren and 20 (14 percent) were pentecostal; so over 50 percent were either Mennonite or pentecostal.

A similar ethos among local Mennonites and Apostolic Faith included war resistance. The Apostolic Faith were evangelistic, and for a moment saw the good news as including love for enemies. In 1921, three years after WWI, members of the Apostolic Faith were holding street meetings in downtown Portland. A veteran in the crowd tried to shout them down with, "How many of you served in France?"[26] In my home town, Medford,

25. Kostlevy, "Perfecting Mennonites."
26. "Religion and Bonus Booster Clash."

Apostolic Faith folks were stopped by the police during the war for handing out tracts against going to war. The tracts contained the doctrinal statement of the Apostolic Faith, complete with a statement against going to war. The newspaper reported, "Patriotic people of Medford are considerably worked up over a four-page religious publication, 'The Apostolic Faith' . . . being distributed about the city . . . by two women. . . . In the publication are several seditious utterances." Right in the doctrinal statement of the Apostolic Faith was the statement, "It is our firm conviction, supported by the word of God, our consciences bearing us witness, that we cannot take up arms against our fellow man, however great the provocation or however just the cause might seem, it being the spirit of the gospel presented by Christ in His sermon on the mount, Matt, 5:39-46." One soldier was, "quoted as thanking God for having heard his prayer to be transferred from a machine gun company to the hospital service: . . . 'In that branch of service, I will not have to kill anyone.'"[27] Looking through my records of early Apostolic Faith, I have counted eight former Mennonite family units among the Earliest Apostolic Faith.[28] Many of these Mennonite families were converted to the Apostolic Faith through revivals in the Dallas, Oregon among Mennonite communities. Not far from Dallas, Oregon in Albany was one of the largest Assemblies of God Churches, pastored by Rev. Earl Book. Rev. Book was also the state superintendent for the Assemblies of God in Oregon and I went to college with his son, Jim Book. Although I did not discover this until recently, Rev. Book's uncle and other close relatives from Kansas were religious objectors to WWI, members of the River Brethren, and likely associates to the Zooks and other Holiness Mennonites I have described from Kansas already.[29]

In my youth in Oregon, vestiges of these connections could be found. In Ashland, Oregon, we had a pentecostal radio preacher, Leo Wine. We regularly listened to him on the radio and I had visited and met him at his church, Faith Tabernacle. Leo Wine was a close relation to a large group of WWI religious objectors from Church of the Brethren in Virginia. His

27. "Apostolic Faith," 2.

28. Families of Abraham Flaming, George C. Friesen, John L. Friesen, Abraham K. Janzen, George Kliever, Cecil Robert Lambert (son of Mary Regier), Jacob W. Penner, Henry Toews Ratzlaff, Peter S. Richert, John Sawatsky, and John Newman Wiebe.

29. See "Book, David Earl—WWI"; "Book, Isaiah E."; "Book, Monroe M." The 1910 Census for David Earl Book shows he is brother to Isaiah E. Book and Jessee Eyster Book; uncle to Raymond Earl Book, pastor Albany, OR, Assemblies of God and District Supt. AG OR; and father of Raymond Earl Book. See "Book, David Earl—1910."

family had come to Oregon by way of McPherson, Kansas, a Holiness Mennonite and Brethren community, and later by way of Nampa, Idaho, another Holiness community. Leo Wine, the pentecostal radio preacher, had a brother, Victor Keith Wine, also a pentecostal, who was a WWII religious objector.[30]

In deconstructing my pentecostal youth I have discovered what was all around me. Was it accidental that I have come full circle to the Mennonites at this point, or have they been all around me all the time? I hope by bringing the geneology of these two strands to light I pay homage and appreciation to both streams from which I have drunk deeply. Interestingly, Mennonites have reflected how Holiness and pentecostal folks have been in their midst for well over a hundred years. In the 1960s as Mennonites were participating in the communitarian and charismatic renewal, especially in Fellowship of Hope and Rheba Place Fellowship, they reflected on this set of relationships in one of the *Concern* series pamphlets.[31] Their reflection was largely about the 1960s charismatic movement in Mennonite congregations, and whether it was valid and useful. In that conversation, they gave credence to the Holiness movement among the Anabaptists, especially in the United Missionary Church, for example.[32]

I believe this explains a profound cultural bridge that was developed and which offered a way of being in the world to a young pentecostal movement, largely through a common Holiness ethos. Mennonites, it seems to me, were searching for any safe harbor to renew their sectarian sensibilities and lives of non-conformity. Mennonites were looking for cultural renewal and thus needed to be sanctified. Some of them would ultimately follow the bridge to the other side and reside there. I was blessed for their presence on my path. I hope, to my Mennonite friends, my mediated Anabaptist faith will not be diminished even though it is proved to be an alloy. There aren't many Mennnonites out west, but a fair portion of the Oregon Mennonites I worship with, sing, and pray in a Kansas dialect that is faintly familiar to me.

---

30. See "Wine, Victor K."; "Wine, V. Keith." Victor Wine's funeral in 2009 was at Living Praise Tabernacle, Central Point, OR.

31. See Voght, *Concern*.

32. Horst, "Historical Estimate."

BIBLIOGRAPHY

"1921 Census of Canada Results." *Ancestry.com.* https://www.ancestry.com/search/collections/cancen1921/?birth=_waterloo-ontario-canada_1654341.

"Apostolic Faith Prints, Circulates Disloyal Paper." *Medford Mail Tribune,* May 28, 1918, 2.

Beaman, Jay. *Pentecostal Pacifism: The Origin, Development, and Rejection of Pacific Belief among the Pentecostals.* 1989. Reprint, Eugene, OR: Wipf and Stock, 2009.

Beaman, Jay, and Brian K. Pipkin. *Pentecostal and Holiness Statements on War and Peace.* Eugene, OR: Wipf and Stock, 2013.

"Book, David Earl—1910 US Federal Census." *Ancestry.com.* https://search.ancestry.com/cgi-bin/sse.dll?dbid=7884&h=175906367.

"Book, David Earl—WWI Draft Card." *Ancestry.com.* https://www.ancestry.com/search/collections/ww1draft/?name=David+Earl_Book&keyword=draft+card&name_x=1_1.

"Book, Isaiah E.—WWI Draft Card." *Ancestry.com.* https://www.ancestry.com/search/collections/ww1draft/?name=Isaiah+E._Book&keyword=draft+card&name_x=1_1.

"Book, Monroe M.—WWI Draft Card." *Ancestry.com.* https://www.ancestry.com/search/collections/ww1draft/?name=Monroe+M._Book&keyword=draft+card&name_x=1_1.

Cain, Eric. "Former Governor Tom McCall's Message to Visitors." *Oregon Public Broadcasting,* March 19, 2013. http://www.opb.org/artsandlife/article/former-governor-tom-mccall-message-visitors.

"Deceased Ministers—Hoffman, B. E. A." Flower Pentecostal Heritage Center. https://ifphc.org/index.cfm?fuseaction=research.showArchiveDetails&ArchiveGUID=ad53d5af-ab73-4c6a-936c-98d5010363f7.

"Emma Youngs Becomes Bride Of W. R. Clark." *Des Moines Register,* August 6, 1946, 7.

Erb, Paul. *South Central Frontiers: A History of the South Central Mennonite Conference.* Scottdale, PA: Herald, 1974.

Erdel, Timothy Paul. "United Missionary Church." In *Historical Dictionary of the Holiness Movement,* edited by William C. Kostlevy, 257–58. Lanham, MD: Scarecrow, 2001.

Frank, Thomas. *What's the Matter With Kansas?: How Conservatives Won the Heart of America.* New York, NY: Henry Holt, 2004.

Horst, Irvin B. "A Historical Estimate of the Charismatic Movement." *Concern* 15 (1967) 45–50.

King, Ezra W. *The Diaries of Ezra W. King: From 1907–1933.* Spokane, WA: Byron David King, 1994.

Koslevy, William C. "Hephzibah Faith Missionary Association." In *Historical Dictionary of the Holiness Movement,* edited by William C. Kostlevy, 128. Lanham, MD: Scarecrow, 2001.

"Quiring, David—WWI Draft Card." *Ancestry.com.* https://search.ancestry.com/cgi-bin/sse.dll?dbid=6482&h=10677300.

"Quiring, George [Gerhard]—WWI Draft Card." *Ancestry.com.* https://search.ancestry.com/cgi-bin/sse.dll?dbid=6482&h=1069011.

"Quiring, Jacob Henry—1900 US Federal Census." *Ancestry.com.* https://www.ancestry.com/search/?name=jacob+henry_Quirring&name_x=_1.

"Quiring, John Cornelius—WWI Draft Card." *Ancestry.com.* https://search.ancestry.com/cgi-bin/sse.dll?dbid=6482&h=27928966.

"Religion and Bonus Booster Clash on Corner; Call Police." *Oregon Daily Journal,* June 5, 1921, 4.

Storms, Everek R. and Richard D. Thiessen. "Eby, Solomon (1834–1931)." *Global Anabaptist Mennonite Encyclopedia.* November 2011. http://gameo.org/index. php?title=Eby,_Solomon_(1834-1931)&oldid=102370.

"US World War I Draft Registration Cards 1917–1918." *Ancestry.com.* https://www. ancestry.com/interactive/6482/005243520_04345?pid=27053060.

Voght, Virgil. *Concern* 15 (1967).

"Wine, Victor K.—US Army Enlistment Records." *Ancestry.com.* https://search.ancestry. com/cgi-bin/sse.dll?dbid=8939&h=2484723.

"Wine, V. Keith—1930 US Census." *Ancestry.com.* https://search.ancestry.com/cgi-bin/ sse.dll?dbid=6224&h=33236087.

8

Why I Like the Quiet Peace of Mennonites and Loud Liberation of Pentecostals

*The Transformative Possibility
of Mennocostal Ethics and Praxis*

RYAN R. GLADWIN

THE CALL FOR HOLINESS and an alternative ethic that confronts the principalities and powers was one of the driving reasons that I, a former cradle Methodist, opened myself up to the influence of pentecostalism[1] and chose to become an Anabaptist-Mennonite.[2] The simple living and "quiet" commitment to peace and justice of the Mennonites resonated with my Wesleyan pursuit of social holiness.[3] In like manner, I was attracted to the

---

1. I use the small 'p' pentecostalism/pentecostals to refer to Pentecostal-Charismatic movements, broadly speaking, as does Yong, *Spirit Poured Out*, 18–22. Under this term, I include the following pentecostal-charismatic three-fold Pentecostal typology (Classical Pentecostals, Charismatics, and Neocharismatics) laid out in Burgess and Van Der Maas, *New International Dictionary*, xviii–xxi.

2. I prefer to call myself an Anabaptist rather than a Mennonite, being that Anabaptist is a more encompassing term that includes other Anabaptist non-Mennonite churches. Moreover, I would include the burgeoning neo-Anabaptists as a subset of Anabaptism. However, for reasons of facility, I will use the terms Mennonite and Anabaptism synonymously throughout this chapter, unless otherwise noted.

3. John Wesley famously wrote in the preface to the 1739 version of *Hymns and*

mitochondrial power of pentecostals and the potential of the pentecostal convictions and practices to "loudly liberate" individuals and communities from sin and empower them for social transformation. However, I came to realize that these two ecclesial traditions, that over time had become part of my spiritual DNA, have often been maligned in the academic study of religion and ethics.

In this chapter, I examine the commonalities between Mennonite and pentecostal "social" ethics and how both traditions are keenly concerned with social transformation, although they have tended to focus first and foremost on personal and communal transformation, individuals and local churches being prophetic, and pneumatological witnesses of the ethics of God's reign.[4] In short, Mennonites and pentecostals have tended to focus on the formation of an alternative communal social ethos and accompanying alternative ecclesial practices rather than macro-social, structural changes.

A PERSONAL NARRATIVE

Although the Christian faith became personal for me at age ten, it had gestated from long before in the lessons, stories, songs, and experiences I heard, repeated and lived in a local United Methodist Church in Southeast Florida. From my earliest memories, the church and Christian faith and practice have been central to my life. For this reason, the story of my faith is best told through the successive engagement in different communities of faith. Growing up in the evangelical wing of the United Methodist Church that embodied the strengths of the holiness and evangelical traditions, I learned the importance of conversion and the pursuit of sanctification as a second work of grace. I keenly remember that indelible mark that was made upon me by the grace-empowered possibility of Christian perfection ("Be perfect, therefore, as your heavenly Father is perfect" Mt. 5:48)[5] instilled through years of Methodist liturgy, songs, and sermons. As an aspiring ministerial student, I unwittingly attended an academic institution

---

Sacred Poems, "The gospel of Christ knows of no religion but social; no holiness but social holiness" (Wesley, *Hymns and Sacred Poems*, iii). The context of the passage means that Wesley was saying that there is no solitary holiness, but instead all holiness is social—an activity lived out with others.

4. I prefer to use the term 'reign of God' to 'kingdom of God' because it implies the dynamic and multifaceted ontology of God's reign as compared to the static implications of the term kingdom.

5. All quotations of Scripture will be the NRSV version unless otherwise stated.

(Messiah College)[6] rooted in the *Anabaptist* tradition because it was also linked to Wesleyanism, had a solid NCAA wrestling program, and offered me a generous academic scholarship. In that context I was challenged to form a Christian worldview that questioned aspects of my prior faith with a call to renounce violence and seek reconciliation in the name of Jesus. As a missionary and pastor in Latin America, my faith was once again probed as I learned to preach from a Colombian Brethren in Christ pastor whose oratory style was more pentecostal than Anabaptist. The roots of pentecostalism seeped deeper into my Wesleyan soil as I served and pastored in a thoroughly pentecostalized ecclesial context.[7] It was also in Latin America that my understandings of sin, salvation, and Christian ministry were confronted by the reality of systemic poverty, oppression, and violence. I learned that Christians cannot escape the influence of the oppressive structures of society and are called to confront the structures through practices of liberation, justice, and peace with and for the poor and oppressed. I began to search for theological sources that responded to these realities, so I began seminary studies at Duke Divinity School. To my dismay, I found that most of the theological sources—broadly Methodist—focused on issues of justice, especially in the North American setting, formed theories of social transformation that often ignored the path of transformation of Mennonites and pentecostals. This perplexed me because I knew that I had served among Anabaptists and pentecostals working for peace and justice.[8] As my desire to examine mennocostal forms of social transformation continued to grow amid a passion to train ministry students, I completed my doctoral degree at the University of Edinburgh, an institution rooted in the Reformed tradition.

THE WAY THAT PENTECOSTALS AND MENNONITES HAVE BEEN IGNORED AND MALIGNED

Although we are taught as children that "sticks and stones will break your bones but words will never hurt you," we learn as adults that words are more powerful and enduring than sticks and stones. Words are symbols that have

6. The Brethren in Christ Church, a denomination with Anabaptist, Wesleyan, and Pietistic roots, founded Messiah College in 1909.

7. See Gladwin, "Pentecostalization of Latin American Evangelicalism," 199–214.

8. I have been in many slums in different parts of Latin America and never found one where there is not a pentecostal church or pastor.

the power to create but are themselves also created. The power to use words to create and form the image and likeness of another endures: caricatures die slow deaths, sometimes fading only after many centuries. The magisterial traditions[9] have a long history of ridiculing Anabaptists. This goes all the way back to Martin Luther, who disparagingly called them *Schwärmer* (fanatics) and eventually justified the use of capital punishment to silence what he considered a dangerous and growing heretical tradition among the poor and working classes. In like manner, early depictions of pentecostals frequently characterized them as enthusiasts that preyed on the poor and uneducated. Through most of their history, Anabaptists and pentecostals have been at best ignored and at worst maligned, disparaged as "sectarian enthusiasts"[10] who apolitically reject the world and culture around them. It has only been since the latter half of the twentieth century that the "sectarian" Anabaptist and "enthusiast" pentecostals have been welcomed at the ecumenical table[11] and become subjects of interest and dedicated scholarly study within the academy.

However, even the gaze of academia has not been free from the prejudice of the past. Early historical and theological studies of Anabaptism tended to categorize them as "step-children of the Reformation."[12] The situation has been even more contentious in Christian ethics and, in particular, Christian social ethics, where Anabaptists have been branded as sectarians with little to add or paradigmatically offer to questions surrounding the engagement of public spaces, political systems, or social structures. The Christian social imaginary in the field of Christian social ethics continues to be dominated by the condescending guise of the magisterial traditions. In the modern context, this can be seen in the lasting influence of H. Richard Niebuhr and Ernst Troeltsch and their typologies of the relationship

9. I use this term to refer to the Protestant traditions (Lutheran, Reformed, and eventually Anglican) that advocated, similar to Roman Catholicism, for interdependence between the church and state and for secular authorities (princes, magistrates, or city councils) to have role in the enforcing of church discipline.

10. Pavel, "Correlating," 35.

11. Anabaptists and, in particular, Pentecostals have a checkered past with ecumenism. On the one hand, the magisterial traditions have tended to dominate the ecumenical movement and, as a result, define Christian faith and practice in ways that make it difficult for inclusion of Free Church traditions. On the other hand, Anabaptists and pentecostals have been slow to appreciate ecumenical dialogue because of their 'minority' ecclesiological stances.

12. Church historian J. Lindeboom referred to the Anabaptists as such. See Williams and Mergel, *Anabaptist Writers*, 26.

between Christ and culture (Niebuhr)[13] and church and sect (Troeltsch).[14] In like manner, Max Weber and his development of the concepts of "social" and "political" failed to account for "peripheral, marginal, and microsocial political options,"[15] and concepts of social change continue to influence Christian "social" ethics and isolate Anabaptists.

Much the same can be said about pentecostals, both in North America and globally, in that early studies pictured pentecostals as apolitical and sectarian.[16] For example, the early studies of Emilio Willems and Christian Lalive d'Epinay formed the general perception of Latin American pentecostalism as an apolitical and popular religion of the masses. Not surprisingly, the work of d'Epinay depended heavily on the same Niebuhrian and Troeltschian categories cited above.[17] Similarly, the exponential growth of pentecostalism has often led to confusion with Latin American Liberation Theology (LALT), as noted in the well-known quote, "Liberation theology opted for the poor and the poor opted for Pentecostalism."[18] LALT was one of the most significant theological developments of the twentieth century because of a theological method that not only analyzed social problems but also aspired to make real, historical change. However, at the twilight of the twentieth century it became clear that liberation had not arrived and, as a result, the quote above has often been used against LALT as proof of failure since millions of Latin America's poor opted for pentecostalism.[19] Accordingly, pentecostalism has functioned as a foil of LALT: the poor chose a new incarnation of popular religion instead of social transformation.

13. Niebuhr, *Christ and Culture*. The text was originally published in 1951.

14. Troeltsch's two-volume *Social Teaching of the Christian Churches*, was first published in 1912 in German and then translated and published in English in 1931.

15. Gladwin, "Pentecostal-Charismatic Social Ethics," 55.

16. Wacker, "Early Pentecostals," 141–60; Lalive d'Epinay, *Haven of the Masses*; Willems, *Followers of the New Faith*.

17. Gladwin, "Pentecostal-Charismatic Social Ethics," 54–57.

18. Miller and Yamamori, *Global Pentecostalism*, 17. The original source of this quote is not known, but nonetheless it has been repeated again and again.

19. The confines of this chapter do not allow for more commentary on the supposed "failure" of LALT. I will simply note that large-scale liberation did not arrive in Latin America because of the failure of LALT but rather because of the violent oppression of radical movements with the rise of rightist dictatorships and authoritarian governments. For a good analysis, see Gladwin, *Liberating Latin American Ecclesiology*. For an excellent study on the success of pentecostalism and in contrast to liberation theology in the Brazilian context, see Vasquez, *Brazilian Popular Church*.

How should one make sense of the rise of pentecostalism with the global poor? Is pentecostalism simply a foil for social change or a pernicious popular religion that consoles people's pain without authentic social transformation? In my opinion, there are profound problems with such a negative depiction of pentecostalism. First, this interpretation fails to account for the "agency" of the individuals who choose pentecostalism precisely because it offers the possibility of transformation in *lo cotidiano*.[20] Second, pentecostalism as a popular religion[21] has transformative potential precisely because it is popular, that is something that the people actively practice and influence themselves. Third, recent studies have demonstrated the significant social changes that pentecostals are bringing today around the world.[22] As a result, it is possible to speak in a positive way about the poor exercising agency and choosing pentecostalism because it provides a cosmology that makes sense of a contemporary world that integrates both pre- and post-modern[23] patterns of life and forms of understanding. Likewise, it is possible to speak of pentecostalism as a popular religious experience that provides a set of religious practices that bring some level of "liberation" to the poor within their immediate context.

MENNONITES, PENTECOSTALS, AND SOCIAL TRANSFORMATION

Moving beyond the caricatures of Mennonites and pentecostals, we still find challenges surrounding how these two traditions are received in the academy, in particular, the field of Christian social ethics. One of the struggles of speaking to mennocostal social ethics is that the field of study has long been dominated by the social imagination of the magisterial traditions and

20. Spanish term for 'the everyday.' It is a theological term used by Latin American and Latino/a theologians to refer the theological priority of transformation and the necessity to focus theology on the everyday reality of the poor.

21. Popular religion is a difficult term to define and is often used with a negative connotation. I use the term here to refer to religion as actually practiced by people in the context of their lives and their local ecclesial communities.

22. Just to name a few: Attanasi and Yong, *Pentecostalism and Prosperity*; López, *Pentecostalismo y Transformación*; *Pentecostalismo y Misión Integral*; Miller and Yamamori, *Global Pentecostalism*; Wilkinson and Studebaker, *Liberating Spirit*.

23. I have reservations with these terms because they presuppose the existence of a 'modern' age and body of thought that is somehow at the center of the pre- and post-, demonstrating that modernism has not really passed by or, on the other hand, was never as monolithic as has been supposed.

modernist conceptions of society, culture, and social change. As mentioned above, the effects of Niebuhr, Troeltsch, and Weber influence the field of social ethics through key concepts such as society, culture, and politics. The principal problem is that Mennonites and pentecostals have historically spoken of and worked for transformation in ways that do not conform to the matrix of macro-social transformation. Pentecostals and Mennonites have tended to view individuals and the church instead of society and the power of the state as "the" nexus of transformation. The magisterial Protestant traditions, like Roman Catholicism, have historically justified the use of the power of the "state" (princes, magistrates, or councils) to guarantee doctrinal purity and enforce ecclesial discipline. In contrast, the early Anabaptists understood ecclesial discipline as the non-violent work of the local church community and not the magisterium. For Anabaptists, Christian ethics served not to change society-at-large through the will and power of the state, but to form alternative cruciform-communities that embodied the ethics of the kingdom, typically marked by behavior that contrasted with society-at-large. This is evident in the development of Anabaptist sacramentology and community ethics. Anabaptist insistence on believer's baptism was not based on modernist commitments to individualism and the need for an "individual" testimony of conversion (faith), as is the case in most believers' churches today, but instead the need for baptism to be a symbol of the voluntary faith and submission of an individual's will (*gelassenheit*)[24] to Christ and his church. In like manner, the ecclesial practices of communion and the ban also served for the formation of cruciform-community that was distinct from the world in that Christian community embodied Christ's own submission of his will to the Father.

Pentecostals, for their part, have tended to speak of transformation in more individualist terms, often tied to outward manifestations of the transforming presence of the Spirit. Thus, classical pentecostals have emphasized that Baptism of the Spirit is a second work of grace that is outwardly manifested with speaking in tongues. However, much of the same is true for the battery of empowered practices among Charismatics and neo-Charismatics: physical healing, inner healing, the anointing, spiritual warfare, etc.[25] Although these practices are often understood as individual and per-

24. German term used by Anabaptists to refer to self-surrender, resignation, or the yielding of one's will to God's will.

25. An exhaustive list would be much longer and would differ from one cultural context to another.

sonal experiences of God's liberating presence through the Holy Spirit, they find meaning through shared experience and application in the laboratory of local churches.[26] The dominant model of social transformation among pentecostals is microsocial, from the community to society-at-large.[27]

The individualistic and communal focus of pentecostals and Mennonites is not surprising given their historical status as marginal minorities. Both groups began as movements on the fringes of society and developed theories of social transformation and social interaction to prioritize the micro-social, both personal and communal. In contrast to the larger guild of Christian social ethics with a lengthy concern for the development of a public theology, pentecostals and Mennonites have focused first and foremost on local transformation. Although much ink has been spilled concerning Mennonite and pentecostal rejection of the larger society—it is precisely this rejection of the "ways of the world" that stands at the center of Mennonite and pentecostal social ethics and their alternative vision for society based on the witness of the early church in the scriptures and the eschatological hope and expectation of the reign of God. Antonio González has noted that the early, "Christian communities insist on distinguishing themselves from the rest of society, precisely because they seek to be an alternative social order."[28] So it follows, Mennonites and pentecostals tend not to be apolitical sectarians, but ecclesial communities, an alternative *polis* for social transformation. For pentecostals, this alternative vision converges by way of a cosmological, pneumatological and eschatological anticipation of the imminent return of Jesus Christ and God's reign. A classical pentecostal cosmology typically employs dualistic theologies where the world is a composite of spiritual and physical realities amid forces of good and evil; the individual Christian is transformed through the power of the Spirit and thereby seeks to resist the forces of evil and live a righteous life in anticipation of Christ's return. For Mennonites, this alternative vision converges by way of ecclesiology, pneumatology, and sacramentology, and

---

26. I do not mean by this to ignore the significant influence that extra-ecclesial events such as evangelistic crusades and/or mass gatherings have had in the formation of pentecostal belief in practice, but instead simply to say that the primary space for the practice of pentecostal belief and practice has been and continues to be the local church.

27. Miller and Yamamori, *Global Pentecostalism*, 5.

28. González, *God's reign*, 218. See also the original Spanish version, *Reinado de Dios e Imperio*, 250. González demonstrates how the first Christians transformed social relations within the context of the local church, making the argument that this was transformational although it did not necessarily transform the larger structures of society.

the church functions as a kingdom-community marked by a priesthood of all believers that embodies an alternative society that lives according to the reign of God.

MOVING TOWARDS A MENNOCOSTAL SOCIAL ETHOS

What do these two traditions offer to the field of Christian social ethics? Is it possible to speak of a mennocostal social ethic? To begin, it is crucial to recognize that both Mennonites and pentecostals are radically driven by a primitivist desire to return to the ways of the early church and, at the same time, live in light of the eschatological hope and expectation of the already-but-not-yet kingdom of God. They are both renewal movements that believe strongly in the *charismata*, particularly outward manifestations of the presence of the Spirit. While this is self-evident in the name and history of pentecostalism, the same has not always been true of contemporary Mennonites. Indeed, there has been a concerted effort among mainstream Anabaptists to distance the tradition from the soil of renewal that it shared with spiritualists during the Reformation. This is clearly seen in the work of Harold Bender and his influential *Anabaptist Vision* in which he attempted to define an Anabaptist "core" for modern Mennonites. He enunciated an Anabaptist identity focused on traits and practices that fail to mention *charismata* or a radical eschatological anticipation of Christ's return. This can also be seen in the historiographical narrative of scholars such as William Estep,[29] who argues that the true Anabaptists were "biblical" Anabaptists in that they were shaped by a robust commitment to the Bible as the ultimate authority. This historiography prioritizes the biblical-Anabaptism of the Swiss and Southern German Anabaptists as well as the influence of Menno Simons and his attempts to distance Anabaptism from the spiritualists after the infamous Münster debacle. However, it is clear that the nascent Anabaptist movement had an openness to the Spirit and *charismata,* and that the distinction between the spiritualists and the Anabaptists is not at clear as some would claim.[30] For example, Anabaptist hermeneutics was distinct from that of the magisterial traditions not because of their emphasis on the authority of the Bible, but because they understood hermeneutics as a

---

29. See Estep, *Anabaptist Story,* 9–28, 158–70. Estep's typology uses the terms Anabaptists, inspirationists, and rationalists.

30. Byrd, "Pentecostalism's Anabaptist Heritage," 49–61; Snyder, *Anabaptist History and Theology,* 299–364.

pneumatological and communal process; they "anticipated involvement of the Spirit within the community when it gathers around the Scriptures."[31] Accordingly, it is not an overstatement to say that pentecostalism is "in our century the closest parallel to what Anabaptism was in the sixteenth century."[32] Further, I would contend that one might speak of pentecostalism as an extension of Anabaptism[33] or part of a larger believer's church and/or baptistic tradition.[34] It may be true that the global and numerical expansion of pentecostals makes them, not Anabaptists, "the most vital contemporary expression of the modern believer's church tradition."[35]

Since these two traditions have much in common, not least the soil of charismatic renewal, pentecostals and Mennonites would do well to till that soil; radical and continual renewal is necessary for the formation of communal and social transformation. The powerful convictions, ecclesial practices, and anticipation of the action of the Spirit of early Mennonites and pentecostals mentioned above are potential mitochondria for the formation of transformative communities.

As such, a mennocostal worldview calls into question the methodology and calibration of mainstream Christian social ethics. A mennocostal social ethic envisions transformation and social change from below, from the grassroots of local communities. Though Niebuhr (and others) describes the modern canon of contemporary Christian ethics in the North American setting and beyond, his conception of the church and social ethics are inadequate; he fails to address the complexity of cultures and subcultures that exist in the context of any given society and instead depicts culture as a monolithic whole to which Christ and the church respond.[36] According

31. Heidebrecht, "Mennonite Brethren Peace Theology," 230, cited in Fleming, "Holistic Pneumatology," 14.

32. Yoder, "Marginalia," 78, cited in Davis, "Anabaptism," 221.

33. Durnbaugh, Believers' Church, 18–33.

34. James McClendon has most succinctly made this assertion in his call for a baptistic vision. He lists what he sees as the 'marks' of this radical and baptistic tradition: biblicism, liberty, discipleship, community, and mission. He also provides a list of denominations or movements that are baptistic, including Anabaptists and pentecostals. See McClendon, Ethics, 26–34. For further comments on this baptistic vision, see McClendon, Doctrine, 45–46, 144.

35. In 1955, H. P. Van Dusen, the then president of Union Theological Seminary, made this declaration. This was cited in Davis, "Anabaptism as a Charismatic Movement," 219–34.

36. Niebuhr lays out a fivefold taxonomy—against, of, above, in paradox, or transforming—of ways in which Christ (and in turn the church) responds to culture.

to this view, Mennonites and pentecostals are apolitical, sect-like traditions that envision Christ as against the monolithic culture of "society." However, as I have shown, Mennonites and pentecostals do in fact impact the shape of their surroundings, and thereby provide at the least a mennocostal social ethics not "against" culture but "for" alternative culture. On the other hand, Niebuhr advocates for a social ethic that envisions Christ as transforming culture through engagement of culture, and the structures of society through the centers of power and socio-cultural production but ignores the possibility of micro-social transformation through local communities. In the decades since Niebuhr first published *Christ and Culture*, there have been numerous critiques and attempts to rectify his work[37] and, as a result, my critique is by no means novel or unique. Having said this, I cannot understate the ongoing dominance of Niebuhrian thought that privileges the politics of macro-social movements, specifically the political structures of the modern nation-state. To the contrary, the politics of Mennonites and pentecostals have not historically been the politics of official parties and institutions of the nation-state, but instead communal practices carried out on the margins of society. For this reason, it may be better to speak of a Mennonite and pentecostal *social ethos* instead of a social ethic. I borrow this term from the work of the Argentine sociologist of religion Joaquín Algrantí and his development of the concept of social ethos in conversation with Weber.[38] According to Algrantí, the concept of social ethos is better suited than social ethics when speaking of the vision of the social transformation of pentecostals because it is open to micro-social, peripheral, and popular expressions of politics. He stresses that a pentecostal social ethos is not concerned with the formation of a pre-politics or pseudo-politics, but with the grassroots politics from below. Moreover, this social ethos is not rooted in macro-social and structuralist theories of the social, but in the pentecostal cosmology and pnuematologically-infused practices. This idea of a localized, communally-formed politics founded on a social ethos has similarities to a Mennonite ethos of a cruciform-community rooted in practices such as baptism, communion, and the ban. A Mennonite social ethos is focused on the construction of communities that through the Spirit are intended to be prophetic examples of God's reign. Such a social ethos

---

37. Just to name a few: Stassen et al., *Authentic Transformation*; Carson, *Christ and Culture.*

38. Algrantí, *Política y Religión*, 319–20. Algrantí develops this concept in conversation with Max Weber and Weber's concept of religious ethos.

represents small, but nonetheless significant, steps of transformation for those who live on the margins, as it did for the first Anabaptists (as well as for the Anabaptists in the Global South, which makeup the numerical majority of Anabaptists today).[39]

Conclusion

While Christian social ethics frequently undervalues the significance of micro-social transformation, small instances of transformation prove critical for those on the margins of societies, indeed often the margin between life and death. Much the same could be said for the early Christians who represented only a small minority on the fringes of the Roman Empire and could not begin to imagine substantive structural changes to larger society, such as equality to the poor, liberation of slaves, and possibilities for fairness and justice; nonetheless they made small but similar steps toward egalitarian relationships within the contexts of local churches. "For the poor," transformative local churches meant that "Christianity represented the real possibility of escape from the most abject poverty."[40] Similarly, Paul speaks to the strides offered by early Christian communities to break down the social and cultural division between Jews and Gentiles, men and women, and slaves and free persons (Galatians 3:28). As Antonio González has argued, "The first and most radical denunciation of evil is a simple establishment of people who have banished oppression, inequality, and injustice from their midst."[41] I must add that he is not saying that Mennonites and pentecostals should not be concerned with the transformation of macro-social structures and society-at-large. Even though the proponents of a mennocostal social ethic express a reasonable hope that local and communal transformation can serve as catalysts for larger social change, they must listen to and engage the valid critiques that point out that the social structures also condition the formation of local cultural alternatives and the possibility of micro-social transformation. Any mennocostal social

---

39. Today, the majority of Anabaptists are in Latin American and Africa and not North America and Europe. Moreover, even in the United States, the largest amount of growth that is occurring among Anabaptists is among Latinos/as and other people of color.

40. González, "God's reign," 205.

41. González, "God's reign," 218. González examines these three social changes in the context of early Christians in this book.

ethic must humbly acknowledge the inevitable imprint that larger social structures have, even on local ecclesial communities that aspire to offer alternative and transformative forms of living: mennocostal transformation comes not through hopelessly seeking to abstain from the influence of the structures, but through engaging and confronting the social structures with alternative forms of community.

A Personal Note

As a trained academic theologian who is committed to not only talking about what the church should do (ethics), but also engaging what the church is actually doing (practical theology), I often grow tired of the enduring caricatures of Anabaptism and pentecostalism. Although the magisterial model of church and society is in ruins with the crumbling of Christendom, and the face of the global church today is predominately Free Church and pentecostal, the power of the magisterial traditions and modern social theory continues to influence our social imagination. Although in places like Latin America all Protestants function as Free Churches and roughly 75 percent are pentecostal we continue to find a dominant matrix of social change that ignores the socially transformative possibilities of the new face of the global church.[42] As a result, I see a vital part of my ministry as a teacher and scholar is that of being an apologist for Mennonite and pentecostal theological perspectives because I believe a mennocostal social ethic offers direction for both what the church is today and should be in the next century.

BIBLIOGRAPHY

Algrantí, Joaquín. *Política y Religión en los Márgenes: Nuevas Formas de Participación Social de Las Mega-Iglesias Evangélicas en La Argentina*. Buenos Aires, Argentina: Ciccus, 2010.

Attanasi, Katherine, and Amos Yong, eds. *Pentecostalism and Prosperity: The Socio-Economics of the Global Charismatic Movement*. 1st ed. New York: Palgrave Macmillan, 2012.

Burgess, Stanley M., and Eduard M. Van Der Maas, eds. *The New International Dictionary of Pentecostal and Charismatic Movements*. Grand Rapids: Zondervan, 2002.

42. Pew Research Center, "Spirit and Power."

Byrd, Charles H. "Pentecostalism's Anabaptist Heritage: The Zofingen Diputation of 1532." *Journal of the European Pentecostal Theological Association* 28.1 (2008) 49–61.

Carson, D. A. *Christ and Culture Revisited.* Grand Rapids: Eerdmans, 2012.

Davis, Kenneth R. "Anabaptism as a Charismatic Movement." *MQR* 53.3 (1979) 221.

Durnbaugh, Donald F. *Believers' Church: The History and Character of Radical Protestantism.* New York: Macmillan, 1968.

Estep, William R. *The Anabaptist Story.* 3rd ed. Grand Rapids: Eerdmans, 1995.

Fleming, Jody B. "Holistic Pneumatology in Mission: Anabaptism and the Pentecostal-Charismatic Movement." *Anabaptist Witness* 4.1 (2017) 14.

Gladwin, Ryan R. "Charismatic Music and the Pentecostalization of Latin American Evangelicalism." In *The Spirit of Praise: Music and Worship in Global Pentecostal-Charismatic Christianity*, edited by Monique M. Ingalls and Amos Yong, 199–214. University Park, PA: Penn State Press, 2015.

————. *Towards a Liberating Latin American Ecclesiology: The Local Church as a Transformative Historical Project.* Princeton Theological Monograph Series. Eugene, OR: Pickwick, forthcoming.

————. "Toward a Transformative Latin American Pentecostal-Charismatic Social Ethics: Argentine Perspective." In *Pentecostals and Charismatics in Latin America and Latino Communities*, 49–63. New York: Palgrave Macmillan, 2015.

González, Antonio. *God's Reign and the End of Empires.* Miami: Convivium, 2012.

————. *Reinado de Dios e Imperio: Ensayo de teología social.* Santander: Sal Terrae, 2003.

Heidebrecht, Doug. "Toward a Mennonite Brethren Peace Theology: Reading the Bible through an Anabaptist Lens." *Direction* 43.2 (2014) 230.

Lalive d'Epinay, Christian. *Haven of the Masses: A Study of the Pentecostal Movement in Chile.* London: Lutterworth, 1969.

López, Darío. *Pentecostalismo y Misión Integral.* Lima: Puma, 2009.

————. *Pentecostalismo y Transformación Social.* Buenos Aires, Argentina: Kairós, 2003.

McClendon, James W. *Doctrine.* Nashville: Abingdon, 1994.

————. *Ethics.* Nashville: Abingdon, 2002.

Miller, Donald E., and Tetsunao Yamamori. *Global Pentecostalism: The New Face of Christian Social Engagement.* Berkeley, CA: University of California Press, 2007.

Niebuhr, H. Richard. *Christ and Culture.* New York: Harper Collins, 2001.

Pavel, Cheb. "Correlating the Anabaptist and Pentecostal Traditions." *Communio Viatorum* 55.1 (2013) 35–56.

Pew Research Center. "Spirit and Power: A 10-Country Survey of Pentecostals." *Pew Research Center.* October 5, 2006. http://www.pewforum.org/2006/10/05/spirit-and-power.

Snyder, C. Arnold. *Anabaptist History and Theology: An Introduction.* Kitchener, Ontario: Pandora, 1995.

Stassen, Glen H., et al. *Authentic Transformation: A New Vision of Christ and Culture.* Nashville: Abingdon, 1995.

Troeltsch, Ernst. *The Social Teaching of the Christian Churches.* Louisville: Westminster John Knox, 1992.

Vasquez, Manuel A. *The Brazilian Popular Church and the Crisis of Modernity.* Cambridge: Cambridge University Press, 2008.

Wacker, Grant. "Early Pentecostals and the Almost Chosen People." *Pneuma* 19.2 (1997) 141–60.

Wilkinson, Michael, and Steven M. Studebaker, eds. *A Liberating Spirit: Pentecostals and Social Action in North America*. Eugene, OR: Pickwick, 2015.

Willems, Emilio. *Followers of the New Faith: Cultural Change and the Rise of Protestantism in Brazil and Chile*. Nashville: Vanderbilt University Press, 1967.

Williams, George H., and Angel M. Mergal, eds. *Spiritual and Anabaptist Writers*. Louisville: John Knox, 1957.

Yoder, John H. "Marginalia." *Concern for Christian Renewal* 15 (1967) 78.

Yong, Amos. *The Spirit Poured Out on All Flesh: Pentecostalism and the Possibility of Global Theology*. Grand Rapids: Baker Academic, 2005.

9

First say, "Peace" (Luke 10)

Spook and Spirit in Cold War Eastern Europe

GERALD SHENK

I WRITE THESE LINES on the day after we learned that our friend and partner in Anabaptist and pentecostal dialogue, Alan Kreider, has taken his
final leave from our earthly consultations[1]. I can envision him eagerly making his way to the corner where the earliest of Christ's followers may be
congregating, preparing some questions he's been pondering about them
for several recent decades. Two weeks ago I asked him what we can know
of early Christian understandings about those who have departed this life.
Are they wakeful and keeping watch? Or perhaps more in a dormant state,
awaiting the full and final resurrection? He engaged the question with de-
light, and then declared, "They mostly didn't know!" But with Alan, we
know that he'll maintain his eager life-long learning, long into the life that
is to come.

My life along the interface between Anabaptists and pentecostals is
most significantly tied to three decades during which I interacted intensely
with the peoples and faith communities of the former Yugoslavia. During
the 1970s I was a student in a university while President Josip Broz Tito
ruled a socialist experiment with a strong communist party and an atheist

---

1. Alan Kreider was Professor Emeritus of Church History and Mission at Anabaptist
Mennonite Biblical Seminary in Elkhart, Indiana. See Ringenberg, "History."

ideology that always viewed religious people with caution and sometimes outright suspicion. In the 1980s I worked by invitation with local efforts in theological education, hosted by Baptists and pentecostals as they found their way through the decline of the socialist regime and used newly expanding freedoms to build their programs and resources in outreach to their neighbors (most of whom were traditionally Catholic and Orthodox Christian, along with a significant population of European Muslim heritage).

In the 1990s the whole communist project fell into chaos and genocide and hideous inter-group atrocities, while the small evangelical faith communities struggled to provide light in the dark despair, hope in a time of catastrophic violence, and glimmers of basic humanity when real hell broke loose around them. My work during this season, along with intensive teaching sessions at the Evangelical Theological Seminary in Osijek, Croatia, included a mission to connect with local peacemaking efforts, where persons of faith would step up to bind the wounds of war, offer shelter to refugees, and seek healing for those whose souls, bodies, and spirits were deeply harmed by the inter-communal violence that engulfed their society.

But how does a young Mennonite Christian, raised in rural farmlands of Pennsylvania during the throes of the deadly cold war struggle between East and West, arrive on the other side of the proverbial iron curtain and find fellowship with small, beleaguered evangelical communities on the ground there? The simple and straightforward answer is peace. The Shalom of God's reign calls us out, sends us forth, and flings us into situations we would never otherwise enter. When Jesus of Nazareth sets up the first experiment with his early followers in witness on their own (according to Luke 10), a rehearsal if you will for the Great Commission (of Matt 28), he instructs them to travel in pairs, take no baggage, and then "whatever house you enter, first say, 'Peace to this house.'" (Luke 10:5)

Fear of communism was rampant in the years of my youth; the mighty forces rebuilt after World War II lost no time in scaling up for confrontations and clashes via proxies around the globe. Even though the primary contestants did not engage each other directly with deadly force in their home territories, other lands quickly became battlegrounds for testing troops and weapons and strategies.

I had already tasted that real fear when Soviet missiles and US warships faced off near Cuba in the month when I turned nine years old; soon I also heard the deep hostilities when domino theories took conscripts to fight in remote corners of Southeast Asia. I saw my peers clash in the streets with anti-war protests during the 1960s. Raised in a household without television, I nevertheless had exposure to radio preachers and even the Reader's Digest warnings about baleful communist influences on the civil rights agitators of our times. Godless communists constituted a threat to our entire way of life, especially to our much loved and hard-won religious freedoms. God and country, according to most public rhetoric back then, must inevitably align and pull in tandem to confront and defeat such daunting foes. What else is a decent human being supposed to do about enemies like these?

I must admit that I did hear even some Mennonite voices echoing these fears during those turbulent years. I believe the points of resonance reach back into our memories of having been persecuted for our faith in many places along the five centuries since Anabaptist radicals in the sixteenth century moved beyond the settled versions of established Christian communities (whether Catholic or Protestant Reformed). Even more poignantly, we knew that some Mennonite groups long resident in lands of Russian and Ukrainian society had suffered harm during the years of Stalinist communist regimes.

And so our peace-minded people of sincere Christian faith were drawn in two directions during my formative years. With a natural suspicion that the ways of the world were not in keeping with the ways of Christ's kingdom, we were reluctant to embrace the bellicose rhetoric and the militant propaganda of the Cold War period; yet, our people also identified with the narratives of suffering Christians across history and around the world.

Our church leaders in the 1970s perceived that popular culture and the dominant news sources could profoundly undermine our traditional commitment to making peace in the way of Jesus.[2] Even in the 1950s and '60s, they had arranged for exchange visits and study tours across the enemy lines, bringing regional church leaders to bear witness among us from their life under communist rule. One event during my childhood made a vivid impression on me when preachers in a delegation came from the All-Union Council of Evangelical Christians—Baptists in the Soviet Union.

Fear and tension were crackling as we arrived in the large city church where the Russians were introduced. An angry radio preacher named Carl

---

2. Mennonite church leaders designed a program in the 1970s and 1980s to place North American students in universities of Eastern Europe who would seek fellowship with other existing faith communities as part of a long-term peacebuilding strategy. See Jantzen, "Tenuous Bridges."

McIntire was outside parading in the street with a bullhorn, denouncing all who participated as spies and agents of communism. Echoes of Senator Joe McCarthy's anti-communist conspiracy charges still resonated in the cultural memory, and it took little imagination to mark the occasion as a visible clash between loyalty to the state and the spiritual integrity of the church's public witness.

Our faith had taught me from youngest years that even if these strangers were enemies, the Gospel urges us to show them love rather than fear. And if they had a plausible claim to holding the same faith as ours, even more so would we want to treat them as a family, kindred in Christ. I began to discern unholy fire in the mean spirit and verbal violence of the agitator in the street. It would not be the only test of loyalties to unfold as I emerged from teen and young adult years while kingdoms and empires continued to clash.

Some years later a renewed spiritual quest led me to California, where I enrolled for studies at Fuller Theological Seminary. Theological diversity and range of denominational variants there was a providential preparation for the challenges I would encounter in subsequent assignments. Among the particular blessings was a stint as assistant to future provost Russell Spittler, who not only taught a formative course on Corinthian correspondence but also introduced me to the young, dynamic pentecostal leader from Yugoslavia, Peter Kuzmič.

Then director of the Biblical Theological Institute in Zagreb (Croatia; now Dean, Evangelical Theological Faculty), Kuzmič readily welcomed me and my wife Sara into a collaboration that became quite a remarkable journey together. With his colleagues, he was launching a building program for many dimensions of holistic ministry and outreach, across the divides within the ethnic mosaic that was Tito's Yugoslavia. His ties also reached far afield in the orbit of international evangelical organizations at their heyday. Book publishing, mission, education, social ministry, counseling, evangelism, inter-religious dialogue, public theology engaging socialist society and an agile Marxist ideology—these and many other endeavors grew organically from the soil in which the early pentecostal seeds had been planted by several previous generations.

Eventually, I would recognize that the pentecostal and other neo-Protestant movements in Yugoslavia of the 1970s and '80s were coming into a new engagement with their society, training their youth for multifaceted contemporary ministry in the world. Emerging from a more sheltered existence largely avoiding public scrutiny, they now began to envision themselves as not merely tolerated but eligible for full-fledged participation in the tumultuous and contentious arenas of their nation.

Along with singing in the congregations, engaging in Bible studies, some preaching and a growing course load in teaching, I pursued university studies in the sociology of religion (Zagreb and Sarajevo). The Yugoslav complexity was a prime laboratory for tracking inter-religious dynamics in a strenuously secular socialist order, in what proved to be late in the communist era. With a mix of national Orthodox churches, Catholic Christians, scattered minorities in classic Protestant communions, plus neo-Protestant evangelical groups, alongside several ethnic Muslim communities and with an overlay of Marxist rule, even secular sociologists had begun to find religion significant for comprehending contemporary social dynamics.

My learning curve was steep indeed. I began to understand that much of what I had taken for granted in the life of the church was culturally conditioned, depending in large part on structural patterns and traditions that had been accumulating in layers over many decades and centuries. Rural and urban dynamics in a rapidly modernizing society meant changes to religious life, often with unintended consequences.

During a period of relative tranquility between church and state, for example, a helpful newspaper article would highlight the growing use of electronic devices in the local Catholic parish. Can a priest or nun operate a video camera? Will a fax machine in the church office lead to better communication across differences and distance?

What if a foreign film portrays religious dynamics that the official censors find objectionable? I was privileged to watch a private screening of the film "The Exorcist" with 800 Catholic priests and nuns at Kaptol in Zagreb, right after the public cinemas had seen it withdrawn. I should note that the religious audience also found much of the film's portrayal difficult or objectionable, although for their own reasons, of course.

With the sociologists, I could see these movements in their context, stretching with considerable difficulty between rural roots and modern city life. Previous generations had been viewed as suspect, almost like immigrants for their faith that had a certain foreign imprint (in contrast to the centuries of settled patterns in the larger historic traditions). But now, with gradually increasing access to higher education, young believers could enter more of the professions (even though ideological restrictions persisted).

At the same time, advanced theological training was long held in suspicion by more traditional parts of the pentecostal and other laity-led movements. Respect for elders and deference to the founders of congregations who had struggled with keen opposition and suffering during early periods of repression (both official and informal) were key components of the heritage. Internal resistance meant that progress and change were always contested.

In the wider society, bureaucratic regulations tended to swamp every initiative, blocking creative ventures and ensuring that ideological control would prevail. Firebrands in Christian witness would regularly get into trouble, sometimes landing in prison. Many would eventually emigrate, finding the paths to easier postings abroad. Those who chose to remain, working within the ongoing restrictions, had to find patient ways to accomplish the changes prompted by bringing the gospel to their neighbors.

I've long cherished the legacy of Brother Andrija Sabo, pentecostal pastor in Osijek, eastern Croatia. He would take promising young believers and send them in pairs to unreached areas across the country: "You two go to this town; you head to that region." You'll be getting into some difficulties if you preach the gospel there, he acknowledged, and you may be detained. But I will come and help set you free again. There is no law against the Bible. You must use your freedom if you want to keep it.

And they went out. Some of them later became pastors and gave many years in faithful service while starting new congregations. Their early fervor and zeal would be tested in many severe ways during the turmoil that awaited them all in the Balkan wars of the 1990s. But for a small and struggling movement, that passion to share the good news of Jesus led to the formation of many capable and creative young leaders.

Many of them, if they made faith commitments early in life, were practically limited in the choice of careers or professions. University training was largely reserved for persons not deemed overly religious. Quiet participation in standard religious rites did not automatically disqualify a believer for some trades and vocations, but the more responsible and rewarding paths were simply not available to any whose faith was too outspoken.

This resulted in a very gifted set of alert, eager, and competent young disciples ready for training for church vocations, just as the objective conditions for providing theological education came into view. It took remarkable courage and vision to bring this together, but many persons were drawn to that vision and began to accomplish it. We worked at theological education by extension, taking the studies into provincial settings and local congregations. Journals and magazines aimed to lift the level of biblical awareness and sense of calling in everyday life. Summer camps provided intensive reframing in the patterns of thought that belong to faith. Pastors' conferences kept pace for continuing education. Noteworthy teachers from afar came to volunteer their wisdom and encouragement.

In several contexts, we deemed it significant to introduce values of conflict mediation and training to deal explicitly with substantive differences in values and priorities. A small but influential cadre of youth was prepared to handle disputes and tensions with new skills. At the time, nobody could foresee the sudden breakup and demise of the communist social order, but some of the fault lines were becoming more perceptible.

Bear in mind, if you will, that these neo-Protestant evangelical groups constituted less than one-half of 1 percent of the Yugoslav population as a whole, scattered amid the far larger communities of Serbian Orthodox, Croatian Catholic Christians, and several groups of Muslims long resident in the Balkans, alongside traditional ethnic communities of Reformed, Lutheran, and Methodist heritage. Even the sociologists found it difficult to take these small groups into view.[3]

These small groups, carrying a different social DNA than their larger neighboring faith communities, showed a potential for work and witness that would rapidly transcend the fragmentation that loomed ominously once the socialist order fell into chaos. Thus, when pentecostal witness did begin to step up, meeting the challenges of brutality and terror in the collapsing regimes of the Balkans in the early 1990s, I saw them asserting some very contrary perspectives.

They made it clear that they saw each as bearing the imprint of God's creative intentions, as capable of responding to the calling of God in ordinary life. They focused on the importance of personal commitment, asserting that the experience of the Holy Spirit in one's life can take precedence over formal structures and legitimation schemes. They showed that direct participation in spiritual reality is available to ordinary believers, with or without official mediating structures.

In their prayers, their fervent sermons and their impassioned singing, they bore testimony to the sacred in-breaking of God's actions among human beings, in ways that do not always flow through official and authorized channels alone.

---

3. I pursued these topics with my subsequent doctoral dissertation at Northwestern University on the "Social Roles of Religion in Contemporary Yugoslavia (1987)."

In an age of scientism and rationalism (late modern era), they showed that the truths of immediate experience are sometimes more persuasive than the lengthy abstractions of traditional teaching. And although my connections to the movement were mediated largely through the rising educational initiative as I described above, these pentecostal communities harbored some of the same misgivings toward higher education that my faith tradition exhibited in pockets of rural America (continuing to the present).

Throughout this journey together, I found some aspects of the pentecostal experience to be instructive for my social awareness and reflection. First, these groups knew that they were too small to present a complete and comprehensive agenda for their whole society. They couldn't lay claim to wrestling control of the body politic; they could not pretend to have solutions for every successive crisis overwhelming their troubled lands as the socialist system ground toward dissolution.

But the last group of students whom I was privileged to mentor and train, in the late 1980s before I ended my years of residence among them in the Balkans, were no doubt the most attentive to the potential and growing impact of their faith in an increasingly turbulent society fraught with the strains of impending collapse.

I had long advocated for a self-awareness on the part of would-be leaders in the small Christian communities, a recognition that they would someday be seen as pillars of their local society, as people who help to hold things together in a world coming apart. Whereas earlier generations of students had found the very notion of Christian social responsibility almost laughable ("the Marxists will never let us have that kind of importance!"), this last cohort of what we may designate the Christian response to the collapse of state socialism seemed to be drawn toward the tough social and political realities. As demagoguery and deadly partisan rivalries intensified across the region, these young Christian leaders in training were asking how churches might respond to the needs of the weakest, the alienated, the most repressed in their communities.

Along with apprehension about the impending cataclysms, they seemed determined to concentrate on core tasks for faithful living amid a contrary society. While structures and institutions began to unravel (inflation would soon reach 30,000 percent—per month!), they renewed their commitments to the church being the church. They soon showed a willingness to rise above recent denominational divisions in favor of broader evangelical cooperation.

Even after I moved to a new teaching post in Virginia in 1989, I kept in touch with some of my former students, now scattered across the region. With brief return visits, I was able to track some of the stories. "Pastor, can you help us at this orphanage? All the social funds have dried up, and we don't have food!" Waves of refugees began flooding across the region, washing up on church doors with a clamor for food, medicine, shelter, and clothing.

The needs were far too great for these small groups to meet. They typically gave all they had and then reached out for assistance from their contacts abroad. This help was very difficult to organize, but spontaneous and eventually more coordinated responses began to arrive. Ministries of compassion earned a hearing for their preaching like never before. Some churches folded and vanished under the onslaught of unbearable pressures, but others sprang up anew, sometimes amid warehouses and distribution points for the material aid that reached very large numbers of folks in dire distress. Collaboration in networks across deep divides and earnest theological differences became the new norm.

I interviewed some very ordinary believers, unlikely prospects for leadership roles, who became front-line aid workers and agents of such good news that dozens of new congregations emerged from their witness. Their scriptural faithfulness in everyday life became a very bright light amid the immense darkness.[4]

I think it is fair to observe that, after the outright warring madness subsided, these church workers who had become such pillars in their local society found their roles somewhat more circumscribed again as civil society was restored. For a while, they personally and as a group constituted almost the only or last structures of credibility left standing, the only kind of people their fellow citizens in extreme distress could turn to for help. But it was a relief when some semblance of normalcy was restored, and goods and essential services could be secured in more ordinary ways.

The enduring impact of these small faith communities, I am convinced, is still very large and beyond the proportion of their actual size. There is nothing to romanticize about faithful Christian compassion in times of war for fellow human beings caught up in injustice, violence, starvation, and even genocide. But the toughest chapters of a pentecostal witness in the Balkans constitute, in my limited apprehension at least, quite a saga of measuring up under severe testing and distress.

4. Shenk, *Hope Indeed!*

This review of my journeys with pentecostals in the Balkan context has prompted many precious memories for me. I am also moved to reflect on the unique witness of faith in times of turmoil and rapid social change. What I learned with my students and from their elders was that the contemporary Christian witness is often at its best when under great stress, challenged by enormous tests and facing directly into severe opposition. Forged in fire, many of these modern followers of Jesus reached back into the depths of Christian history, attempting to model their faithfulness on the patterns of the earliest disciples. With natural, organic responses to human need around them, they began to find ways to flesh out the gospel so that everyone could understand it. And their rugged commitment to the humanity present in each of God's children became a shining testimony, not only to basic humanitarian values, but to the love of God made manifest in Christ and his enduring body here on earth.

And so their story recapitulates many of the features from the wider Christian movement in its many chapters and voices over two millennia. With the earliest disciples of Jesus, they learned to speak peace first when encountering situations of human struggle and despair. In the power of the Spirit, they went boldly where ordinary human prudence would have counseled caution, reaching into war zones and refugee camps and keeping company with wretched castaways in the storms of life. And in those paths, good news produced fruits, sometimes with whole new congregations following Jesus in the ways that lead to life.

Since my participation began in the years of Cold-War tensions and clashing empires East and West, I was often faced with questions about my reasons for spending years in obscure provinces and lovely but remote towns and cities across Eastern Europe. The natural suspicion went straight to espionage, and possible nefarious purposes for which a foreigner might seek to gain access to such intriguing people. Outside of church circles, where I enjoyed ready acceptance and extraordinary hospitality, the secular mindset was often baffled about what would make a stranger come and stay here, even learning the local languages. My studies at the university notwithstanding, a visible tension would haunt many introductory conversations. Only when I came clear about studying the sociology of religion and my enduring passion for understanding the life of faith communities in a socialist society could my newfound acquaintance suddenly relax. Seizing on a category not valid for visas but perfectly comprehensible in ordinary discourse, the frequent response was, "Oh, you're a missionary! I was afraid the only other explanation was work for the CIA!"

Indeed, there were spooks aplenty throughout the Balkans in those years, but the best spirits were those I found giving tribute to the Spirit of Jesus at work for God's reconciling mission in the world. And for the privilege of sojourning among them in nine years of residence and further decades of fruitful interaction, I am profoundly grateful.

BIBLIOGRAPHY

Jantzen, Mark. "Tenuous Bridges over the Iron Curtain: Mennonite Central Committee Work in Eastern Europe from 1966 to 1991." *Occasional Papers on Religion in Eastern Europe* 31.1 (2011) 16–32. http://digitalcommons.georgefox.edu/ree/vol31/iss1/2.

Ringenberg, Jessica. "History for the Sake of Mission: A Tribute to Alan Kreider." *The Mennonite*, May 9, 2017. https://themennonite.org/history-sake-mission-tribute-alan-kreider.

Shenk, Gerald. *Hope Indeed! Remarkable Stories of Peacemakers*. Intercourse, PA: Good, 2008.

10

Stories We Live By

Convergences in Community Narratives
of Mennonites and Pentecostals

NATASHA WIEBE

INTRODUCTION

THE MOST TALKED-ABOUT BOOKS among scholars of Mennonite literature
include Miriam Toews's novel, *A Complicated Kindness*, narrated by the
fictional Nomi Nickel; and Rhoda Janzen's memoirs, *Mennonite in a Little
Black Dress* and *Does This Church Make Me Look Fat?* For me, the appeal of
these books lies in how they blend storylines familiar from my Mennonite
family and pentecostal upbringing. When Nickel and Janzen mention
Mennonite history in Russia, I am reminded of family stories of escape
from the Ukraine in the 1920s.When Nickel and Janzen catalogue rules
for good Mennonite living, I recall similar expectations for youth in the
Pentecostal Assemblies of Canada. When Nickel writes about the rapture,
and Janzen about her childhood fear of the Antichrist, I remember being
frightened by pentecostal movies on the end times. Nickel's and Janzen's
narratives bring together Mennonite and pentecostal elements, a blending I call *mennocostal.*[1] In celebration of my rich and quirky mennocostal

---

1. Wiebe, "mennocostal 1," 39; "Mennocostal Musings."

heritage, this chapter explores several convergences among pentecostal and Mennonite storylines.

"Life is a story," says novelist Yann Martel. "You can choose your own story; a story with God is the better story."[2] What stories do Mennonites and pentecostals choose to tell? How do these choices affect our lives? This study describes three storylines I learned during pentecostal church services and youth activities in southwestern Ontario in the 1970–80s. It compares these storylines to Mennonite counterparts expressed by family and creative writers who share our Russian Mennonite heritage. Finally, the study discusses some ways the storylines shaped interactions with others, both within our communities and without.

My approach is not theological. Rather, this study is a narrative inquiry. Narrative researchers assume that people, and their literary characters, "are storytelling organisms who . . . lead storied lives. . . . The study of narrative is the study of the ways humans experience the world."[3] To study my mennocostal experience, this study draws from my narratives, told through examples and vignettes. This is in keeping with narrative inquiry, in which the researcher's story always has a place to varying degrees.[4] To provide context for and further develop points drawn from my experience, I turn to scholarship on narrative inquiry, conservative Christianity, and Mennonite literature. I also make connections to other personal narratives with pentecostal or Mennonite settings. These narratives are set in different times and places, and by referencing them, I do not mean to suggest that all pentecostal and Mennonite communities are the same. Rather, I reference others when their experience echoes, and therefore deepens understanding of, my own.

VIGNETTE 1: SINGING IN TONGUES

every summer my family travelled to a revival meeting in Mennonite country and my sister and me ran through the gravel parking lot and pointed at cars painted black and squealed when we saw horses and buggies standing near the door inside we played *where's menno* the women were easy to find because they wore print dresses like laura ingalls and we counted their hairnets

2. Laity, "Yann Martel."
3. Connelly and Clandinin, "Stories of Experience," 2.
4. Clandinin and Connelly, *Narrative Inquiry*, 121.

during the sermons except those by our favorite speaker mr yutzi he used to be mennonite like dad was once in fact mr yutzi used to be *amish* (he must have been really old fashioned) sometimes during the singing he would start to dance a little hop hop that charged the crowd and my sister and me danced with him and mom too but dad kept his eyes closed and talked to jesus who lived in his heart

best of all was the singing in tongues back home we didn't sing in tongues we talked in them speaking in tongues was a gift from god and in our church you got your prayer language like you got your moustache or period but if you were slow you didn't have to worry because we had starter sentences to help you let go and let god (*sell me a hyundai he bought a bow tie* say them a few times and you were off) speaking in tongues was noisy like altar calls when we rushed forward after Sunday night service to scrub sin with tears and glossolalia and like tongues & interpretation when mr lear wailed a message from the holy ghost in *gullamashundalla* his face ripening like a tomato and his arms stretched and flapping like kite strings in the wind (and mom translated in english *thus saith the lord* and my sister and me didn't know where to look) but singing in tongues was different you could tell it was coming when everything got real still (even the babies were quiet) it was that holy

hushshhh when you could feel the spirit slide on by *sssssssssshhhhhhhh*

then a high voice would begin to sing like icicles in the sunlight and willow leaves in the wind and soft ice cream in the dish the narnia voice would sing and mr yutzi would join it and mom and dad and my sister too and then we were a choir our voices *ris*ing and falling and *ris*ing and falling and *ris*ing and falling and i hear mom for a moment before she's swallowed by the sound and i hear dad and then he is gone i hear mr yutzi and my sister i hear everyone and no one and our voices are *ris*ing and

falling and *ris*ing and falling and we're like my school-trip symphony but without a conductor and we're *crash*ing and quiet *crash*ing and quiet we're *crash*ing and quiet and my skin my skin tingles because we sing parts from a blizzard's hymnbook we sing we sing we sing in a tuning orchestra's gooseflesh harmony.[5]

---

5. Wiebe, "mennocostal 1," 39; "Mennocostal Musings," §3.

Exuberance and quiet

While the Bible describes several gifts of the Holy Spirit, including "the ability to heal, to give prophecies, to speak in tongues . . . and to perform miracles,"[6] for my pentecostals, *the* gift was speaking in tongues. Growing in your faith included suddenly beginning to pray in a language given by the Spirit, just as in Acts 2 (although the above "starter sentences" suggest the experience wasn't spontaneous for everyone). I learned the importance of speaking in tongues from participating in pentecostal services. The services that enthused the adults, the ones that made me cry and feel clean inside, often concluded with the congregation moving to the front of the church to pray, an activity during which *glossolalia* was prominent:

> during a
>
> good altar call mr lear gets worked up and begins to wail just like when my sister and me get spanked but he's feeling the fire of the spirit and not a burn on the bum and soon everyone begins to pray as loud as he does and your tongues-talk turns into a chant like you imagine the africans do around their fires in the bush before the missionaries save them and back and forth mr lear's *shundais* dance with your *lallamatikas* back and forth you go and your body begins to rock with the rhythm of your talk and maybe you fall back from the power of the spirit.[7]

Our noisy and communal practice of *glossolalia* is no doubt partly why we were occasionally called holy rollers and teased about swinging from chandeliers. We were the rowdy kids on the Christian block. This reputation served me well as a teenager, when I learned to deflect unwanted romantic attention from non-pentecostal boys by asking if they, too, spoke in tongues.

Even as a child, I was aware that pentecostals were known for exuberance in church.[8] However, occasional visits to Opa's (Grandpa's) United Mennonite church suggested Mennonites were more staid. Hymns were sung, but no faster songs with drums and bass guitar. There was no *glossolalia*. And there was definitely no dancing (Why don't Mennonites believe in premarital sex? Because it might lead to dancing!). As Rhoda Janzen jokes, "in a Mennonite church . . . you sit very still and worship Jesus with all your heart, mind, and soul, only as if a snake had bitten you, and you are now in

6. Dann, "Introduction to Christian Fundamentalism," 11.
7. Wiebe, "Mennocostal Musings," §5.
8. Dann, "Introduction to Christian Fundamentalism," 11.

the last stages of paralysis"[9] Such restraint is fitting for a community that has been defined by the "old axiom [of] 'Quiet in the Land' . . . of keeping to ourselves, intentionally separated from a dominant culture."[10] However, the vignette challenges the storyline of quiet. It describes a recurring event during which a group of charismatic Mennonites were noisier and more spontaneous than pentecostals. The vignette takes the community storylines of pentecostal exuberance and Mennonite quiet, and flips them to tell a personal story that "run[s] counter to expectancy" and "breach[es] a canonical script."[11]

Vignette 2: Sword drill

On Wednesday nights, my sister and me dress in our uniforms with the knights and horses on them and go to church group called *Crusaders*. We bumper-car around the gym with the other kids until Mr. Lear blows his whistle and calls

at-TEN-shun!

Mr. Lear is our commander but he's not the commander-in-chief because that's Jesus. Jesus sits on the red velvet throne by the gym wall. We all stand tall and salute him, and I feel a big balloon blow up inside. We march by invisible Jesus and put our quarter tributes in the collection plate. Sometimes, after Crusaders, the little boys take turns sitting on his invisible lap, but they jump up real quick because he might not like it (and Mr. Lear sure doesn't).
Best of all are the sword drills.
First we kneel with our Bibles
   the sword of the spirit
         against our left sides.
Then Mr. Lear says a verse like *Ephesians six verse thirteen*
and we wait
   a really
      long
         time.

9. Janzen, *Mennonite in a Little Black Dress*, 3.
10. Janzen, "Teaching Peace Studies."
11. Bruner, "Narrative Construal of Reality," 139.

Finally Mr. Lear says
charge! and everything smears like a fingerpainting because we're flipping pages as fast as we can and I'm real fast because I've memorized all of the names of the books of the Bible but Grace is fast too and I know she's gaining on me because I can't hear her pages turning anymore and oh no she's starting to stand up and I'm on the right page but I haven't found the right verse but *stand up stand UP* says the voice inside and I jump up and sing out *The Lord says* to pretend I'm starting to read and get a head start.

Soldiers and peacemakers

My second vignette is informed by the storyline of the Christian soldier who fights alongside Jesus to rescue unbelievers from Satan. I absorbed this storyline during eight years in a pentecostal children's group called *Crusaders*. We knights, ladies, maids, and squires earned badges for such things as building campfires and leading someone to Jesus. Our military theme was based on Ephesians 6:13–18:

> Therefore put on the full armour of God, so that when the day of evil comes, you may be able to stand your ground, and after you have done everything, to stand. Stand firm then, with the belt of truth buckled around your waist, with the breastplate of righteousness in place, and with your feet fitted with the readiness that comes from the gospel of peace. In addition to all this, take up the shield of faith, with which you can extinguish all the flaming arrows of the evil one. Take the helmet of salvation and the sword of the Spirit, which is the word of God. And pray in the Spirit on all occasions with all kinds of prayers and requests.[12]

The first vignette describes the soldier's duty to "pray in the Spirit," which we equated with *glossolalia*. The second vignette focuses on the sword. By describing the sword drill, or competition of "who can find the Bible verse first," the vignette shows the emphasis we placed on knowing the Bible. We believed that simply hearing scripture could cut someone to the quick and convince them of wrongdoing. Ironically, the narrator cheats at sword drill; the competition has overshadowed the purpose of better acquainting her with God's word.

---

12. Unless otherwise noted, Bible verses are from the New International Version.

As an adult, I learned that if good pentecostals were soldiers, good Mennonites were peacemakers. As Rhoda Janzen writes, the "central tenet of [the Mennonite] faith was nonviolence. Mennonites refused to fight. This position . . . arose out of the deeply held conviction that Jesus modeled a different kind of life, one that would turn the other cheek, even to martyrdom." When describing a conversation about Jesus driving the moneylenders from the temple, Janzen observes she had

> never heard a single sermon preached on the Jesus whip. . . . I had imagined Jesus pitching a harmless hissy fit in the middle of the temple, cracking his whip for cranky emphasis. . . . Jesus wasn't actually *hurting* anybody. When I explained this vision to [my Pentecostal boyfriend], he laughed . . . "Jesus *drove* those money changers out of the temple," he said.[13]

From other writers, I learned that non-violence or non-resistance meant more than not physically fighting. Poet Patrick Friesen says where he grew up, "Pacifism meant that you didn't argue or confront each other very often . . . so you found . . . subtle ways of getting around that. And I think that's where a lot of Mennonites learned how to write."[14] Miriam Toews agrees, saying that "Mennonite stuff" like non-resistance got "under the skin," leading her to attach the anger she was not supposed to express to her characters.[15] The essays and poetry of Di Brandt also challenge non-resistance by speaking out about such potentially-divisive issues as the silencing of women, abuse, and religious contradictions in her conservative Mennonite community.[16]

Like the different Mennonite communities of the aforementioned writers, my pentecostal church avoided conflict. Although we were soldiers, our fight was with the devil, not each other. Good soldiers don't question their orders, and so it was common to curtail a conversation expressing religious doubt by saying, "God's ways are higher than our ways, and his thoughts are higher than our thoughts" (Isaiah 55:8–9). Jacob Shelley says that when he raised difficult questions with pentecostal churchmates, they "did not want to discuss things . . . they wanted to set me straight."[17] This

13. Janzen, *Does This Church*, 212.
14. Tiessen, "Introduction," 18.
15. Wiebe, "It Gets Under the Skin," 121.
16. Wiebe, "Di Brandt's Writing," 479–89.
17. Shelley, "Life Stages," 131.

recalls one of Brandt's poems in which the Mennonite narrator unwittingly identifies a contradiction in community beliefs. The father responds, "when are you / going to learn not everything has to make sense your brain is not / the most important thing in the world what counts is your attitude /& your faith your willingness to accept the mystery of God's / ways."[18] Most communities manage dialogue about controversial matters to varying degrees; without harmony, a community may cease to exist. In my pentecostal church and greater Mennonite community, two different storylines that helped maintain conversational boundaries included pentecostal soldier (raise the shield of faith against the arrows of doubt) and Mennonite peacemaker (remain quiet about issues that could disturb community harmony). As sociologist Laurel Richardson observes, "Participation in a culture includes participation in the narratives of that culture. . . . Cultural stories . . . instruct the young and control the adult. . . . They are not 'simply' stories but are narratives that have real consequences."[19]

Vignette 3: Military parade

On Saturday we pack into the church bus and sing *Oh bus driver speed up a little bit* and *100 bottles of Coke on the wall* and drive to another town for a rally with Crusaders from all over.

We cram into the hockey arena and compare badges and have sword drills and tie knots and watch the bible-quiz kids compete and then it's time for the

parade. The grown-ups sheepdog us out to the parking lot and into our ranks and give bibles to my sister and other kids who forgot their swords. Some of us get to be in front and hold the church banner. The little boys point and the big boys shove and the big girls roll their eyes and put on lip gloss but

we all stand tall when we hear the drums call.

Dum. Dum.
Dum, dum, dum.

18. Di Brandt, *Questions i asked my mother*, 6.
19. Richardson, "Narrative Knowing and Sociological Telling," 32.

Thump says the pavement
under our feet.

Left. Left.
Left, right, left.

My stomach dances as
we mark time.

Left. Left.
Left, right, left.

Onward Christian soldiers
marching as to war

with the cross of Jesus
we pass the grocery store.

People honk, and point at us,
as through the town we tread.

My sister waves, and stares right back,
But I look straight ahead.

God's chosen people

By describing the energetic Crusader parade, the above vignette carries forward two storylines discussed previously: those of pentecostal exuberance and militarism. The vignette also hints at another storyline: God's chosen people. My church expressed this storyline through songs that compared us to the Jews of the Old Testament, including "We're marching through Canaan's land." Moreover, there were sermons that positioned us born-again Christians as chosen, including those on 1 Peter 2:9, "But ye are a chosen generation, a royal priesthood, a holy nation, a peculiar people; that ye should shew forth the praises of him who hath called you out of darkness into his marvellous light" (KJV). Showing awareness of our apartness, we referred to non-Christians as "the world," basing this expression on verses like "you do not belong to the world, but I have chosen you out of the world" (John 15:19), and "anyone who chooses to be a friend of the world becomes an enemy of God" (James 4:4). The vignette expresses the storyline of God's chosen people by depicting the Crusaders as set apart: their procession is physically separate from the watching townspeople; they are dressed differently; and the narrator looks straight ahead, not engaging with onlookers.

To help us "be in the world, but not of it," my pentecostals developed a set of guidelines that included no alcohol, secular music, movie theatres, missionary dating (dating unbelievers), and divorce. In *A Complicated Kindness*, Nomi Nickel shares similar rules for her Mennonite hometown:

> Five hundred years ago in Europe a man named Menno Simons set off to do his own peculiar religious thing and he and his followers were beaten up and killed or forced to conform all over Holland, Poland and Russia until . . . some of them, finally landed right here where I sit. . . .
>
> Imagine . . . a breakaway clique of people whose manifesto includes a ban on the media, dancing, smoking, temperate climates, movies, drinking, rock 'n' roll, having sex for fun, swimming, make-up, jewellery, playing pool, going to cities, or staying up past nine o'clock. . . . Thanks a lot, Menno.[20]

When Nickel describes the Mennonites' "peculiar religious thing," she alludes to 1 Peter 2:9, the same verse my pentecostals used to establish themselves as chosen. Di Brandt is more direct, saying Mennonites were

> not unlike the Jewish people in our wanderings, like the wanderings described in the biblical book of Exodus. . . . The Chosen People of the Wilderness. . . . That was our big story. We were like this tribe in the wilderness, surrounded by alien cultures.[21]

In keeping with this tribal theme, my opa playfully referred to outsiders as "Philistines," an arch-enemy of the ancient Jews. His Mennonite neighbours were more polite, referring instead to *dee Enjlanda* (the English), and this expression shows the importance that speaking German had in maintaining cultural separation from outsiders.[22]

---

20. Toews, *Complicated Kindness*, 5.

21. Di Brandt quoted in Wiebe, "Restorying," 214.

22. Paetkau, "Separation or Integration?," iii.

Remaining apart from the world could be challenging. The vignette shows this tension in my pentecostal community. The children's activities are shaped by outside influences: Crusaders is akin to Guides and Scouts, and the children sing a dealcoholized version of "100 bottles of beer on the wall." The characters also challenge the notion of separation: The sister doesn't take the parade too seriously, forgetting her Bible and engaging the worldly onlookers. Moreover, an alternate reading of the ending suggests the narrator stares straight ahead not because she is a good and focused soldier, but because she is embarrassed; the sound of the drums ("dum") and the trite concluding rhymes build toward this interpretation. In these ways, the vignette strains against the pentecostal storyline of being separate. Similarly, there are numerous examples that challenge the ideal of Mennonite separation. For instance, Rhoda Janzen writes that in Russia, Mennonites assisted with restructuring Jewish and Russian villages[23] and sold wagons to well-to-do Russians.[24] Moreover, Di Brandt suggests that Mennonite food—Dutch *Zweiback,* German *Sauerkraut,* Ukrainian *Borscht*—shows the countries that hosted Mennonites over the centuries "can't have been all that hostile if we learned nearly all our recipes from them!"[25] When Opa and other Mennonites immigrated to Pelee Island, Ontario in the 1920s, sharing their mother tongue with German American islanders made it difficult to maintain cultural apartness, compelling the Mennonites to relocate to mainland communities with larger Mennonite populations.[26]

Today, most North American Mennonites are urban and assimilated.[27] For some, this means the loss of a distinct Mennonite identity; to others, it is the opportunity for Mennonite churches to reclaim defining principles like non-resistance and welcome newcomers from outside the heritage.[28] Since my youth, pentecostals in southwestern Ontario have also redefined some ways they maintain apartness, tolerating such things as movie theatres, secular music, and divorce. Community boundaries shift. When the world outside changes, so does the community trying to maintain its apartness. Signals of community change can be found within the personal

---

23. Janzen, *Black Dress,* 229.

24. Janzen, *Black Dress,* 233.

25. Brandt, "In Praise of Hybridity," 125–42.

26. Wiebe, "Mennonite Memories," 417–19.

27. Loewen, "Mennonite *Fin de Siècle*," 37–38.

28. Loewen, "Mennonite *Fin de Siècle*," 40, 49.

narratives of (former) members because individual experiences often differ from community expectations.

Conclusion

This study explores a trio of interrelated storylines constructed from my mennocostal experience: from memories of services and activities in my childhood pentecostal church; from stories told by Mennonite family; and from writing and reflections of authors who share my Russian Mennonite heritage. These storylines are: (1) pentecostal exuberance and Mennonite quiet; (2) pentecostal soldiers and Mennonite peacemakers; and (3) pentecostals and Mennonites as God's chosen people. The storylines blend together to make up bigger ones. In my pentecostal community, the overarching story was that of salvation through Jesus:[29] the Christian soldier fights in God's army against Satan (2) to bring people in the world over to the side of Jesus (3), and to help us in this quest, the Spirit gives the gift of *glossolalia* (1). In my greater Mennonite community, one story that has preoccupied creative writing is that of historical Mennonite diaspora,[30] the 500-year search for a home (3) in which Mennonites could quietly practice their faith (1), away from mainstream sin and violence (2). The storylines are not just stories; they provide frameworks through which we act, shaping our worship as noisy or quiet; offering practices for "being in the world, but not of it"; and determining how we converse—or not—about subjects that challenge community beliefs or potentially disrupt community harmony. The stories we tell about experiences in pentecostal and Mennonite communities may express and perpetuate official storylines, but also push back against their constraints.[31] One-size stories don't fit all. Contrary to traditional storylines, the "gift" of tongues may be coaxed into being rather than received spontaneously; radical worship practices may be learned from churches historically considered conservative; peacemaking may be redefined as non-violent activism rather than passive non-resistance[32]; and moving into the mainstream may renew, rather than destroy, churches once defined by shared ethnicity.

29. Rattigan, "Fantastic Voyage," 55.
30. For example, see Zacharius, *Rewriting the Break Event*.
31. Chase, "Narrative Inquiry," 667–69.
32. Janzen, "Teaching Peace Studies."

BIBLIOGRAPHY

Brandt, Di. "In Praise of Hybridity: Reflections from Southwestern Manitoba." In *After Identity: Mennonite Writing in North America*, edited by Robert Zacharius, 125–42. Winnipeg: University of Manitoba Press, 2015.

———. *Questions i asked my mother*. Winnipeg: Turnstone, 1987.

Bruner, Jerome S. "The Narrative Construal of Reality." In *The Culture of Education*, by Jerome S. Bruner, 130–49. Cambridge: Harvard University Press, 1996.

Chase, Susan E. "Narrative Inquiry: Multiple Lenses, Approaches, Voices." In *The Sage Handbook of Qualitative Research*, edited by Norman K. Denzin and Yvonna S. Licoln, 651–79. Thousand Oaks: Sage, 2005.

Clandinin, D. Jean, and F. Michael Connelly. *Narrative Inquiry: Experience and Story in Qualitative Research*. San Francisco: Jossey-Bass, 2000.

Connelly, F. Michael, and D. Jean Clandinin. "Stories of Experience and Narrative Inquiry." *Educational Researcher* 19 (1990) 2–14.

Dann, G. Elijah. "An Introduction to Christian Fundamentalism." In *Leaving Fundamentalism: Personal Stories*, edited by G. Elijah Dann, 1–24. Waterloo: Wilfrid Laurier University Press, 2008.

Janzen, Randy. "Teaching Peace Studies from a Mennonite Perspective: Quiet in the Land Revisited." *Conrad Grebel Review* 32 (2014). https://uwaterloo.ca/grebel/publications/conrad-grebel-review/issues/spring-2014/teaching-peace-studies-mennonite-perspective-quiet-land.

Janzen, Rhoda. *Does This Church Make Me Look Fat? A Mennonite Finds Faith, Meets Mr. Right, and Solves Her Lady Problems*. New York: Grand Central, 2012.

———. *Mennonite in a Little Black Dress: A Memoir of Going Home*. New York: Henry Holt, 2009.

Laity, Paul. "Yann Martel: 'My children aren't impressed that I won the Booker or that I wrote *Life of Pi*.'" *Guardian*, March 4, 2016. https://www.theguardian.com/books/2016/mar/04/books-interview-yann-martel-the-high-mountains-of-portugal.

Loewen, Royden. "A Mennonite *Fin de Siècle*: Exploring Identity at the Turn of the Twenty-First Century." In *After Identity: Mennonite Writing in North America*, edited by Robert Zacharius, 37–51. Winnipeg: University of Manitoba Press, 2015.

Paetkau, Henry. "Separation or Integration? The Russian Mennonite Immigrant Community in Ontario, 1921–1945." PhD diss., University of Western Ontario, 1986.

Rattigan, David L. "Fantastic Voyage: Surviving Charismatic Fundamentalism." In *Leaving Fundamentalism: Personal Stories*, edited by G. Elijah Dann, 55–68. Waterloo: Wilfrid Laurier University Press, 2008.

Richardson, Laurel. "Narrative Knowing and Sociological Telling." In *Fields of Play: Constructing an Academic Life*, by Laurel Richardson, 26–35. New Brunswick, NJ: Rutgers University Press, 1997.

Shelley, Jacob. "Life Stages." In *Leaving Fundamentalism: Personal Stories*, edited by G. Elijah Dann, 121–35. Waterloo: Wilfrid Laurier University Press, 2008.

Tiessen, Hildi Froese. "Introduction." In *Liars and Rascals: Mennonite Short Stories*, edited by Hildi Froese Tiessen, xi–xiii. Waterloo: University of Waterloo Press, 1989.

Toews, Miriam. *A Complicated Kindness*. Toronto: Knopf Canada, 2004.

Wiebe, Natasha G. "Di Brandt's Writing Breaks Canadian Mennonite Silence and Reshapes Cultural Identity." In *German Diasporic Experiences: Identity, Migration, and Loss*, edited by Matthias Schulze et al., 479–89. Waterloo: Wilfrid Laurier University Press, 2008.

———. "'It Gets Under the Skin and Settles in': A Conversation with Miriam Toews." *Conrad Grebel Review* 26 (2008) 103–24. https://uwaterloo.ca/grebel/sites/ca.grebel/files/uploads/files/CGR-26-1-W2008-11.pdf.

———. "mennocostal 1: singing in tongues." *Rhubarb: A Magazine of New Mennonite Art and Writing* 13 (2007) 39.

———. "Mennocostal Musings: Poetic inquiry and Performance in Educational Research." *Forum: Qualitative Social Research* 9 (2008). http://www.qualitative-research.net/index.php/fqs/article/view/413/898.

———. "Mennonite Memories of Pelee Island, Ontario, 1925–1950: Toward a Framework for Visual Narrative Inquiry." *Narrative Inquiry* 23 (2013) 405–23. http://www.jbe-platform.com/content/journals/10.1075/ni.23.2.10wie.

———. "Miriam Toews's *A Complicated Kindness*: Restorying the Russian Mennonite Diaspora." *Journal of Mennonite Studies* 28 (2010) 33–54. http://jms.uwinnipeg.ca/index.php/jms/article/view/1358/1349.

———. "Restorying in Canadian Mennonite Writing: Implications for Narrative Inquiry." PhD diss., University of Western Ontario, 2010.

Zacharias, Robert. *Rewriting the Break Event: Mennonites and Migration in Canadian Literature.* Winnipeg: University of Manitoba Press, 2013.

11

How the Holy Apostles Practiced Baptism in the Water

By Menno Simons

[Editorial Note: Though we, and our fellow contributors, will undoubtedly disagree with various elements of this sermon, we felt it serves as an appropriate addition to this volume. On the one hand, the author captures the countercultural passion of the early Anabaptists. Menno Simons, founder of the Mennonites, embodies the zeal, courage and tenacity of a protest movement. On the other hand, while we may not share his harsh tone and sectarian exclusivity, he represents well the urgency of upstart and resistance movements. This sermon is taken from Simons's larger work, *An Explanation of Christian Baptism in the Water from the Word of God.*[1] Originally in Dutch, we have followed the 1871 translation by John F. Funk of Elkhart, Indiana.]

IN THE THIRD AND last place we are forced to assert the Christian baptism of the believing, even at the risk of life and blood for the reason, that the holy apostles of God baptized none but those alone who desired to be baptized, as Christ expressly and plainly commanded them, saying, "Go ye into all the world and preach the gospel to every creature; he that believeth and is baptized shall be saved" (Mark 16:15). This commandment the apostles received from the mouth of the Lord and have proclaimed the

---

1. For the complete works of Menno Simons, see van Zanten, "Menno Simons."

holy gospel, the glad tidings of grace, throughout the world (Rom 10) and preached it to every creature which was under the heavens (Col 1). They baptized all who accepted this gospel by faith, and no others as is shown and perceived in many Scriptures treating of the Acts of the Apostles; some of which Scriptures I shall place before the reader, by which all the rest of the Scriptures will be easily explained.

When Philip was led by the angel of the Lord, to the chariot of the eunuch, who was come from the land of Ethiopia, and read the gospel of Jesus Christ from Esaias the prophet, "Philip preached unto him Jesus and as they went on their way, they came unto a certain water; and the eunuch said, See here is water; what doth hinder me to be baptized? And Philip said, If thou believest with all thine heart thou mayest. And he answered and said, 'I believe that Jesus Christ is the Son of God'" (Acts 8:35–37).

My chosen, beloved brethren, If all the earth were full of learned orators or highly renowned doctors, and these were, by sharp subtlety and human philosophy, exalted as high as the stars; yet, by the grace of God, the word will never be wrung from us, namely this: That where there is no faith, no baptism should be administered, according to the word of God, or else we must admit, first, that the command of Christ Jesus is wrong. Secondly, that the holy apostles have taught wrongfully; thirdly, that the holy Philip here asked wrongfully; fourthly, that the eunuch was concerned about this matter more than all the rest of humanity.

No, kind reader, no. But as Peter and Paul, together with all the pious witnesses of Christ always had their eyes fixed upon the commandment of the Lord Jesus Christ and did not act in opposition thereto, so also the holy Philip, the true servant of God who preached and taught with the same spirit, would not baptize until the illustrious and famous man had sincerely confessed his faith; for it was thus commanded him of Christ Jesus, his true Master, our Redeemer and Savior (Matt 28:19; Mark 16:15).

As the holy apostles required of those that were to be baptized, first, to make a confession of their faith before baptism, so I ask you, beloved reader, how can we require a confession of faith of infants before they are baptized, and who shall confess for them? If you should say the godfathers, then I would reply that the godfathers were first gotten up by Pope Higinius, as we have shown above. Inasmuch as Higinius is the getter up of them, and as infant baptism has been practiced ever since the time of the apostles as Origen and Augustine write, and as I believe, because those who do not rightly confess Christ, ever seek their righteousness in wrought ceremonies, notwithstanding it is no divine command nor apostolic usage, as may be particularly proven by the holy Scriptures, and also by Tertullian and Ruffinus and others—therefore I verily do not see who, by the faith of infants, has answered for them in their baptism which were baptized during the period between the apostles and Pope Higinius, inasmuch as the godfather were first gotten up by Higinius who was either the ninth or tenth pope, and as the infants which were before him had as little doctrine, hearing, voice or understanding as the children of the present day, as they plainly prove by their fruits.

Observe, kind reader, that all their doing with children, such as catechism, godfathers, baptism, crisma, and such like things, is nothing but open hypocrisy, human righteousness, idolatry, useless fantasy and opinion.

Inasmuch as Christ Jesus has commanded but one baptism on the confession of faith, and as the apostles have taught and practiced it—therefore the infant Baptists must consent and admit, by virtue of the word of God, that infant baptism is not by the commandment of Christ, not by the teaching and practice of the holy apostles, but by the doctrine of anti-Christ and by the practice of his preachers.

I repeat that the holy apostles baptized none but those that desired it, or those who confessed the most holy faith either verbally or proved it by their walk, as did holy Peter; for although he was previously informed by a heavenly vision that he might go amongst the Gentiles to teach them the gospel, yet he refused to baptize the pious, noble and godly centurion and his consorts, so long as he did not see that the Holy Spirit was descended upon them, that they spoke with tongues, and glorified God. But when Peter plainly saw that they were truly believing and that the Spirit was descended on them, he said, "can any man forbid water, that these should not be baptized which have received the Holy Ghost as well as we? And he commanded them to be baptized in the name of the Lord" (Acts 10:47–48).

Behold, kind reader, here you are plainly taught that Peter commanded that those only should be baptized who had received the Holy Ghost; who spoke with tongues and glorified God, which only pertains to the believing and not the unconscious infants. Thus the practice of Peter was in accordance with the commandment of Christ (Mark 16:16). Therefore, Peter did not command infant baptism; for the Holy Ghost does not operate in them, as may be plainly seen. This may also be understood from a passage of Paul; for he says, "When they believed Philip preaching the things concerning the kingdom of God, and the name of Jesus Christ, they were baptized both men and women" (Acts 8:12). Observe, nothing is said of infants.

Paul, a preacher and apostle, also baptized upon the confession of faith and truth. He required faith before baptism to such perfection that he regarded the baptism of the holy John the Baptist as useless and vain among the disciples at Ephesus, because they knew not the Holy Ghost, saying:

> Unto what then were ye baptized? And they said Unto John's baptism. Then said Paul, John verily baptized with the baptism of repentance, saying unto the people, that they should believe on him which should come after him, that is, on Christ Jesus. When they heard this, they were baptized in the name of the Lord Jesus. And when Paul had laid his hands upon them, the Holy Ghost came on them, and they spake with tongues and prophesied; and all the men were about twelve. (Acts 19:3–7).

Hear, most beloved readers; for I would here present to you and to all the world three points, which you should impartially consider and judge according to the word of God. First, was the baptism of John not of God? I know you will give an affirmative reply. If now the baptism of John is of God, as it is indeed, and if Paul yet considered this baptism which was from above as insufficient and imperfect in these disciples because they did not acknowledge the Holy Ghost, and as he, after preaching to them Christ, again baptized them with the baptism of Jesus Christ, as is mentioned in Luke, for what purpose must we consider the baptism of children that are naturally unable to understand the divine word, and therefore they acknowledge neither Father, Son, nor Holy Ghost; neither can they distinguish between truth and lies, righteousness and sinfulness, good and evil, right and wrong? Does not this prove infant baptism to be useless, vain and unfruitful? And as administered and received without the ordinance of God? And if we acknowledge this by the word of God through faith, is it therefore not necessary to be baptized with the baptism of Jesus Christ as Christ has commanded and as Paul has administered to these disciples? I say, verily, if we do not, there is, according to the word of God, neither faith, regeneration, obedience, nor Spirit in us, and therefore no eternal life, as we have frequently shown above.

Let all the learned garble this invincible Scripture and practice of Paul as subtlety as they please, yet it will never be asserted by virtue of the word of God but that these disciples, notwithstanding that they were baptized with the baptism of John, were again baptized, after they were taught by

Paul, with the baptism of Jesus Christ; because they knew not that there was a Holy Ghost; that is, if baptism is to be baptism according to the word of God. But, brethren, the preaching of the cross is ever opposed because it is to them that perish, foolishness (1 Cor 1:18).

Again, judge for yourselves kind readers, since Christ Jesus himself and also the holy apostles, Peter, Paul, and Philip, have commanded and taught no other baptism in all the Scriptures of the New Testament, but upon the confession or proof of faith, and as the whole world in opposition thereto, teaches and practices a different baptism, which is founded neither in the command of Jesus nor in the teaching and practice of the holy apostles, namely, infant baptism, and asserts it not by the word of God, but solely by the opinion and long usage of the learned; and forces it upon the world by the cruel, bloody sword; therefore, judge, I say, which of the two we should follow. The divine truth of Christ Jesus, or the lies of the ungodly world? If you answer, Christ, your judgment is right; but the consequence according to the flesh is anxiety, being robbed, apprehension, banishment, poverty, water, fire, sword, the wheel, shame, cross, suffering and temporal death; yet, in the end, eternal life. But if you answer the world, then you verily judge wrongfully; notwithstanding, on the contrary according to the flesh, the consequence is honor, peace, ease, liberty, temporal life and such perishable advantages; yet the end is eternal death.

Thirdly and lastly, judge rightly whether the ordinance of Jesus Christ which he commanded into his church, and which the holy apostles learned and administered from his blessed mouth, can ever be changed and broken by human wisdom or excellency. If you answer in the affirmative, you must prove it by the divine and evangelical Scriptures or else we should not believe it. But if you answer in the negative, as it should be, you must acknowledge that those, no matter who they are, whether they lived at the time of the apostles, and were even their disciples, who say that the apostles baptized infants, shamefully misrepresent the apostles and load falsehood upon them, yea, that they speak their own opinion and not the word of God, for the most holy apostles, the true witnesses of Christian truth, never taught two different baptisms in the water; neither did they act contrary to the command and ordinance of Christ, nor administer it contrary to their own doctrine.

O, had the educated and learned men, Origen, Augustine, Jeronimus, Lactantius, and others, not soared so high in their smartness and philosophy; and had they been satisfied with the clear, chaste, and plain doctrine of Jesus Christ and his apostles, and had they conformed their intelligence and subtle reasoning to the word of God, then the heavenly doctrine and unchangeable ordinance of our beloved Lord Jesus Christ would not have been subjected to such shame and change! And in particular has the great Origen, by his philosophy and self-conceit, so shamefully treated with the Holy Scripture that Martin Luther in his book called *Seruum Arbitrium*, calls him *Spercissimus scripturarum interpres*, that is: *The falsest explainer of the Scriptures*. And besides, it is annotated in the Lutheran New Testament that this Origen is the great star which fell from heaven, burning like a lamp, and that his name is Wormwood (Rev 8:11). Therefore we will leave it to God who and what he is. Notwithstanding he has treated the word of God so shamefully and has erred so terribly, yet because he pleases the world in regard to infant baptism—the holy doctrine of Christ Jesus and the apostles must stand back; and Origen is heeded, accepted and followed as a sure testimony to this idolatrous ceremony. O, abominable blindness! O, shameful foolishness! That we do not believe the sure word of our Lord Jesus Christ, the word of truth, and the true witnesses who were sent by him! but that we would rather follow, to the loss of our souls, those who teach to please us, notwithstanding it is plain from their writings that they have so often stumbled and erred, and been mistaken in regard to the truth of Almighty God!

Therefore I beseech you all, beloved brethren in the Lord, by the grace of God to open your understanding, that you may be no longer deceived, and that you may perceive, you who are made uneasy by the writings of the learned, that all the writers, both ancient and modern, have ever sought righteousness in wrought ceremonies, which we should only seek in Christ Jesus. And again, that, because they have not the word of God on their side they do not follow the same path in regard to this matter, do not speak of one accord nor write unanimously. For as their writings show, some seek the washing away of inherent sin. Others teach that they should be baptized on account of their faith. Again, to train them in the word and commandments of God. Still, others, to have them included into the covenant with God; and, again, to baptize them into the church of Christ. Behold, kind readers, thus each of the before mentioned writers follows his own course, and does not follow the same way. If they were supported by the word of God, in regard to this matter, they would all be unanimous. But because they have not the word of God—each one follows his own inclination, thinking that he can, under a scriptural appearance, palm off pernicious falsehood as being the truth. Yea, he tickles his vision so long with garbled Scriptures that his mind becomes so obscured that he can no more conceive that he teaches, follows and administers accursed falsehood for the blessed truth of God.

Thus, most beloved children, because the learned have ever sought and yet seek righteousness in infant baptism, you can easily surmise that these infant Baptists have, by that means, made this innovation. For with the ancients it was not the common practice, I say common, as may be deduced from Tertullian, Ruffin, and others; but as appears, just after the demise of the apostles or perhaps yet in their times, they commenced to abuse the true, Christian baptism, which solely belongs to the believing. As some of the Corinthians already in the time of Paul suffered themselves to be baptized for the dead (1 Cor 15:29), so, also, through the false doctrine and opinions of foolish bishops, the abominable serpent of infant baptism crept in, and was so confirmed by long usage that, at last, it was thought and accepted by all the world as an apostolic institution for the sake of righteousness which they all seek therein. Therefore you must acknowledge, beloved brethren, notwithstanding infant baptism is of old date, that it is still not by the command of Jesus Christ, and by the teaching and practice of the holy apostles; and is therefore idolatrous, useless and vain.

And because the true, Christian baptism has such a great promise, namely, the remission of sins, and other promises (Acts 2:38; Mark 16:16; 1 Cor 12:13; 1 Pet 3:21; Eph 4:5), the pedo-baptists apply the same baptism to infants; never once observing that the before mentioned promises are solely to those who show obedience to the word of God; for Christ Jesus has so commanded it. Inasmuch as pedo-baptism is not commanded, therefore it is not required of children as obedience. For where there are no commandments there are no transgressions. Again, baptism is not commanded to infants, by God; and therefore they have no promise in their baptism, from which it follows that infant baptism is idolatrous, vain, useless and void, before God, as was said above; for God, the Lord, has no pleasure in the ceremonies, unless they are administered according to his divine and blessed word.

But the little children, and particularly those of Christian seed, have a peculiar promise which was given them of God without any ceremony, but out of pure grace, through Christ Jesus our Lord, who says, "Suffer little children, and forbid them not, to come unto me; for of such is the kingdom of heaven" (Matt 19:14; Mark 10:14; Luke 18:16). This promise makes glad

and assures all the chosen saints of God in regard to their children or infants; being assured that the true word of our beloved Lord Jesus Christ can
never fail. Inasmuch as he has shown such great mercy towards the children
that were brought to him, that he took them up in his arms, blessed them,
laid his hands upon them, promised them the kingdom of heaven and has
neither done nor commanded them anything more; therefore they have
in their hearts a sure and firm faith in the grace of God, concerning their
beloved children, that they are children of the kingdom, of grace, of the
promise and of eternal life through Christ Jesus our Lord, to whom alone
be the glory; and not by any ceremony. Yea, by this same promise they are
assured that their beloved children, so long as they are not of understanding years, are clean, holy, saved and pleasing unto God, be they alive or
dead. Therefore they give thanks to the eternal Father through Jesus Christ
our Lord, for his inexpressibly great love to their children, and train them
in the love of God and in wisdom, by correcting, chastising, teaching and
admonishing them, and by walking before them with an unblamable life
until they may hear the word of God, believe it and fulfill it in their works.
Then is the time, of whatever age they may be, that they should receive
the Christian baptism which Christ Jesus has commanded, in obedience to
his word, to all Christians; and which his apostles have thus practiced and
taught.

Behold, brethren, if it should be said that we thus rob the children of
the promise and of the grace of God, you will observe that they contradict
us out of hatred and envy, and do not tell the truth. Say, who has the stron-
gest ground and hope of the salvation of their children? Is it he who places
his hopes upon an outward sign? Or is it he who bases his hopes upon the
promise of grace, given and promised of Christ Jesus? Still, the evangelical truth must, in all respects, be blasphemed and belied by the ignorant
and light minded. But, notwithstanding this, the just and impartial Judge,
Christ Jesus, will some time pass the true sentence between them and us,
although they do not fear it now. I am forced to think that then it will be
acknowledged by many, too late, that they did not believe and follow the
truth of Christ Jesus but the falsehood of anti-Christ. Take heed and watch.

Again, it is sometimes, and very foolishly too, asserted by the pedo-
baptists, "That the apostles baptized whole households, as the household
of Cornelius (Acts 10:48); the household of Stephanus (1 Cor 1:13); the
household of Lydia, and of the jailer (Acts 16:15, 33); from which, they say,
it may be presumed that there were also small children among them." From

this allegation, beloved brethren, they show, although not intentionally, that they cannot produce Scriptures to prove infant baptism. For whenever we must follow (build on) presumption, there is evidently no proof of the assertion.

To such opponents I would reply, in plain language, thus: Three households, namely, of Cornelius, Stephanus and of the jailer, were all believing. Of the first household it is written, "There was a certain man in Cesarea, called Cornelius, a centurion of the band called the Italian band; a devout man and one that feared God with all his house, which gave much alms to the people, and prayed to God always" (Acts 10:1–2). If they all served and feared God, as Luke writes, then they were not baptized without faith, as is plainly shown in the same chapter; for Peter commanded that those should be baptized who had received the Holy Ghost, as they had who spoke with tongues and glorified God; which are all fruits of faith, as every intelligent person will admit.

Again, of the household of Stephanus it is written, "I beseech you, brethren (ye know the house of Stephanus, that it is the first fruits of Achaia, and that they have addicted themselves to the ministry of the saints); that ye submit yourselves unto such, and to everyone that helpeth with us, and laboreth" (1 Cor 16:15–16). I repeat it to serve the saints is a work of faith. Since the house of Stephanus served the saints, as Paul writes, therefore they showed by their fruits that they had faith.

Again, of the house of the jailer, it is written that Paul and Silas spake unto him and said, "Believe on the Lord Jesus Christ, and thou shalt be saved and thy house; and they spake unto him the word of the Lord, and to all that were in his house. And he (the jailer) took them the same hour of the night, and washed their stripes; and was baptized, he and all his, straightway. And when he had brought them into his house, he set meat before them and rejoiced believing in God with all his house" (Acts 16:31–34); or as Erasmus says, "He has rejoiced because he believed in God with all his house." Beloved reader, observe first, that they spake unto him the word of the Lord, and to all that were in his house. Secondly, he rejoiced with all his house. To hear the word is something which pertains to those of understanding minds, and spiritual rejoicing is a fruit of the believing or of the spiritual (Gal 5:18). Inasmuch as they all heard the word and rejoiced in God, therefore it incontrovertibly follows that the holy apostles did not baptize them without faith.

In the fourth place, in regard to the house of Lydia, I reply: Because the world tries to establish their cause on presumption, therefore we would say first, that presumption ought not to establish faith; and if it were so that it could avail before God, then still the presumption in the case of the house of Lydia would not be in favor of the world but against it; because it is the custom in the Holy Scriptures and also with the world, that a house is named after the man and not after the woman, so long as the husband lives, because the husband is the lord of his wife and household. As in this case, the house is named after the woman, and as there is no mention made of the man, therefore it follows that she, at the time, was not married. If she was a young woman or widow, as appears, then the presumption of the world is contradictory; and it is probable that she had no children, and still more probable that she had no infants since she at that time had no husband.

Again, we would further say in reference to this Scripture, that if it were that Lydia had infants, they would not be counted among the baptized of the house. For Christ commanded that the believing should be baptized and the holy apostles taught and practiced such baptism; from which it may be safely deduced that when the holy Scriptures speak of houses being baptized, or houses being subverted that it has reference to those of understanding years, who may be taught or subverted, as Paul shows in another Scripture, that some "subvert whole houses, teaching things which they ought not, for filthy lucre's sake" (Titus 1:11). If you take the term whole houses as applying also to infants; and as whole houses were subverted, as Paul says, then it would follow that infants were subverted by false doctrine. No, beloved reader, no. An infant without understanding can be neither taught nor subverted; therefore they are not counted in the number of baptized, or those who were subverted, of which the Scriptures speak. But the Holy Scripture teaches and admonishes, both by words and sacraments, as they are called, those alone who have ears to hear and minds to understand, as we have frequently shown above.

If anyone would like to have more information about the ceremony of baptism and about the objections made to it, let him read our first treatise on baptism which we published; and by the grace of the Lord, he will be enlightened upon the subject from the word of God.

Brethren, I conclude this treatise on baptism in the water in these words: Inasmuch as God, the merciful Father, has graciously sent into this miserable, blind and erring world his chosen, beloved Son, Christ Jesus, who has taught us the holy will of his Father, in great clearness; and as he has, in his great love, offered up his precious and most holy flesh and blood for us, and as to him the eternal Father has not only pointed us through his holy prophets but also from high heaven, saying, "This is my beloved Son in whom I am well pleased; hear ye him" (Matt 17:5); therefore we say and testify that we should hear this Christ Jesus; that we should believe in him and follow him in all things which he has taught and commanded us; and that we should also hear and follow his holy apostles who by his own divine command were sent out with the most precious word of grace, namely, with the holy gospel or else we have neither God, promise, nor eternal life, as is plain and intelligible to all mankind, from the New Testament.

As this Christ Jesus has given us this express and incontrovertible command in this wise: First to teach the gospel and then to baptize those who believe, and those that are thus baptized shall be saved (Mark 16:16; Matt 28:19; Acts 2:38; 10:48; 16:33; 19:5). And as the holy apostles have taught and used no other baptism than baptism on faith, according to the command of Christ, as shown and proven by many reasons (Acts 2; 8; 10; 16; 19; Rom 6:4; Col 2; 1 Cor 12:13; Titus 3:5; 1 Pet 3:21); therefore we again declare before you, before all the world and before God, that we are prompted by nothing but by the fear of God, being so taught by his word, thus to teach this Christian baptism, and thus to receive it upon the confession of faith, for the remission of sins (Acts 2:38), as said before, and are thus baptized with the washing of water, by the word (Eph 5:26) and by a Holy Spirit which quickens our hearts, into one body (1 Cor 12:13); of which body Christ Jesus is the head (Col 1:18; Eph 1:22). Nor do we know of any other baptism, of which God is a witness than this alone; of which, by the grace of God, we have so much taught and written.

I herewith beseech you, kind reader, not to do like the angry, blind and bloody world, who condemn everything from an envious, rebellious, refractory and raving heart before they have thoroughly perused and understood it; who reject all good, Christian doctrine and usage; sometimes because of fashion, again, because of the cross, and sometimes because of the plainness of the person. Do not thus; but judge this and all our writings according to the Spirit and holy word of the Lord, and you will plainly see whether we have written and taught you truth or falsehood; whether we teach two baptisms or one; whether we seek to save your souls or destroy them; whether we seek the praise and honor of the Lord or his dishonor. For I trust, by the grace of God, if you are desirous of your own salvation, and if you peruse what we have written and judge it with a spiritual judgment, that you will find nothing in it but the teaching which is of God; the eternal, heavenly, true and saving will of God and the very strait way of truth which the ever blessed Jesus Christ and his apostles have, in the most holy gospel taught and shown all mankind.

Take heed, ye illustrious, noble and pious lords! Take heed ye judges and keepers of the law, against whom your cruel, bloody sword is sometimes sharpened and drawn. I tell you in Christ Jesus that we seek nothing but what we have here told you, as you may clearly see by many, namely, that there is not a false syllable nor deceitful word heard from their mouths or found in them, and these are forced and led by you to the sword, fire and water, as poor, innocent sheep to the slaughter. And if you should point me to the abominable actions of the corrupted sects, and say that you must, therefore, oppose baptism, by the sword, that such ungodly doings may be averted and hindered; then I would again reply, first: Christian baptism belongs not to corrupted sects, but it is the word of God. Secondly, the holy, Christian baptism does not cause mutiny nor shameful actions; but it is caused by the false teachers and false prophets who boast themselves to be baptized Christians, and yet, before God, are not such. Thirdly, there is nothing under heaven at which I am more alarmed than I am at the ungodly actions of the false, corrupted sects. They frighten me more than death; for I know that all men must once die (Heb 9:27). More than the tyrannical sword; for if they take my body, it is all they can do (Matt 10:28). More than Satan; for I have vanquished him through Christ. But in case the terrible doctrine of the corrupted sects adhered to me, then I would verily be lost; eternal woe would be to my poor soul. Therefore I would rather die the temporal death (that he knows who knows all things) than to eat, drink, commune, greet or converse with such, if I knew that they would not be helped by my conversation or admonition; for it is forbidden in the word of Christ to keep the company of such (Matt 7:15; 1 Cor 5:11; 2 Thess 3:14; Phil 3). And, by the grace of God, I know to a certainty, that they are not in the house of the Lord, in the church of the living God and in the body of Jesus Christ. Therefore I say, if you find in me or in my teachings, which is the word of God, or among those who are taught by me or by my brethren, any thieving, murdering, perjury, mutiny, rebellion or any other criminal acts, as were formerly, and are yet found among the corrupted sects—then punish all of us; as we would be culpable if this were the case. I repeat, if we are disobedient to God in religious matters, we are willing to be instructed and corrected by the word of God; for we mean diligently to do and fulfill his most holy will. Or if we are not obedient unto the emperor in matters belonging to him as he is called and ordained of God, I say in matters belonging to him, then we will willingly submit to such punishment as you may inflict upon us. But if we sincerely fear and seek our Lord and God, as I trust we do, and if we are obedient unto the emperor in temporal matters, as we should be according to the word of God (Matt 22:21; Rom 13:7; 1 Pet 2:13; Titus 3:1), and are yet to suffer and be persecuted and crucified for the sake of the truth of the Lord—then we should consider that "the disciple is not above his master nor the servant above his lord. If they have called the master of the house Beelzebub, how much more shall they call them of his household?" (Matt 10:24–25). Yet you should know and acknowledge, O ye beloved, noble, illustrious, pious lords, ye judges and keepers of the law, that as often as you take, condemn and put to the sword such people, that you put your tyrannical sword into the blessed flesh of the Lord Jesus Christ, and that you break the bones of his holy body; for they are flesh of his flesh and bone of his bone (Eph 5:30); they are his chosen, beloved brethren and sisters, who are with him, born from above, of one Father, (John 1:13); they are his sincerely beloved children who are born of the seed of his holy word; they are his holy, spotless and pure bride whom he, in his great love has wedded as his consort. Why? Because they have, by the operation of their faith, and led by the Holy Spirit, cordially committed themselves to the service of our beloved Lord Jesus Christ, and do not live any more according to their lusts, but agreeably to the will of God, alone, according to the direction of his holy, blessed word. Yea, they would rather surrender everything which they possess, and suffer envy, slander, scourging, persecution, anxiety, famine, thirst, nakedness, cold, heat, poverty, imprisonment, banishment, water, fire, sword or any other punishment than to forsake the gospel of grace and the confession of God and be separated from the love of Christ Jesus (Rom 8:35). But they will never accept the vain doctrine and commandments of men.

Therefore we pray you, as our beloved and gracious rulers according to the flesh, by the grace of God, to consider and realize, if there is any reasonableness about you, in what great anxiety and suspense we poor, miserable people are placed. For if we abandon Christ Jesus and his holy word, we fall into the wrath of God; and if we remain firm in his holy word, we are put to your cruel sword. O, Lord! if it were true that this large church were thy holy church, bride, and body, as they boast it to be, then we might truthfully assert that thou art the prince, bridegroom and head of an abominable, detestable band of murderers, who thirst after the innocent blood of those who sincerely seek, fear, love and serve God. For the ignorant, blind people go about like a backsliding heifer, as the prophet says, seeking nothing but the persecution, imprisonment, and destruction of God's saints and children.

All the priests and monks, who seek and fear nothing but their gluttonous, greedy belly, and their avaricious, pompous flesh, do nothing but upbraid, slander, lie and persecute; the judges and magistrates, who seek to live of the bloody labor of the miserable; take them and deliver them into the hands of the tyrants, that they may become favorites of the rulers, as the prophet says (Mic 7); "The prince asketh and the judge asketh for a reward." The lords and keepers of the law, as a body, are after nothing but the favor and friendship of their prince to whom they are sworn; after authority, good wages and aggrandizement. They are those who torture, banish, confiscate and murder, as the prophet says, "Her princes within her are roaring lions; her judges are evening wolves; they gnaw not the bones till the morrow" (Zeph 3:3). At another place, "Her princes in the midst thereof are like wolves, ravening the prey to shed blood, and to destroy souls, to get dishonest gain" (Ezek 22:27). O, how just was the revelation of holy John, when he saw that the Babylonian woman was drunk with the blood of the saints and with the blood of the martyrs of Jesus (Rev 17:6). O, beloved lords and judges of the land, observe once, how all the righteous, the prophets, Christ Jesus himself, together with his holy apostles and servants, have been treated from the beginning; and today you still treat those thus, who in purity of heart seek the truth and life eternal. Therefore we must run the risk; for in case you do not fear God, and do not sheathe your murderous sword against Christ Jesus and against his holy church, then we esteem it of less consequence to fall in the hands of worldly princes and judges than to fall into the hands of God. I repeat it, take heed, awake, and be converted, that the innocent blood of the pious children of God, which calls for vengeance in heaven, may never more be found on your hands.

Take heed, also, ye wise and learned and ye common people! For such a people are they and such is their doctrine and faith whom you daily ridicule and mock as fools; whom you slander as heretics and deceivers; and whom you take and deliver, and murder in your hearts, as thieves, murderers, and criminals. Yet, God's word shall never be broken (1 Pet 1:24; Jas 1:10; Ps 90:6). O ye miserable people, what will become of you! that you are not ashamed daily to mock and ridicule the blessed Christ Jesus; to trample upon him and thus ravingly tear to pieces his most holy and glorious body, notwithstanding you boast of his divinity, word, death, grace, mercy, and blood.

Say, beloved, if you are the church of Christ, why are you not obedient unto him? If you are the body of Christ, why destroy its holy members? If you are the children of God, why trample upon your brethren? If you are the servants of Christ, why not do the things he has commanded? If you are the bride of Christ, why not hear his holy voice?

If you are the truly regenerated, where are, then, the fruits? If you are the true disciples of Christ, where is your love? If you are the true Christians, where are your Christian ordinances of baptism, Supper, deacons, ban, and life as commanded in his word? If you are the truly baptized ones of Christ where is your faith, your new birth, your death unto sin, your unblamable life, your good conscience, your Christian body into which you were baptized and your Christ whom you have put on?

O beloved brethren, an error has been rampant long enough! Christ Jesus will be no longer mocked as a fool. I tell you as truly as the Lord lives, that so long as you are thus earthly, carnally and devilishly-minded; so long as you oppose God and his holy word; so long as you live without the fear of God, according to the lusts of your flesh, so long you are not the true church of Christ, even if it were that you were using the true sacraments, which, however, is far from being so. Beloved brethren, first our hearts must be cleansed and afterward our outward actions will show; or else it is hypocrisy before the eyes of God. I repeat it, so long as you live thus ungodly, as you have done hitherto, Christ Jesus was, verily, born in vain, died in vain, arose and ascended in vain. He is no Lord, Deliverer or Savior of the willful, obdurate, unrepenting and disobedient sinners, but he is a Lord, Deliverer and Savior of those who willingly hear his divine word; who sincerely renounce evil, and walk diligently according to his holy commandments, all the days of their lives.

May God, the gracious Father, who lives in mercy forever, grant you all true knowledge to comprehend all divine truth; and a heart, mind, and will to fulfill that which you now confess by faith from the word of God, through Christ Jesus our beloved Lord. To him be the honor, praise, kingdom, power, and glory forever and ever, Amen.

Let the bride of Christ rejoice.

HEREIN, reader, you have most devoutly what the mode of God's baptism, which perished through the long degeneracy of the ages, in the church ought to be, being restored whole by the unspeakable gift of God. Therefore let the writers oppose as they please; let the learned oppose by their shrewdness as they know how; let all the world under the heavens oppose in every way in which they are able, this is the only mode of baptism which Christ Jesus himself instituted and the apostles taught and practiced.

The invincible truth will ever abide, although powerfully opposed by many. He who reads the teachings of Christianity and considers well will welcome this divine truth, of Christ, though for many ages lost, and now thus made to appear, because it is not without merit by its favor toward us.

May the reader give thanks to the infinitely great and good God.

Mayest thou be well, be humble, read, obtain, believe and live, and may the lord be with thee.

BIBLIOGRAPHY

van Zanten, Machiel, ed. "Menno Simons: Life, writings, doctrine, images, and links." *Menno Simons.net.* http://www.mennosimons.net.

Index